# BEYOND COUNSELING AND THERAPY

# BEYOND COUNSELING AND THERAPY

**Robert R. Carkhuff**
**Bernard G. Berenson**

State University of New York, at Buffalo

**Holt, Rinehart and Winston, Inc.**
New York • Chicago • San Francisco
Atlanta • Dallas • Montreal
Toronto • London

## Contributors

Frederick C. Thorne     University of Miami

John Douds     Brandeis University

Richard Pierce     State University of New York at Buffalo

Winni Barefoot     University of Florida

Raphael Vitalo     University of Massachusetts

Printed in the United States of America
3456   038   98

# PREFACE

As committed counselors and therapists, we feel that we have something to say concerning theory and practice, training and research in counseling and psychotherapy. In the following pages, we attempt to say it.

We have organized the book around our own experiences in counseling and training, and our research and theorizing concerning facilitative interpersonal processes in general. In the first section we attempt to describe the present state of conditions for the human in trouble, the man in need of help. The hope that we see is in the attitudinal disposition of the whole counselor, a whole person who views counseling as a way of life.

In the second section, we describe our attempts to develop a comprehensive model of facilitative interpersonal processes, a model in which both therapist and client are assessed on the same core dimensions of interpersonal functioning. A variety of potential preferred modes of treatment are constructed around these core dimensions. The potential preferred modes of treatment are studied in the third section in order to determine the unique contributions of each; that is, the contributions that each might make to constructive client process movement and outcome over and above those changes accounted for by the central core of facilitative conditions.

In the fourth section, we attempt to make application of the model of core conditions and preferred modes of treatment to clinical practice. Of necessity, any theoretical model does not translate easily to clinical practice. Therefore, attention is given to what is unknown to us as well as what is known. Phases of therapy are hypothesized and described. The implications of crisis therapy, "the crossroads for both client and therapist," and the need for confrontation at the crisis point in counseling and real life are described and the preferred modes of treatment blended fully into therapeutic processes. Finally, the thread which holds the entire book together, the whole person—"the goal of training and counseling" is considered.

In the last section, counseling and therapeutic processes are viewed again in their relation to society at large, and a summary and overview of the book is presented.

We have written this book with all persons concerned with effective human relations in mind. In particular, we have been concerned with those in the helping and teaching profession: counselors and psychotherapists; guidance and rehabilitation specialists; educators, psychologists, and social workers, as well as the intelligent and interested and concerned lay public.

We wish to acknowledge the helpful stimulation of Dr. David Aspy, Dr. Ralph Bierman, and of John Douds, M.S.W., who also had the primary responsibility for organizing Chapter II, a collaborative effort with the authors to which Richard Pierce also made a contribution. We would like to acknowledge the continuing support of Dr. Frederick C. Thorne, among the first of the eclectic theorists and practitioners, who also contributed a meaningful chapter on client dimensions to this book. In addition, we recognize the contribution of Raphael Vitalo on psychoanalysis and Mrs. Winni Barefoot to our research on therapeutic crises and to tape excerpting. Finally, we wish to acknowledge the typing and administrative assistance of Mrs. Robert R. Carkhuff and, in general, the support and encouragement from our wives, students, clients, and colleagues, particularly Dr. Myron Manley.

R. R. C.
B. G. B.

Buffalo, N.Y.
June 1967

# CONTENTS

# SECTION ONE

# Counseling and Life

In the first section of the book, we attempt (1) to establish the present state of resources available to the
human in need of help, and (2) to set the tone for the
remainder of the book. In Chapter 1, we consider those
dimensions of human encounters which lead to the
constructive change of one or both of the parties to
a relationship. Then we proceed to attempt to establish
the levels at which these conditions are available from
both nonprofessional and professional sources. The low
levels of human nourishment available to the distressed
person lead us to a consideration of the implications
for counseling and therapy and, indeed, all constructive
human encounters. The hope, it would appear, lies in
the development, through both training and constructive personal change, of the whole person/counselor,
the person who does not view counseling and therapy
as distinct from life, but, rather, counseling as a way of
life. The only reasonable starting point from which to increase the quality and quantity of nourishment in all
human relationships is the whole counselor, a person
acutely aware of his own experience.

# Chapter 1

. . . If counselors and psychotherapists
functioned in real life the way most
of them do in the therapeutic hour
they would be patients. . . .

## Man and His Nourishment

An unhealthy society is one in which only 20 percent of its people are free of signs of emotional distress (Srole, Lagner, Michael, Opler, and Rennie, 1962). An unhealthy society is one in which one third of its members demonstrate distressing psychiatric symptomatology (Leighton, 1956). An unhealthy society is one in which half of the hospital beds are occupied by mental patients, and in which one third of these are second admissions (Department of Health, Education and Welfare, 1960; Schofield, 1964). American society, in which all of these conditions exist, is not healthy.

An unhealthy society cannot provide human nourishment to its members. Ours does not. The clients and patients who seek out our inpatient and outpatient treatment centers are largely people who cannot find sources of human nourishment in their everyday life environments. Indeed, they are most often the broken and disabled products of a social system which has disallowed or made difficult their emergence as constructive and potent persons.

The clients and patients who seek out treatment are so desperate for nourishment that many of them are willing to (and must) pay for the devoted attention of another human being. The "more knowing" roles prescribed by society, that of parent, teacher, minister, guidance counselor, coach, and perhaps even spouse, while seemingly incorporating the notion of providing human nourishment, have obviously left their principal functions undischarged. They have left their "less knowing" counterparts impotent and unfulfilled. They have ceded their own special voids to their children, students, and partners, for they have very little to offer.

## THE DIMENSIONS
## OF HUMAN NOURISHMENT

There is an extensive body of evidence suggesting that all human interactions between persons designated by society as "more knowing" and "less knowing" may have facilitative or retarding effects upon the "less knowing." Thus, in significant counseling and psychotherapy, teacher-student, or parent-child relationships, the consequences may be constructive or deteriorative on intellective as well as psychological indexes. In addition, there is extensive evidence to indicate that, to a large degree, the facilitative or retarding effects can be accounted for by a core of dimensions which are shared by all interactive human processes, independent of theoretical orientation; that is, patients, clients, students, and children of persons functioning at high levels of these dimensions improve on a variety of improvement criteria, while those of persons offering low levels of these dimensions deteriorate on indexes of change or gain (Aspy, 1966; Carkhuff, 1967; Carkhuff and Truax, 1966; Truax and Carkhuff, 1964, 1966).

Those core dimensions which receive the most imposing support are those involving the levels of empathic understanding, positive regard, genuineness, and concreteness or specificity of expression, offered by those persons designated as "more knowing." In turn, these dimensions are related to the degree to which the "less knowing" person can explore and experience himself in the relationship, a dimension which also is shared by all interactive processes between "less knowing" and "more knowing" persons. Additional dimensions, such as those involving the levels of appropriate self-disclosure, spontaneity, confidence, intensity, openness, flexibility, and commitment of the "more knowing" persons have been posited (Carkhuff, 1967a). However, the empirical evidence in support of these dimensions is sparse and, in a very real sense, movement toward these dimensions represents movement to the unknown from the known—a very necessary movement, but one for which at present we have very little demonstrable effects. Nevertheless, we can make inferences concerning these less-established dimensions from the data that we have on the researched dimensions.

The core dimensions related to constructive change or gain may be operationally defined.[1] On five-point scales developed to assess the facilitative dimensions related to improved functioning in all interpersonal processes (Carkhuff, 1967a), the following operational definitions emerge:

On all scales, level 3 is defined as the minimally facilitative level of interpersonal functioning. At level 3 of the *empathic understanding* scale, the verbal or behavioral expressions of the first person (the counselor or therapist, teacher, or parent) in response to the verbal or behavioral expressions of the second person (the client, student, or child), are essentially *interchangeable* with those of the second person in that they express essentially the same affect and meaning. Below level 3, the responses of the counselor detract from those of the client. Thus, at level 1, the lowest level of interpersonal functioning, the first person's responses either *do not attend to* or *detract significantly* from the expressions of the second person in that they communicate significantly less of the second person's feelings than the second person has communicated himself. At level 2, while the first person does respond to the expressed feelings of the second person, he does so in such a way that he *subtracts noticeably* from the affective communications of the second person. Above level 3, the first person's responses are additive in nature. Thus, at level 4, the responses of the first person *add noticeably* to the expressions of the second person in such a way as to express feelings a level deeper than the second person was able to express himself. Level 5, in turn, characterizes those first person responses which *add significantly* to the feelings and meaning of the second person in such a way as to express accurately feelings levels below what the person himself was able to express or, in the event of ongoing deep self-exploration on the second person's part, to be fully with him in his deepest moments.

*Respect* or positive regard in interpersonal processes is defined at

[1]The scales, themselves, present many limitations, most obviously a high degree of subjectivity on the part of the raters or judges. This subjectivity could not be avoided, even if it were undesirable. In actuality, counseling and psychotherapy are highly subjective experiences, and the scales are merely attempts to assess the levels of the dimensions involved in these experiences. In operation, research emphasis is placed upon a high degree of relationship between the ratings and reratings by the individual raters as well as a high degree of relationship between the ratings of different raters. Perhaps the major limitation of the scales is a kind of middle-class quality. Only the verbal material of therapy can be rated, and often unorthodox communications by the therapist may have a constructive impact upon the client. The communications which do not fall within the range of definitions of the scales may not receive high ratings. In the end, heavy reliance is placed upon the overall average levels of conditions throughout therapy as assessed by the ratings of random selected excerpts. For example, at a crisis point in therapy, responses by both therapist and client may be made which are rated at low levels, but which, nevertheless, enable the client to become further involved in therapeutic process movement. If both therapist and client function at high levels during the ensuing process, the overall average ratings will be much higher. The scales and those from which they are derived (Truax and Carkhuff, 1966), with all their limitations, emerge as important instruments with repeated replication in the same and different settings.

minimally facilitative levels by the first person's communication of a *positive respect* and concern for the second person's feelings, experiences, and potentials. Levels below 3 are characterized by a lack of respect or negative regard. Thus, at its lowest level, level 1, there is a communication of a clear *lack of respect* or *negative regard* for the second person, whereas at level 2, the first person responds to the second person in such a way as to communicate *little respect* and concern for the feelings and experiences of the second person. Levels above 3 are characterized by the communication of deepening levels of respect. Thus, level 4 describes first person communications carrying a *deep respect* and concern for the second person, while level 5 characterizes a facilitator who communicates the *very deepest respect* for the second person's worth as a person and his potential as a free individual.

*Facilitative genuineness* in interpersonal processes is defined at minimally facilitative levels by the first person's providing *no discrepancies* between what he verbalizes and what other cues indicate he is feeling, while also providing *no positive cues to indicate really genuine responses* to the second person. Below level 3, there are cues indicating discrepancies in the first person's expressions and cues for ingenuine responses. At level 1, the first person's expressions are *clearly unrelated* to what other cues indicate he is feeling at the moment, and/or the first person's only genuine responses are *negative* in regard to the second person and appear to have a totally destructive effect upon the second person. At level 2, there are indications that the first person's responses are *slightly unrelated* to what other cues indicate he is feeling at the moment, or when his responses are genuine, they are negative in regard to the second person; the first person does not employ his negative reactions constructively as a basis for further inquiry. Above level 3, there are indications of deepening genuine responses. Level 4 characterizes the facilitator when he presents *positive cues indicating genuine responses* (whether positive or negative) in a nondestructive manner to the second person. At level 5, the facilitator's expressions indicate that he is *freely and deeply himself* in his relationship with the second person; he is completely spontaneous in his interaction and open to experiences of all types, both pleasant and hurtful; in the event of hurtful responses, the facilitator's comments are employed constructively to open further areas of inquiry for both the facilitator and the second person.

*Personally relevant concreteness,* or specificity of expression in interpersonal processes, is defined at minimally facilitative levels by the first person's enabling the second person to discuss personally relevant material in *specific and concrete* terminology. Below level 3, varying degrees of vagueness and abstractness dominate the conversations. Thus, at level 1, the first person leads or allows *all* discussions with the second person to deal only with *vague and anonymous generalities,* while at level 2, the first person *frequently* leads or allows even discussions of material personally relevant to the second person to be dealt with on a *somewhat vague and abstract level.* Above level 3, specificity and concreteness dominate the problem-solving activities. Level 4 describes the facilitator's frequent helpfulness in enabling the second person to develop fully in *concrete and specific* terms almost all instances of concern; level 5 characterizes the communications of the facilitator who is *always* helpful in guiding discussion so that the second person may discuss fluently, directly, and completely specific feelings and experiences.

Depending upon the levels of the facilitative dimensions offered by the "more knowing" person, the "less knowing" person might engage in a variety of activities. Perhaps the most significant of these activities involves the second person's ability to be openly and deeply himself in his relationship with the first person. Thus, the second person may feel free to explore, experience, and experiment with himself in a facilitative relationship, or he may restrict his activities in a relationship offering low levels of conditions. Again, the client's ability to explore himself—perhaps the central focus of all therapeutic processes—has been related to constructive change or gain.

*Self-exploration* in interpersonal processes is defined at level 3 by the *voluntary* introduction by the second person of *personally relevant material,* although he might do so in a *mechanical* manner *without the demonstration of emotional involvement.* Below level 3, the second person either does not voluntarily introduce personally relevant material or responds only to the introduction of personally relevant material by the first person. Thus, at level 1, the second person *does not discuss personally relevant material,* either because he has had no opportunity to do so or because he actively evades the discussion even when it is introduced by the first person. At level 2, the second person responds with discussion to the introduction of personally relevant material by the first person, but does so in a mechanical manner without the demonstration of emotions. Above level 3, there is a voluntary introduction of personally relevant material by the second person with increasing emotional proximity. Thus, at level 4, the second person *voluntarily introduces* discussions of personally relevant material with both *spontaneity and emotional proximity,* and at level 5 the second person *actively and spontaneously* engages in an *inward probing* to discover feelings or experiences about himself and his world.

## THE LEVELS OF HUMAN NOURISHMENT

The levels of human nourishment available to the person at a crisis point are grossly inadequate. Most environments simply cannot support and sustain an individual in trouble. The individual in society is not allowed either to emerge as an individual or to resolve the conflicts which result from the frustration of his attempts to emerge, (see Table 1, page 9).

The person in need of help is unable to find facilitative agents in his everyday environment. Individuals from the general public, when cast in the helping role, function midway between levels 1 and 2 (Martin and Carkhuff, 1967); that is, at this index of their maximum level of interpersonal functioning, they are essentially oblivious to the feelings and experiences of the person before them. In effect, they are immune to constructive human encounters. They provide a level of interpersonal functioning not significantly different from neuropsychiatric patients under outpatient care, or counseling center clients, who are cast in a helping role (Pagell, Carkhuff, and Berenson, 1967). In addition, those members of the general population who are oriented toward helping do not function at significantly higher levels than the public in general (Pierce, Carkhuff, and Berenson, 1967).

The data from the college environment is similar, although there is a trend toward improved interpersonal functioning (in the helping role), when the students are oriented toward helping or choose to major in one of the helping professions. Thus, college freshmen function at levels of facilitative dimensions similar to the levels of the general public (Carkhuff, Piaget, and Pierce, 1967), while sophomores with an interest in dormitory counseling, demonstrate slightly higher levels of functioning (Berenson, Carkhuff, and Myrus, 1966), and senior psychology and education majors function still higher, almost at level 2 (Carkhuff, Piaget, and Pierce, 1967; Holder, Carkhuff, and Berenson, 1967; Piaget, Berenson, and Carkhuff, 1967).

It is important to note that few of the groups of persons cast in the helping role attained an average of level 2 overall, a summary description of which follows. Thus, in our assessments of the general population, the first person, *at a maximum*, responds to the superficial feelings of the other person, not only infrequently, but also continuing to ignore the deeper feelings; he communicates little positive regard, displaying a lack of concern or interest for the second person; his verbalizations are somewhat unrelated to what he is feeling, and most often he is responding according to a prescribed "role" rather than by expressing what he personally feels or means; he frequently leads or allows discussions of material personally relevant to the second person to be dealt with on a vague and abstract level. Furthermore, *at a maximum*, the second person responds with discussion to the introduction of personally relevant material by the first person, but does so in a mechanical manner and without the demonstration of emotional feeling.

It is significant that from within the nonprofessional population, a person under duress can receive the highest levels of facilitative condi-

Mean Levels of Facilitative Interpersonal Functioning Available from Nonprofessional and Professional Helpers

| STUDY POPULATION | N (NO. OF INDIVIDUALS) | EMPATHY | COUNSELOR RESPECT | GENUINENESS | CONCRETENESS | CLIENT SELF-EXPLORATION | OVERALL AVERAGE | AUTHORS |
|---|---|---|---|---|---|---|---|---|
| 1. Outpatients | 9 | 1.43 | 1.57 | 1.79 | 1.66 | 1.68 | 1.59 | Pagell, Carkhuff, and Berenson, 1967 |
| 2. General Public | 10 | 1.44 | 1.84 | 1.72 | 1.47 | 1.42 | 1.58 | Martin and Carkhuff, 1967 |
| 3. Lay Helpers | 17 | 1.46 | 1.55 | 1.48 | 1.47 | ** | 1.49 | Pierce, Carkhuff, and Berenson, 1967 |
| 4. College Freshmen | 32 | 1.24 | 1.85 | 1.91 | 1.19 | 1.38 | 1.51 | Carkhuff, Piaget, and Pierce, 1967 |
| 5. College Dormitory Counselors | 36 | 1.54 | 2.03 | 2.19 | 1.79 | 1.60 | 1.83 | Berenson, Carkhuff, and Myrus, 1966 |
| 6. Upper Class Students (Education majors) | 24 | 1.66 | 1.96 | 1.94 | 1.93 | ** | 1.87 | Kratochvil, Aspy, and Carkhuff, 1967 |
| 7. Upper Class Students Juniors and Seniors) | 11 | 1.92 | 1.86 | 2.20 | 2.16 | ** | 2.03 | Holder, Carkhuff, and Berenson, 1967 |
| 8. Upper Class Students (Juniors and Seniors) | 16 | 1.97 | 2.01 | 2.11 | 2.17 | ** | 2.06 | Piaget, Berenson, and Carkhuff, 1967 |
| 9. College Seniors (Psychology Major) | 24 | 1.90 | 1.95 | 2.05 | 2.00 | 1.95 | 1.95 | Carkhuff, Piaget, and Pierce, 1967 |
| 10. Best Friends (College) | 16 | 2.06 | 2.11 | 2.05 | 1.82 | 2.06 | 2.02 | Martin, Carkhuff, and Berenson, 1966 |
| 11. Graduate Students (Psychology) | 25 | 2.07 | 2.39 | 2.32 | 2.13 | 2.82 | 2.35 | Carkhuff, Piaget, and Pierce, 1967 |
| 12. Teachers (In Classroom) | 13 | 2.00* | 2.30* | 2.00* | ** | ** | 2.10 | Aspy, 1966; Aspy and Hadlock, 1966 |
| 13. High School Guidance Counselors | 14 | 1.76 | 2.02 | 2.07 | 1.64 | 1.90 | 1.89 | Martin and Carkhuff, 1967 |
| 14. Experienced Counselors and Therapists | 32 | 1.86 | 2.04 | 2.20 | 2.08 | 2.48 | 2.13 | Carkhuff, 1967b |

*Part of this data is constituted by approximate transformations from other related scales.
**Not appropriate in the particular study involved.

tions, an overall average of level 2, from his best friend (Martin, Carkhuff, and Berenson, 1966). The implication, then, is that an individual in trouble seeks out his best available friend in order to have a less retarding interaction. Even with his best friend, however, the level of interpersonal functioning is inadequate. Nevertheless, his chances of improvement are increased with a motivated friend who has some understanding of him as opposed to a random selection of neighbors or associates.

Graduate students in the helping professions, in turn, enter graduate school at a level slightly higher than level 2 overall (Carkhuff, Piaget, and Pierce, 1967). Counseling psychology students function at levels slightly higher than clinical students (this perhaps reflects a selection factor of its own). Following graduate training, however, the results are very distressing. On at least one dimension, empathic understanding, the trainees, in an essentially traditional psychoanalytic program, demonstrated very low levels of functioning following completion of their studies and internships. (Bergin and Solomon, 1963). The transformed data indicates that, after training, the trainees were functioning at level 1.75 on empathy (Pierce, 1966). The direct suggestion is, then, that in graduate school something very deleterious happens to the functioning of graduate students on one of the critical effective ingredients of therapeutic processes. It is also important to note that in the Bergin and Solomon study, empathy once again related positively to judgments of therapeutic competence involving patient benefits, and negatively to overall and practicum grade point averages; that is, *those students who communicated the highest level of understanding and whose patients, in effect, had the greatest opportunity to gain or change constructively in therapy received the lowest grades in their training programs.*

## THE LEVELS
## OF PROFESSIONAL NOURISHMENT

The person at a crisis point in his life is so desperate for the help that he cannot find in his environment that he turns to professional helpers. In some cases his desperation reaches the point at which he is willing to pay for the kind of nourishment he cannot find elsewhere. However, the professionals as a whole cannot deliver—even for money.

The inference that something deteriorative happens to trainees in the helping profession is supported by the base data of professional helpers. While there is a slight upward trend from the low level immediately following training established in the Bergin and Solomon study (Pierce, 1966) —a trend which is perhaps a correlate of experiences in the field—*there is a direct suggestion that the professional teachers, counselors, and therapists*

*involved never again achieve the level of functioning on the relevant thera-*
*peutic process variables that they had on entering graduate school.*

Teachers in a classroom setting function at approximately level 2 in spite
of the fact that it has been long known experientially, and is now known
empirically that the facilitative dimensions of empathy, positive regard, and
genuineness are related to intel!ective achievement as well as to more
psychological indexes (Aspy, 1966; Aspy and Hadlock, 1966). School
guidance counselors, the persons to whom the students should be able to
turn in a time of need, function slightly below level 2 in their counseling
(Martin and Carkhuff, 1967).

Again, at best, the professional helpers in the educational setting offer
less than facilitative levels of the effective ingredients of constructive change
or gain. Thus, there is only communication of a superficial understanding,
and little respect for the other person. An ingenuine relationship leads only
to vague, abstract, and mechanical explorations of personally relevant material.

Professional counselors and therapists in the field relate at slightly (but
perhaps not functionally or significantly) higher than level 2, which may
reflect the effect of selection and/or situational variables (Carkhuff,
1967b). A further breakdown of this data indicates that outpatient
counselors and therapists function slightly above level 2, while inpatient
practitioners function slightly below level 2, which may again reflect
selection and/or situational variables. In addition, the more prominent
therapists in the group function slightly higher than the less prominent.
Furthermore, the existentially oriented therapists and the client-centered
counselors function midway between levels 2 and 3; the psychoanalytic
therapists function slightly above level 2; a group of other counselors and
therapists, including vocational counselors, function at approximately level
2; and counselors and therapists with a behavioristic orientation function
below level 2. Again, even when persons are so desperate that they reach
into financial resources to pay for professional help, they do not receive in
return levels of human nourishment sufficient to effect constructive change
or gain.

## THE GAME OF LIFESAVING

If counselors and psychotherapists functioned in real life the way
most of them do in the therapeutic hour, they would be patients. The
professional helpers to whom we turn because human sustenance is not
available in the general environment are themselves functioning at ineffectual levels of those dimensions related to constructive change or gain. Beyond their counseling and psychotherapy, their distorted perceptions and
communications lead to the deterioration of their own significant human

relationships. They find the same lack of personal fulfillment in their daily living that their clients do. Perhaps most important, they cannot allow the clients to find more in life than they themselves have found.

The crises of counseling and psychotherapy may be likened to those of the person floundering in the water several hundred yards off shore. Perhaps the distressed person does not know how to swim or, knowing how, simply does not have enough strength to make it to shore. Our professional lifeguards, it seems, do not know how to swim themselves. To be sure, they have been given extensive training in many lifesaving techniques, all of which they have tested in the children's pool. They know how to row a boat; they know how to throw out a ring buoy; they know how to give artificial respiration. But they do not know how to swim themselves. They cannot save another because, given the same circumstances, they could not save themselves.

In their lifesaving training, our counselors learn instead the game of therapy, an elaborate game involving numerous mazes, many of which are dead-end. The object of the game is to find that path which allows the counselor and client to communicate in some indirect way. In the less fortunate cases, the game takes the form of a counselor's soliloquy, since the counselor already knows which route is the correct one, and the client does not. In the more fortunate cases, the client moves into proper position and receives the benefits of the particular orientation and techniques which are available to him.

The theory and technique are represented by an interrelation in the complex mazes of the roles, *not the "beings,"* of counselor and client. The theory and technique are calculated to prevent direct and honest communication between two parties. Indeed, there is no communication at all unless the client fits his prescribed role. *No human being, client or counselor, can be incorporated in a role.* The communication in counseling and therapy is from the role of the counselor to the role of the client and vice versa, with each groping not so much to "touch" as to protect themselves.

The shortest distance between two points remains a straight line. *The most effective communication between two human beings is direct and honest communication.*

> . . . how pathetic it is to hear the therapist remark that he almost laughed, cried, got angry. What would happen to a child who was raised by a parent who almost expressed his real being. The child might turn out to be *almost* human! (Douds, 1967, p. 5)

A patient is "almost honest." His counselor, unfortunately, is most often dishonest. If the patient were fully honest he would acknowledge the dishonesty of his counselor, and he would not enter the lifesaving game.

## THE GAME OF LIFE

Society's umbrella extends over all areas of human endeavor. In its rules and regulations and in the role models which it presents for emulation, society replaces the individual experience with its collective experience. To be sure, the collective experience contains within itself enough truths to insure its self-perpetuation. However, as counselors and clients become more whole, they learn to discriminate the myths of life from life itself.

The myths tell us that what is neutral is good; what is marginal is bad; what is vulnerable and sensitized is sensitive; what is communicated in low, modulated tones is warm and respectful; and what is rational is genuine. When we look at our collective product, we find only a weak and impotent person no more capable of helping another than he is of helping himself.

The myths tell us that counseling and psychotherapy are most likely to rehabilitate the troubled person. They provide us with impotent role models—the shadowy figure of the analyst and the reflective mirror-image or alter ego of the client-centered practitioner. They provide us with tests which have answers about people, so that the individual takes personality, aptitude, and interest tests in order to determine where he should go and what he should do, and satisfaction inventories in order to find out whether he has made the appropriate choice, all of which should enable him to conclude at the end of his sixty-eight years of existence that he has lived a "reasonable life." When we look at the data, we find that *troubled people, both children and adults, are as likely to be rehabilitated if they are left alone as if they are treated in professional counseling and psychotherapy* (Eysenck, 1952, 1960, 1965; Levitt, 1957, 1963).

The myths tell us that clients can only benefit from experienced and professional practitioners in the human relations areas. When we look at the data, we find that *counseling and psychotherapy can have constructive or deteriorative consequences for clients, and these changes can be accounted for by the level of the therapist's functioning on facilitative dimensions, and independently of the therapist's orientations;* therapeutic processes may be "for better or for worse" (Carkhuff, 1967a; Carkhuff and Truax, 1966; Truax and Carkhuff, 1963, 1964, 1966).

The myths tell us that in order to become effective practitioners we must spend many years and thousands of hours learning all that is learnable in the areas of counseling and psychotherapy. The trainee proceeds to invest himself in a highly intellectual, ritualistic experience, learning by rote one theory or another, and related techniques. When we look at the data, we find that while *there are no training programs which have demonstrated their efficacy in terms of a translation to client benefits, there is a suggestion that on those dimensions related to constructive client change or gain, the trainees deteriorate in functioning* (Bergin and Solomon, 1963; Carkhuff, 1967a; Carkhuff, Piaget, and Pierce, 1967).

The myths tell us that psychology is the science most concerned with human relations and with discovering the answer to man's problems. Instead of human problems in search of an answer, when we look, we find methodology in search of content, working machinery in search of questions to ask.

The myths tell us that our students can only grow intellectually with intellectually resourceful and knowledgeable teachers. When we look at the data, we find that high-level functioning teachers elicit as much as two and one-half years intellectual or achievement growth in the course of a school year, while teachers functioning at low levels of facilitative conditions may allow only six months of intellectual growth over the course of a year: *students may be facilitated or they may be retarded in their intellectual as well as emotional growth, and these changes can be accounted for by the level of the teacher's functioning on the facilitative dimensions and independently of his knowledgeability;* education may be "for better or for worse," (Aspy, 1966, 1967; Aspy and Kratchovil, 1966; Carkhuff, 1967a).

The myths tell us that academic achievement equals creativity. The teacher, taking the school child by the hand, always says, whether explicitly or implicitly, "I am only trying to help you to become a more creative and productive member of society." When we look at the data, we find that *academic achievement is independent of all other real-life indexes of creative achievement and leadership* (Holland and Richards, 1965).

We could go on. There are many other fraudulent myths, some less harmful than others. However, the necessity for seeing and breaking through the myths of counseling and psychotherapy is of life and death urgency.

## TOWARD HUMAN NOURISHMENT

The data on the levels of human nourishment might not be so imposing were it not for contrasting data based upon the selection and/or training of potent and constructive lifesavers. The fact is that we can select—and train—potent therapeutic agents.

The most potent therapists we have been able to bring together average out around level 4 or above on the five-point scales (Carkhuff, 1967b). It is significant that each of these persons was either thrown out of their graduate training programs or led a very tenuous graduate school existence. These therapists have evolved toward higher levels of effective functioning, in large part, through a continuing open and honest, mutual sharing and discovering process with each other. Each therapist has somehow through his experiences learned to swim on his own, and in turn, contributed and received a sharpening of true lifesaving skills. He does not, however, participate in the game of lifesaving, for he knows too deeply the life and death urgency of his counseling encounters. He knows that if counseling is not an effective way of life for him, he will be unable to enable the client to choose life and find fulfillment in it.

In addition, there is extensive evidence to indicate that in relatively short periods of time, both professional and nonprofessional trainees can be brought to function at minimally facilitative levels. The effective training programs incorporate a heavy experiential emphasis with a focus upon the trainee's own constructive change or gain. In this context, research scales which have been related to therapeutic personality change are employed (Truax and Carkhuff, 1966; Truax, Carkhuff, and Douds, 1964). The trainees learn first to discriminate the levels of the dimensions involved and finally to communicate at high levels of these conditions. The difficulties which the trainees encounter in learning to implement and make operational these dimensions in role-playing and clinical encounters and those which are induced by the discrepancies between their evaluations of their own levels of responding and the feedback of the ratings of others, constitute the basis for many therapeutic inquiries.

A contrast with the apparent deterioration in functioning in the four or more years, or several thousand hours, of the usual graduate training is provided by the results of these training programs. In less than twenty-five hours, both prospective undergraduate dormitory counselors (Berenson, Carkhuff, and Myrus, 1966) and experienced guidance counselors (Martin and Carkhuff, 1967), who were functioning as groups at less than level 2, were brought to function at almost level 3. In the case of the college students, the improvement in interpersonal functioning was significantly greater than that in a training-control group which met for the same number of hours and did everything that the training group did with the exception of incorporating the therapeutic experience and employing the previously validated research scales. Significant gains were reflected on a variety of indexes beyond those involving objective tape ratings. The trainees saw themselves as having changed more constructively than the other groups. The "standard" clients, whom they saw before and after training, discerned the same significant differences between groups. Furthermore, in this case their dormitory roommates felt that the members of the training group were functioning at significantly higher levels following training than did the dormitory roommates of the members of the training-control group or those of a control group which did not meet at all. Thus there was a generalization of the training to all areas of interpersonal relationships. In addition, trainee self-change was reflected in a variety of other ways in both programs, including, for example, constructive change as reflected on the MMPI.

Longer term programs with both clinical psychology graduate students and lay hospital attendants established that both groups could be brought to function at minimally facilitative levels in less than 100 hours (Carkhuff and Truax, 1965a), and these conditions translated directly to patient benefits, as assessed by outcome indexes (Carkhuff and Truax, 1965b). We would hypothesize that the gains accomplished by the trainees here would be retained longer than the shorter-term programs, in large part because not enough trainee change has been effected for the short-term trainees to have incorporated the conditions as a way of life. Furthermore, the levels of interpersonal functioning accomplished will be modified by whether or not the environment supported or reinforced the continued communication of these conditions.

In summary, then, personal difficulties evolve in large part because of a social system which precludes the potent and constructive emergence of the individual, and which reinforces the provision of only the lowest levels of human nourishment in the individual's environment. In his distress, the individual cannot turn to anyone in his environment, simply because even his best friends are functioning at less than effective levels of living. He turns finally, in his urgency, to professional helpers, who have, themselves, not yet recovered from the severely handicapping experience of graduate training and life in an empty society. The professional helpers invite the prospective client to become involved in the game of lifesaving, which, if successful, offers the client no more benefits on the average than if he were not treated at all, and which, if unsuccessful, can have severely retarding effects upon the overall functioning of the client. Providing the client with an honest experience, the very experience which the client requires to free himself, is prohibited because the helpers can no longer be honest and open with themselves.

In contrast, we know that with selection and/or training we can produce potent therapeutic agents who can effect significant constructive client change or gain. We know also that our training programs are only as good as the therapists who conduct them. We know that only persons who are, themselves, powerful swimmers can manage the burden of a drowning person, who often has to be helped against the currents of a social system which would prefer the drowning to potent emergence. We know that only persons who are themselves powerful swimmers can teach and free a person to swim by himself, to enable him to live creatively and productively with his own experience, and perhaps, at a later point, to help another person to shore.

## References

Aspy, D. The relationship between teacher functioning on facilitative dimensions and student performance on intellective indices. Unpublished dissertation, Univer. of Kentucky, 1966.

Aspy, D. Counseling and education. In R. R. Carkhuff (Ed.), *The counselor's contribution to facilitative processes*, Urbana, Ill.: Parkinson, 1967. Chapter 12.

Aspy, D., and W. Hadlock. The effects of high and low functioning teachers upon student academic performance and truancy. Unpublished manuscript, Univer. of Florida, 1966.

Berenson, B. G., R. R. Carkhuff, and Pamela Myrus. The interpersonal functioning and training of college students. *J. counsel. Psychol.*, 1966, *13*, 441–446.

Bergin, A., and Sandra Solomon. Personality and performance correlates of empathic understanding in psychotherapy. *Amer. Psychol.* 1963, *18*, 393.

Carkhuff, R. R. *The counselor's contribution to facilitative processes.* Urbana, Ill.: Parkinson, 1967. (a)

Carkhuff, R. R. A survey of the levels of facilitative functioning of counselors and psychotherapists. Unpublished data, State Univer. of New York at Buffalo, 1967. (b)

Carkhuff, R. R., G. Piaget, and R. Pierce. The development of skills in interpersonal functioning. *Couns. educ. superv.* in press, 1967.

Carkhuff, R. R., and C. B. Truax. Training in counseling and psychotherapy: An evaluation of an integrated didactic and experiential approach. *J. consult. Psychol.*, 1965, *29*, 333–336. (a)

Carkhuff, R. R., and C. B. Truax. Lay mental health counseling: The effects of lay group counseling. *J. of consult. Psychol.*, 1965, *29*, 426–431. (b)

Carkhuff, R. R., and C. B. Truax. Toward explaining success and failure in interpersonal learning experiences. *Personnel guid. J.*, 1966, *46*, 723–728.

Douds, J. Counseling and real life. In *The counselor's contribution to facilitative processes*. Urbana, Ill.: Parkinson, 1967, Chapter 13.

Department of Health, Education and Welfare. *Patients in mental institutions*, 1958, Washington, D. C.: Public Health Service, 1960.

Eysenck, H. J. The effects of psychotherapy: An evaluation. *J. consult. Psychol.*, 1952, *16*, 319–324.

Eysenck, H. J. The effects of psychotherapy. In H. J. Eysenck (Ed.), *The handbook of abnormal psychology*, New York: Basic Books, 1960.

Eysenck, H. J. The effects of psychotherapy. *Int. J. Psychother.*, 1965, *1*, 99–178.

Holder, T., R. R. Carkhuff, and B. G. Berenson. The differential effects of the experimental manipulation of therapeutic conditions upon high and low functioning clients. *J. counsel. Psychol.*, 1967, *14*, 63–66.

Holland, J. L., and J. M. Richards. Academic and nonacademic accomplishment: Correlated or uncorrelated? *J. educ. Psychol.*, 1965, *56*, 165–174.

Kratochvil, D., D. Aspy, and R. R. Carkhuff. The effect of absolute level and direction of change in counselor functioning upon client functioning. *J. clin. Psychol.*, 1967, *23*, 216–218.

Leighton, Dorothea C. The distribution of psychiatric symptoms in a small town. *Amer. J. Psychiat.*, 1956, *112*, 716–723.

Levitt, E. E. The results of psychotherapy with children. *J. consult. Psychol.*, 1957, *21*, 189–196.

Levitt, E. E. Psychotherapy with children: A further evaluation. *Behav. Res. Ther.*, 1963, *1*, 45–51.

Martin, J. C., and R. R. Carkhuff. The effect upon personality and interpersonal functioning in a summer practicum for guidance counselors. *J. clin. Psychol.*, in press, 1967.

Martin, J. C., R. R. Carkhuff, and B. G. Berenson. Process variables in counseling and friendship. *J. counsel. Psychol.*, 1966, *13*, 356–359.

Pagell, W., R. R. Carkhuff, and B. G. Berenson. Therapist-offered conditions and patient development. *J. clin. Psychol.*, in press, 1967.

Piaget, G., B. G. Berenson, and R. R. Carkhuff. The differential effects of high and low functioning counselors upon high and low functioning clients. *J. consult. Psychol.*, in press, 1967.

Pierce, R. An investigation of grade-point average and therapeutic process variables. Unpublished dissertation, Univer. of Massachusetts, 1966.

Pierce, R., R. R. Carkhuff, and B. G. Berenson. The effects of differential levels of therapist-offered conditions upon lay mental health counselors in training. *J. clin. Psychol.*, 1967, *23*, 212–215.

Schofield, W. *Psychotherapy: The purchase of friendship.* Englewood Cliffs, N. J.: Prentice-Hall, 1964.

Srole, L., T. S. Lagner, S. T. Michael, M. K. Opler, and T. A. C. Rennie. *Mental health in the metropolis: The midtown Manhattan study.* New York: McGraw-Hill, 1962.

Truax, C. B., and R. R. Carkhuff. For better or for worse: The process of psychotherapeutic personality change. In *Recent advances in the study of behavior change.* Montreal: McGill Univer. Press, 1963, Chapter 8.

Truax, C. B., and R. R. Carkhuff. Significant developments in psychotherapy research. In L. E. Abt and B. F. Reiss (Eds.). *Progress in clinical psychology.* New York: Grune & Stratton, 1964, Chapter 7.

Truax, C. B., and R. R. Carkhuff. *An introduction to counseling and psychotherapy: training and practice.* Chicago: Aldine, 1966.

Truax, C. B., R. R. Carkhuff, and J. Douds. Toward an integration of didactic and experiential approaches to training in counseling and psychotherapy. *J. counsel. Psychol.*, 1964, *11*, 140–147.

# SECTION TWO

# Toward a Comprehensive Model
# of Facilitative Processes

An integral part of viewing counseling as a way of life involves the attempt to develop—both in inductive generalizations from a stable body of phenomena and in the deductive qualifications through hypotheses testing—meaningful, and comprehensive cognitive models. In Chapter 2 we present a model for primary factors, or a central core of facilitative dimensions around which secondary factors involving a variety of potential preferred modes of treatment can be built. The evidence supporting the core conditions' relationship with constructive change is extensive. The implications of the potential preferred modes of treatment are profound. The multidimensional model for counseling and therapy is considered at length in Chapter 3. Counselor, client, and contextual variables are explored. Both client and counselor are assessed on the same dimensions of interpersonal functioning, and differential predictions are generated and research evidence presented for counselor-client differences. Perhaps most important, the effects of the interaction of counselor and client variables are considered in practice. In this regard, we would like to make the reader aware of the fact that Dr. Frederick C. Thorne has generously provided us with his attempt to develop etiological equations from which the reader might draw truly relevant client dimensions (see Appendix A).

Chapter 2

> . . . the intent is not to negate, but
> rather to discern, the potentially
> significant contributions of the various
> orientations to counseling and
> psychotherapy and to put them in
> proper perspective in building
> systematically around a common core
> of interpersonal conditions.

## The Dimensions of Counseling

The greatest part of therapeutic effectiveness can be accounted for independently of the counselor's theoretical orientation and technique. *The clients of those counselors offering the highest levels of facilitative dimensions improve, while those of counselors offering the lowest levels deteriorate* on a variety of indexes; that is, with both inpatients and outpatients, those helping processes involving the highest levels of counselor empathy, positive regard, genuineness, concreteness, and other dimensions, elicit the greatest client therapeutic process movement, and ultimately, the greatest constructive client gains or changes (Carkhuff, 1967a; Truax and Carkhuff, 1964a, 1966).

The substantial body of evidence for the central core of facilitative conditions explains in part the puzzling mass of data challenging the efficacy of the helping professions (Eysenck, 1952, 1960, 1965; Levitt, 1957, 1963): together the constructive and deteriorative outcomes each other out, and we find, as Eysenck and Levitt did, that there are no average differences on the change indexes of the treated and the untreated groups. Furthermore, since the conditions of change are not the exclusive property of professional practitioners, they are available from nonprofessional sources. Thus, if the patients in the untreated or control groups studied sought help from attendants, nurses, and others, the untreated groups may not really have been untreated groups. Finally, *in seeking help from nonprofessional sources, the patients stood an excellent chance of receiving functionally the same levels of facilitative dimensions as they might receive from professional helpers.* However, the range of conditions offered by the professional counselors may be greater than that offered by nonprofessional sources. This greater range may be reflected in a greater range of client changes which, again, when averaged out, are not significantly different from the changes effected by nonprofessional practitioners.

Perhaps most important, and often forgotten, is the fact that between 60 and 70 percent of the client populations studied do improve in functioning over a one- to two-year period. In spite of the evidence of the low levels of conditions offered clients, we must attempt to explain client changes, however minimal and however low their absolute level of improved functioning.

## EFFECTIVE LEARNING

There is evidence to suggest that the model involving the central core of facilitative conditions has implications for all interpersonal processes, including, in particular, teacher-student and parent-child relationships (Carkhuff and Truax, 1966). "Children and students of parents, teachers, and other significant persons who offer high levels of facilitative conditions improve (on a variety of change indexes), while those of persons who offer low levels of these conditions deteriorate" (Carkhuff, 1967). We might add that the changes are not reflected on psychological indexes alone. The changes are reflected on intellective indexes, such as achievement, as well (Aspy, 1967). We might put the interrelationships of this model another way:

> The direct implication . . . is that the same dimensions which are effective in other instances of human encounters are effective in the counseling and therapeutic processes. To be sure, while primary variables may be the same, the weights may vary with the given instances of the interpersonal processes involved. It may be, for example, that the teachers' empathic understanding of their students will not be as significant a source of effect as those dimensions will be in childrearing or counseling (Carkhuff, 1967, p. 3.)

Nevertheless, our model dictates that a primary core condition such as empathic understanding is critical to all learning and relearning processes. In addition, secondary dimensions, peculiar to a particular interaction of first person (therapists, counselors, teachers, and parents), second person (clients, students, and children), and situational variables (environmental settings, atmosphere, and so forth) may operate to facilitate or retard the outcomes of the primary process variables. Here, an outstanding example might involve the differential effects of the application of nondirective techniques, or the implementation of the traditional "shadowy" figure of the orthodox analyst with (1) functioning outpatient neurotic populations, and (2) chronic and regressed hospitalized schizophrenic populations. We know from practice and research that the outcomes would be very different.

In addition, there are some direct suggestions that the effectiveness of the therapeutic processes may be accounted for, in large part, by the presentation in counseling and psychotherapy of the inverse of those conditions which led to the client's difficulty or psychopathology in the first place; that is, the individual's problem evolved in some way in the absence of conditions, or in the context of very low levels of facilitative conditions offered by the significant persons in his environment. Thus, for example, the absence of any real comprehensive understanding, respect, or positive regard, genuineness, and concreteness from the "more knowing" persons in the developing child's environment may have led to his present difficulty, and movement toward amelioration of these difficulties ensues when high levels of these conditions are put into effect.

The generalization to other instances of interpersonal processes has much meaning for our understanding of facilitative conditions. If the parent-child and student-teacher relationships (including relationships in graduate training in the helping professions) can be, as counseling and psychotherapy "for better or for worse," and if the differential levels of the central core of facilitative conditions account for most of the efficacy or inefficacy of these processes, then we are talking not so much about the conditions of counseling and psychotherapy as about the conditions of effective and ineffective living. We are not talking about a series of techniques derived from one particular orientation or another. Rather, we are talking about something much more basic. Indeed, it is likely that it is because more human processes of communication have broken down, both within ourselves as counselors as well as within the client, or between counselor and client, that we turn to the employment of techniques in the first place. Thus, the techniques are in large part rehabilitative in nature, and constitute significant sources of effect largely in the context of a breakdown of more natural processes. However, given the breakdown in communication, the techniques, dependent upon their appropriate employment, may operate to free the person once again to experience and communicate high levels of the dimensions of effective living. In this regard, let us take another look at the central core of facilitative dimensions.

## THE PRIMARY CORE DIMENSIONS

While techniques may be learned and employed to communicate the primary core of facilitative dimensions, the dimensions themselves are integrated parts of the human personality. Although we attend to the dimensions as individual and distinctive units, the dimensions converge at high levels in the healthy personality and at low levels in the unhealthy person. In more moderate ranges, the individuals may function at relatively high levels on some dimensions and low levels on others.

In general, we might hypothesize that the levels at which an individual functions with others reflect the levels of his attitudes and comprehension of himself; that is, the individual is as empathic, respectful, and genuine concerning a wide range of feelings and experiences in others as he is concerning a wide range of feelings in himself. The individual's understanding and attitudes toward himself underscore the need for therapeutic process involvement of those not functioning at self-sustaining levels of minimally facilitative conditions. The individual's understanding and attitudes toward others underscore the need for training in the discrimination and communication of high levels of conditions, even for those individuals who have healthy attitudes and understanding of themselves, and especially for those who wish to function in a helping role.

### Empathy

With empathic understanding, where the first person or counselor strives to respond with great frequency to the other person's deeper feelings as well as his superficial feelings, we find a number of important dynamics that emphasize the underlying understanding of the individual therapist for himself and others, and de-emphasize the techniques employed to communicate this understanding. We find, for example, that the therapist's final, not his initial, level of empathic understanding is related to patient improvement in therapy (Cartwright and Lerner, 1963). The implication is that ultimately, the therapist's effectiveness is related to his continuing depth of understanding rather than to his ability to "technique it" during early phases of therapy. Indeed, too much empathy too early in therapy may have a deleterious effect upon patient development (Truax and Carkhuff, 1963), because it may create too much tension or anxiety in the client. On the other hand, there is a direct suggestion that there exists an optimum amount of empathy beyond which too little psychological tension will exist to initiate a process of constructive change (Bordin, 1955; Wolberg, 1954). Thus, as the therapist proceeds with his client to explore previously unexplored areas of human living and human relationships, it is his communication of his ever-growing awareness of the client, and of himself in relation to the client, which provides the client with the experiential base for change (Carlton, 1967). With communicative skills, the therapist's self-understanding will translate directly to his ability to "tune in" on the client's wavelength and thus overcome the alienation and isolation characterizing the person in need of help. In the context of an understanding relationship, the client is helped to clear up distorted perceptions and their underlying assumptive bases, and ultimately, hopefully, to effect corrective action and constructive change. We must emphasize that empathy is not the client-centered mode of reflection with which it is most often confused. Concerning the effectiveness of techniques of communication, in general, it is important to note that a convergence of client-centered and psychoanalytic thinking has produced the measures of empathic understanding most highly related to the relevant indexes of client change or gain (Truax and Carkhuff, 1964a); that is, the measures of empathy most highly predictive of change integrate the client-centered notion of the reflection of feelings and the analytic emphasis upon diagnostic accuracy. In this regard, there is evidence to suggest that the mode of communicating empathic understanding which approximates the depth reflection of the client-centered school and the moderate interpretation of the psychoanalytic orientation appears to be of the greatest potentially demonstrable efficacy (Bergin, 1966). The emphasis, then, is upon movement to levels of feeling and experience deeper than those communicated by the client, yet within a range of expression which the client can constructively employ for his own purposes. The therapist's ability to communicate at high levels of empathic understanding appears to involve the therapist's ability to allow himself to experience or merge in the experience of the client, reflect upon this experience while suspending his own judgments, tolerating his own anxiety, and communicating this understanding to the client (Fox and Goldin, 1964; Katz, 1963; Truax and Carkhuff, 1966). In sum, Allerand (1964) underscores the point that it is the manner of the therapist, not his theory or technique, which communicates understanding and fosters growth: "The therapist can best convey his understanding of the patient's situation by being fully human himself and not reacting mechanically by reflecting the patient's words or just intellectually understanding problems."

### Respect

Respect or positive regard, in turn, has its origin in the respect which the individual has for himself. He cannot respect the feelings and experiences of others if he cannot respect his own feelings and experiences.

If the significant adult figures of his early environment did not communicate this respect, often the individual must, in his adult years, move through a process of therapeutic personality change involving the communication of respect to attain high self-regard. In addition, the communication of respect appears to shatter the isolation of the individual and to establish a basis for empathy. There are strong indications that the communication of human warmth and understanding are the principal vehicles for communicating respect (Pierce, 1966). In this regard, Raush and Bordin (1957) suggest that there are three critical components involved in the communication of warmth: (1) the therapist's commitment, (2) his effort to understand, and (3) spontaneity. They present evidence to indicate that it is the therapist's effort to understand which communicates respect and is the major tie between the therapist and the client. The work of Norvas and Landfield (1962) indicates that those therapists whose communications of warmth incorporate understanding have the greatest success in therapy. The very deep respect for the other person's worth as a person and his rights as a free individual, is often subsumed under terms such as "unconditional positive regard" or "nonpossessive warmth." However, these constructs appear at least to be superfluous and at most to be misnomers. In this regard, Spotts (Rogers, 1962) has presented evidence to indicate that positive regard accounts for all of the variability or effectiveness of unconditionality. Unconditionality would, instead, appear to be nothing more than the initial suspension of potentially psychonoxious feelings, attitudes, and judgments by the "more knowing" person in all significant interactions with "less knowing" persons. If the person does indeed have respect for his own feelings and experiences and those of others, he will communicate this respect over a continuing period of interaction. In this context, Waskow (1963) has established that under some circumstances with some client populations, the most "judgmental" counselors elicit the greater depth of client self-exploration and experiencing. Again, respect can be communicated in many modalities. We must emphasize that it is not always communicated in warm, modulated tones of voice; it may be communicated, for example, in anger. In the final analysis, it is the client's experience of the expression that counts, and the client may experience the therapist's attempt to share his own experience fully as an indication of the therapist's respect for the client's level of development.

### Genuineness

The distinction between how a therapist says what he says and how much of his own personality he reveals through his statements is made by Barrett-Lennard (1962), and underscores the degree to which the therapist's statements appear to reflect his true feelings. "The degree to which one person is functionally integrated in the context of his relationship with another, such that there is an absence of conflict or inconsistency between his total experience, his awareness and his overt communication is his congruence in the relationship." In short, the base for the entire therapeutic process is the establishment of a genuine relationship between therapist and client (Martin, 1967; Truax and Carkhuff, 1966). The degree to which the therapist can be honest with himself and, thus, with the client, establishes this base. However, a construct of genuineness must be differentiated from the construct of facilitative genuineness (Carkhuff, 1967). Obviously, the degree to which an individual is aware of his own experience will be related to the degree to which he can enable another person to become aware of his experience. However, many destructive persons are in full contact with their experience; that is, they are destructive when they are genuine. The potentially deleterious effects of genuineness have been established in some research inquiries (Truax, Carkhuff, and Kodman, 1965). Hence, the emphasis upon the therapist's being freely and deeply himself in a nonexploitative relationship incorporates one critical qualification: when his only genuine responses are negative in regard to the second person, the therapist makes an effort to employ his responses constructively as a basis for further inquiry for the therapist, the client, and their relationship. In addition, there is evidence to suggest that whereas low levels of genuineness are clearly impediments to client progress in therapy, above a certain minimum level, very high levels of genuineness are not related to additional increases in client functioning (Truax and Carkhuff, 1964a). Therefore, while it appears of critical importance to avoid the conscious or unconscious façade of "playing the therapeutic role," the necessity for the therapist's expressing himself fully at all times is not supported. Again, genuineness must not be confused, as is so often done, with free license for the therapist to do what he will in therapy, especially to express hostility. Therapy is not for the therapist. The therapist does not operate in vacuo. When he crosses the threshold of the conference room, he serves the client and must be guided by what is effective for the client. With a very brittle client leading a very tenuous existence, the therapist may withhold some very genuine responses. Nevertheless, in his therapy he is continually working toward a more equalitarian, fully-sharing relationship. *If there can be no authenticity in therapy, then there can be no authenticity in life.*

## Concreteness

Concreteness or specificity of expression, a variable which is largely under the therapist's direct control, involves the fluent, direct, and complete expression of specific feelings and experiences, regardless of their emotional content, by both therapist and client. This dimension appears to serve at least three important functions. First, the therapist's concreteness ensures that his response does not become too far removed emotionally from the client's feelings and experiences. Second, concreteness encourages the therapist to be more accurate in his understanding of the client, and thus misunderstandings can be clarified and corrections made when the feelings and experiences are stated in specific terms. Third, the client is directly influenced to attend specifically to problem areas and emotional conflicts (Carkhuff and Truax, 1966). In at least one study, concreteness emerged as the most significant contributor to effective therapy, far outweighing the contributions of empathy, positive regard, and genuineness (Truax and Carkhuff, 1964b). Perhaps the most significant qualification upon this variable is that the material must be of personally meaningful relevance to the client (Carkhuff, 1967). In addition, while concreteness is of significant value during the early phases of counseling and psychotherapy, it may be of less or little value when unconscious material is later dealt with. In this context, Pope and Siegman (1962) suggest that therapist specificity may be anxiety-reducing when the content area is neutral, but anxiety-arousing when the material is emotion-laden. Of all of the dimensions, it would appear that we could most easily train therapists to function at high levels of concreteness because it is less tied to the personality makeup or life style of the therapist.

There are a variety of other dimensions for which we have varying support, some related and some unrelated to the core dimensions. These dimensions constitute possible or potential primary dimensions. Their relationship to constructive client change indexes remains, for the most part, to be explored. However, there exists some tentative evidence indicating the effectiveness in some situations of therapist self-disclosure (Barrett-Lennard, 1961; Dickenson, 1965; Jourard, 1964; Martin, 1967), a dimension related to genuineness, in which the therapist (with discriminations concerning the client's interests and concerns), freely volunteers his personal ideas, attitudes, and experiences which reveal him, to a client, as a unique individual. Other dimensions, less easily operationalized in assessment devices, but nevertheless of potentially critical importance to therapeutic processes, include therapist confidence, spontaneity, and intensity (Barnard, 1967), openness and flexibility (Piaget, 1967), and commitment to the client (Berenson and Carkhuff, 1967).

## HIGH AND LOW LEVELS
## OF FUNCTIONING: ILLUSTRATIONS

The following series of excerpts from initial counseling encounters will serve to illustrate examples of minimally facilitative and lower levels

of functioning in counseling and therapy. As the reader will note, each excerpt begins with the client's expression of a similar problem or feeling. In
addition, the excerpts demonstrate and can be rated on all therapist-offered
dimensions: empathy, positive regard, genuineness, and concreteness. The
first excerpt involves a somewhat depressed client in her initial therapeutic
encounter with a therapist functioning at minimally facilitative levels or
above:

CLIENT: Sometimes I just get so depressed I just don't know what to do.
THERAPIST: Sometimes you feel like you're never going to get up again.
CLIENT: Right. I just don't know what to do with myself. What am I going
to do?
THERAPIST: I guess in some ways that—that I've had—I've had the same
kind of experience already . . . I guess there have been points where I
found life hopeless—but I have found that being able to talk with
somebody about this and to talk about some of the specifics involved
has been very helpful to me.
CLIENT: But how is that going to solve my problems? My father hates
me—and he punishes me—and he doesn't trust me and he won't let me
marry the fellow I want to marry. He says he's no good. . . .

This brief excerpt of a helping relationship would be rated at minimally
facilitative levels of interpersonal functioning. As can be seen, the therapist
not only attempts to communicate understanding and respect in a genuine
fashion, but also attempts, in a moderately self-disclosing manner, to lead
the client into a more specific discussion of her difficulties, which she does.
  In the following excerpt, the therapist is not quite so accurate, and as a
consequence does not elicit meaningful self-exploration from a young
woman client.

CLIENT: Sometimes I get so depressed I just don't know what to do with
myself.
THERAPIST: Everyone feels that way once in a while.
CLIENT: Yes, but—but—this time I'm really—really as low as I think I can
ever get.
THERAPIST: You know you don't have to stay this way all the time.
CLIENT: Yes, but—somehow I get the feeling that you don't really want to
hear about what's bothering me.
THERAPIST: Sure I do, but everyone has his ups and downs—maybe you
can tell me about your ups and downs—what experiences you've
had. . . .
CLIENT: (pause): Well, I guess it's true that—that—sometimes I feel better
than at other times—uh—but sometimes I'm way up, then sometimes I
hit the bottom.

The therapist makes generalizations of the client's experience which leave the client, herself, out of the picture. He does not communicate facilitative levels of empathy and respect in his not-so-subtle attempt to shape the client's responses to be congruent with his experience. In response, the client appears confused over whether to continue or not. Finally, she does, but in doing so, she explores herself very cautiously in a very abstract fashion.

In the following excerpt, the therapist functions at an even lower level and elicits only reluctant concessions from the female client in her early twenties.

CLIENT: Sometimes I get so depressed I don't know where I am going.

THERAPIST: Well, you know it's around exam time and lots of kids get feeling a little down at this time of year.

CLIENT: Yea, but this is nothing to do with exams. That's not even bothering me.

THERAPIST: You mean none of the exams are bothering you? Surely one of them must be bothering you!

CLIENT: Well, I'm having a little trouble with French this semester, but it's really nothing to get worried about. I think I'm doing fairly well in it. Uh—it's—that's not really what's bugging me so much.

THERAPIST: Well . . . lots of students have trouble in French—especially here at this school.

CLIENT: Well, I don't know . . . I . . . uh . . . got an A in French last semester and . . . uh . . . I think even if I goof up the exam . . . terribly, I shouldn't get less than a C . . . but . . . uh . . . if you say that's what's bothering me—maybe, maybe it is! But I really don't think so.

The therapist responds only from his own preconceived frame of reference which almost totally excludes that of the client. In so doing, he communicates very low levels of empathy and genuine respect, and is unable to make concrete the client's difficulty in any way. The client momentarily entertains the therapist's persistent argument, for that is what it is, but she does not explore herself in problem areas which are important to her.

The following series of excerpts involve a client functioning at a very different feeling tone level. In the first excerpt, a facilitative therapist is responsive to a young girl in her late teens:

CLIENT: I really can't wait to get out of school. I just want to get out and get started and be on my way. I know I'm going to make it one of these days!

THERAPIST: Hey, you sound like you're really going somewhere!

CLIENT: Yup, I'm gonna make it big—I just know it! I just have that feeling!

THERAPIST: Wow—Sky's the limit, huh?

CLIENT: The future looks so darn bright, I just want to get out of school and—and—get into what I want to be doing. I'm so happy, I can't wait for the semester to be over!

THERAPIST: Boy, I can remember that feeling—it's a wonderful feeling. Maybe you can spell out the possibilities and any other things that maybe we can fruitfully consider here.

CLIENT: O.K.—As soon as I get out of school, I'm going to go into fashion designing and—um—the only thing is I have several different possibilities and—um—in different areas, and I don't really know which one I'm going to take.

Again, a minimally facilitative therapist perceives the client with some degree of accuracy and communicates this understanding in a respecting and genuine way. He is self-disclosing in leading the client into concrete and specific discussions of personally relevant material.

In the next excerpt, the therapist is not as accurate in his perceptions and communications to a young woman:

CLIENT: Gee—I can't wait to get out of school—I can hardly contain myself until this semester is over so I can start on my career—I just know—I just know I'm going somewhere. I just have that feeling.

THERAPIST: Boy, it sure would be nice to finish up with this semester.

CLIENT: Yeah, but I'm really excited about the future too—not just getting out of school.

THERAPIST: Most of us get excited about the end of school—especially that last June—school's all over.

CLIENT: Yeah—I guess it would be nice to finish, but—ah. . . .

THERAPIST: Ah—you remember—ah—the nice feeling when there's no classes—no more pencils, no more books . . .

CLIENT: Yeah—"no more teacher's dirty looks". . . .

The generalizations which the therapist makes on the basis of his experience (whether or not they are accurate for him), do not incorporate the client's experience. He does not communicate the levels of facilitative conditions necessary for the client to become involved in effective therapeutic process movement.

The following excerpt finds the therapist functioning at even lower levels in relation to the client who is a girl in her late teens.

CLIENT: I just can't wait to get out of school—I'm so excited I just want to get out and get started on my career. I know I'm going places!

THERAPIST: What's the matter, don't you like school?

CLIENT: Uh . . . it's not really that—it's just that I . . . I just . . . the future is exciting . . . and school is just a means to an end, and I want to get there.

THERAPIST: Well, you know it's not easy for someone to come to another person in the position of authority and tell them about the things they don't like about school.

CLIENT: I guess not for some people but . . . ah . . . that's never been a problem with me.

THERAPIST: It's pretty easy to say it's not me . . . it's always the other fella . . . I don't know. I just don't know about this.

Again, the therapist's preconceived formulations totally exclude the client. He communicates little understanding and no respect for the client's ability to grapple with *her* own experience. The process deteriorates into a verbal argument, with the client finally asking herself whether or not she wants to continue in this relationship.

The next series of excerpts are at a still different feeling tone level. In the first of the series, the therapist is helpful in involving the female client in meaningful problem-expression and an immediacy of experiencing:

CLIENT: I get so mad at my supervisor . . . every time I try . . . I try to come up with some new ideas he knocks me down. He's a bunch of sour grapes!

THERAPIST: Well, he sounds like a real bastard.

CLIENT: That's it . . . that's just what we call him. Oh . . . sometimes I could . . . I just don't know what I would do.

THERAPIST: Boy, you could really let him have it . . . You could just cut loose.

CLIENT: Yeah . . . sometimes I dream about what I would do to him . . . but I can't . . . doggone it, he's got the power of life and death over me.

THERAPIST: And he'd use it, huh!?

CLIENT: Yeah, I guess he would.

THERAPIST: I guess I've been hit like that myself and maybe in different ways. Maybe you can let me know about your situation . . . what's happened here.

CLIENT: Well, for instance, the other day at work I came up with an idea that everyone thought was great . . . it would have saved hundreds, maybe thousands of hours of work and he cut me to ribbons in front of everybody . . . He—he just—can't stand to have anyone better than he. He made me feel like a nothing . . . just dirt. . . .

The therapist is right "with" the client. He quickly grasps where she is and sees the world through her eyes, and in some ways adds to his initial responses, making it possible for her to get her full feelings out. His communications lead the client easily into a meaningful and specific discussion of relevant material.

The next excerpt finds the therapist's feeble and premature attempts to resolve the client's difficulties ineffective:

CLIENT: I just get so mad at my supervisor . . . he's just a bunch of old sour grapes. Everytime I come up with a creative idea, he cuts me down.

THERAPIST: I don't know—there's bound to be conflict between supervisor and employee once in a while.

CLIENT: Yeah . . . I guess so, but he's really nasty, too. He's just a mean old thing.

THERAPIST: Well . . . you know, sometimes supervisors have to be this way. I guess we have to try to understand them . . . uh. . . .

CLIENT: Yeah, I can understand that, but I've never had any trouble in the past, and it seems everybody has this trouble with him. It just can't be that the world is wrong, and he's right.

THERAPIST: Well . . . maybe some people don't have the trouble with him that you do. What does the trouble mean to you, anyway? What does the word "trouble" mean to you anyway?

CLIENT: Well . . . it's just when there's a strain between people . . . when they fight all the time and don't seem to agree on things and . . . uh. . . .

While the therapist seems to want to be helpful, the client finds herself reacting to his phenomenology rather than developing her own. Thus, the therapist offers low levels of conditions, and the client does not become involved in constructive process movement.

Finally, in the last excerpt, the therapist is functioning at very low levels of facilitative conditions with a young male client:

CLIENT: Oh . . . I get so mad at my supervisor—everytime I come up with a creative idea, he cuts me to ribbons. He's just a bunch of old sour grapes!

THERAPIST: I guess you get angry at a lot of people.

CLIENT: Well—no, not really—just at irrational authority.

THERAPIST: But, don't you find irrational authority everywhere?

CLIENT: No . . . no, I don't think so. I came in here angry, and I think I had a right to be angry . . . But you—you don't seem to understand it.

THERAPIST: Well, that's all I'm trying to do . . . simply trying to understand you here. Lots of people define "angry" differently . . . how do you define it?

The therapist is very inaccurate in his grasp of the client's world, rather, his communications appear to reflect his own distorted experience. The therapist communicates negative regard; he is incongruent in a destructive fashion. He is not constructively self-disclosing. He does not lead the client into specific discussions of personally meaningful material.

We can readily see that, depending upon the therapist's early responses, the process may move in different directions, some moving more deeply into the client's experience and some moving away from the client. The poor therapist brings the focus of his own distorted experience; unfortunately, he is not equipped to handle the difficulties which he creates in the relationship. At minimally facilitative levels of functioning, it appears that the therapist's response is *interchangeable* with that of the client. At higher levels, his response actually adds to the client's response and enables the client to move to deeper levels of self-exploration. We could employ the onionskin analogy here, with the therapist enabling the client to move one level beyond where the client is presently functioning. At lower levels of therapist-offered conditions, the therapist simply does not have anything to offer the client. While he sometimes gets part of the client's message, he most often distorts it in his own perceptual system, and subtracts from the client's response with his communication.

## THE DYNAMIC FUNCTIONS
## OF THE CORE DIMENSIONS

The improvement of clients of therapists offering high levels of facilitative conditions can be understood in the number of ways: (1) the facilitative stimulus complex of high conditions elicits client exploration of anxiety-laden material; (2) the anxiety reduction, which takes place when the client explores himself in the context of high levels of facilitative conditions, is reinforcing; (3) therapists who provide high levels of conditions become personally potent reinforcers for the client; (4) the high conditions elicit a high degree of reciprocally positive affect in the client; (5) in general, the conditions shatter the client's experience of isolation and hopelessness.

The client comes to therapy motivated for something that will allay his anxieties and enable him to function more effectively. In therapy the client responds to a complex of stimuli, some which are essential to the acquisition of improved adjustive behaviors, others which are essential to the extinction of maladjustive behaviors. Among the client responses which high levels of therapist-offered conditions nurture and, indeed, elicit, is the process of self-exploration of thoughts and feelings, which have made for difficulty in past social relationships. The client's verbalizations of anxiety-laden material, and the active and spontaneous engagement in an inward probing about newly discovered feelings or experiences about himself and his world is reinforced by (1) the anxiety reduction which takes place when the material is brought up in the context of genuine warmth and understanding—ameliorating conditions which are viewed as the inverse of those conditions which dominated the client's life and which originally contributed to the acquisition of the anxiety; and (2) the improved prospect for the re-establishment of positive social responsiveness.[1] Thus, therapy involves a social relationship in which thoughts and feelings which have made for past pathological behavior are elicited, and, because the therapist is not rejecting, anxiety extinction takes place.

In addition, the therapist who is offering high levels of facilitative conditions emerges as a potent reinforcer. Since reinforcement is intimately related to motivation, the reinforcement value of social approval or disapproval is itself dependent upon the interpersonal relationship. The reinforcement value of the therapist is based upon the client's need for a protective relationship. The therapist who can establish a high-level emotional relationship can capitalize on the client's initial relief and attachment to the therapist (Murray, 1963). As the relationship becomes for the client (and, we might add, for the therapist), a secure one in which he can experience and experiment fully with himself, the therapist can positively reinforce positive affect or extinguish negative affect and self-destructive activities on the part of the client. On the other hand, therapists who are unable to establish such a facilitative atmosphere and relationship are ineffective, and produce deteriorative client change because they are psychonoxious stimuli and serve as aversive reinforcers.

Finally, the facilitative therapists elicit a high degree of positive affect in the client through the principle of reciprocal affect (Truax and Carkhuff, 1966). This positive affect increases the level of the client's positive self-reinforcement and decreases the client's anxiety. In turn, the client communicates higher levels of positive affect to others and, thus, increases the probability of receiving in return positive affect and positive reinforcement

[1]With some clients, high levels of conditions may not constitute the inverse of those conditions which led to the difficulty or psychopathology in the first place. For example, some clients may come from apparently free and permissive homes, and a structured, disciplinary but concerned approach might be most efficacious, at least initially. Alexander (1963) has a great deal to say about the dimensions of these apparent reversal situations. However, the ultimate hope of the therapeutic effort will be to enable the client to become more congruent, understanding, and respectful of himself. In addition, with delinquents, an approach establishing initially that the therapist can make it in the delinquent's world, but chooses finally to relate in a more fulfilling manner, appears warranted (Carkhuff and Douds, 1966).

from others. Therapists who are functioning at low levels of facilitative conditions elicit negative affect in the client, increasing the level of the negative affect communicated to and received from others.

All interview-oriented therapies share a common core of conditions which both elicit and reinforce the client's exploration of himself in those areas which have presented obstacles to his emotional growth and constructive activities. Even (or perhaps especially) the behaviorists require (1) an extensive and intensive self-exploration of the relevant areas of client functioning and dysfunctioning, and (2) the therapist's emergence as a potent reinforcer in his relationship with the client. In the end, the efficacy or inefficacy of therapeutic processes is in large part contingent upon the level of the relationship established. The evidence establishing that the therapist determines the level of facilitative conditions (Truax and Carkhuff, 1963, 1964a, 1965) leads the "tender-minded," more traditional, and clinically oriented practitioners away from their unrealistic preconceptions and toward the more realistic position of accepting the role of the therapist as an influencer, or, to some degree, a controller of behavior; they are led to a more open stance toward the potential mechanisms and understanding offered by a meaningful social learning theory. For their part, the behaviorists of "tough-minded," impersonal schools must recognize the capacity of the facilitative stimulus complex to establish the therapist as a more potent reinforcer, and to elicit a greater client involvement in the therapeutic process.

## THE SECONDARY DIMENSIONS: POTENTIAL PREFERRED MODES OF TREATMENT

Many of the effects on a variety of outcome criteria, which we employ to assess our counseling and psychotherapy, may be accounted for by the primary core dimensions of interpersonal functioning. Although the weights of these dimensions may vary with therapist, client, and contextual variables, preliminary evidence suggests that in the general case, we may be able to account for approximately 20 percent of the variability of a variety of outcome indexes, and for 33 to 50 percent of quasi-outcome indexes such as insight scales (Truax, 1961; Truax and Carkhuff, 1966).

Secondary dimensions may, for some therapists, clients, and situations, singly or in their various interactions, operate to facilitate or retard the effects of the primary conditions. Many of the dominant and currently available treatment approaches incorporate these secondary dimensions. When these treatment approaches are appropriately employed in the context of the facilitative core dimensions, they may contribute significantly to the efficacy of the counseling and therapeutic processes; that is, given a particular interaction pattern of therapist, client, and contextual variables, brief educational or vocational counseling, nondirective therapy, behavioristic conditioning, psychoanalytic therapy, or any one of the many other available approaches, with their full implications concerning goals and techniques, might be "preferred modes of treatment."

On the other hand, inappropriate application of these approaches may retard the effectiveness of the treatment. For example, a nondirective approach may work very effectively, especially during initial contacts, with a highly motivated college student and not at all with an inpatient psychotic patient. Thus, the appropriate application of the approach may

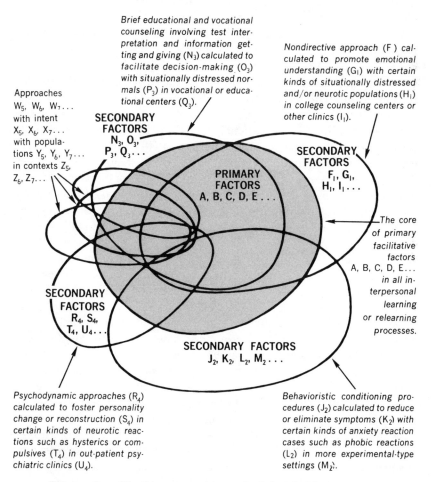

Brief educational and vocational counseling involving test interpretation and information getting and giving ($N_3$) calculated to facilitate decision-making ($O_3$) with situationally distressed normals ($P_3$) in vocational or educational centers ($Q_3$).

Nondirective approach (F) calculated to promote emotional understanding ($G_1$) with certain kinds of situationally distressed and/or neurotic populations ($H_1$) in college counseling centers or other clinics ($I_1$).

Approaches $W_5$, $W_6$, $W_7$... with intent $X_5$, $X_6$, $X_7$... with populations $Y_5$, $Y_6$, $Y_7$... in contexts $Z_5$, $Z_6$, $Z_7$...

**SECONDARY FACTORS**
$N_3$, $O_3$, $P_3$, $Q_3$...

**SECONDARY FACTORS**
$F_1$, $G_1$, $H_1$, $I_1$...

**PRIMARY FACTORS**
A, B, C, D, E...

The core of primary facilitative factors A, B, C, D, E... in all interpersonal learning or relearning processes.

**SECONDARY FACTORS**
$R_4$, $S_4$, $T_4$, $U_4$...

**SECONDARY FACTORS**
$J_2$, $K_2$, $L_2$, $M_2$...

Psychodynamic approaches ($R_4$) calculated to foster personality change or reconstruction ($S_4$) in certain kinds of neurotic reactions such as hysterics or compulsives ($T_4$) in out-patient psychiatric clinics ($U_4$).

Behavioristic conditioning procedures ($J_2$) calculated to reduce or eliminate symptoms ($K_2$) with certain kinds of anxiety reaction cases such as phobic reactions ($L_2$) in more experimental-type settings ($M_2$).

Figure 1. The interpersonal core of primary facilitative factors and some possible examples of secondary factors.

increase the accountable effectiveness, about 10 percent or more, while the inappropriate employment of the approach may contribute nothing or actually detract from the process, and in some way contribute to the deterioration of the client. In the context of high levels of therapist-offered facilitative dimensions, given a meaningful interaction of relevant variables, a variety of treatment approaches may be employed. Figure 1 illustrates the core dimensions and several notable potential preferred modes of treatment. As can be seen, a great part of the effectiveness of any one orientation can be accounted for by the central core of facilitative conditions which each of these orientations hold in common (Carkhuff, 1966; 1967b). Thus, trait-and-factor-oriented vocational and educational counseling, involving information giving and receiving may (with an otherwise functioning client) facilitate and contribute additional effectiveness to a treatment process which involves the need for choice or for decision-making to relieve situational stress. A behavioristic approach involving systematic counterconditioning may be the treatment of choice for the person with an isolated anxiety reaction, such as a phobia, which presents an obstacle to his effective functioning. In other cases, such as with severely disabled inpatients, environmental manipulation from a behavioristic orientation may contribute most effectively. The nondirective and the psychoanalytic approaches seem to make their principal contributions in correcting the distorted perceptions and communications which lead outpatient neurotic-type populations into continual difficulty. An attempt to enumerate the dimensions of the unique contributions, as well as the limitations of each of these approaches, will be made in Section Three.

It is important to note that almost all training programs in the helping professions have built their programs around the secondary dimensions of any one orientation to counseling and psychotherapy. Most clinical psychology, psychiatric, and social work training centers have focused upon psychodynamic thinking and treatment. Very recently, a few psychology and psychiatric programs have come to emphasize the behavioristic approach. Some of the guidance and counseling programs have mistakenly followed one or the other suit. Others have variously concentrated upon the nondirective approach or the trait-and-factor approach to counseling which involves personality, interest and aptitude-testing and interpretation, and "theories" of vocational choice. Given the relevant interaction of variables, each of these orientations may indeed have a unique contribution to make. However, none of these orientations has at this stage demonstrated that they are likely to account for a major part of the variation in the change indexes of most treatment cases.

In addition, while all of the programs must make passing mention of the therapeutic relationship, few devote systematic attention to the primary core dimensions both in (1) the didactic teaching and shaping of behavior, and in (2) providing the experiential therapeutic base for change in their trainees. Again, the intent is not to negate, but rather to discern the potentially significant contributions of the various orientations to counseling and psychotherapy, and to put them in proper perspective in building systematically around a common core of interpersonal conditions.

## References

Alexander, F. The dynamics of psychotherapy in the light of learning theory. *Amer. J. Psychiat.*, 1963, *120*, 440–448.

Allerand, Anne-Marie. Empathy in and out of psychotherapy. Unpublished manuscript, Columbia Teachers College, 1964.

Aspy, D. Counseling and education. In R. Carkhuff (Ed.), *The counselor's contribution to facilitative processes*. Urbana, Ill.: Parkinson, 1967, Chapter 12.

Barrett-Lennard, G. T. Dimensions of therapist response as causal factors in therapeutic change. *Psychol. Monogr.*, 1962, *76*, No. 43.

Barnard, W. M. Counselor spontaneity, confidence and intensity. In R. R. Carkhuff (Ed.), *The counselor's contribution to facilitative processes*. Urbana, Ill.: Parkinson, 1967, Chapter 9.

Berenson, B. G., and R. R. Carkhuff. Counselor commitment. In R. Carkhuff (Ed.), *The counselor's contribution to facilitative processes*. Urbana, Ill.: Parkinson, 1967, Chapter 11.

Bergin, A. E. Some implications of psychotherapeutic research for therapeutic practice. *J. abnorm. soc. Psychol.*, in press, 1966.

Bordin, E. S. Ambiguity as a therapeutic variable. *J. consult. Psychol.*, 1955, *19*, 9–15.

Carkhuff, R. R. Training in counseling and psychotherapy: Requiem or Revielle? *J. counsel. Psychol.*, 1966, *13*, 360–367.

Carkhuff, R. R. *The counselor's contribution to facilitative processes*. Urbana, Ill.: Parkinson, 1967.

Carkhuff, R. R. , and J. Douds. The dilemma of delinquent treatment. Unpublished manuscript, State Univer. of New York at Buffalo, 1967.

Carkhuff, R. R., and C. B. Truax. Toward explaining success and failure in interpersonal experiences. *Personnel guid. J.*, 1966, *46*, 723–728.

Carkhuff, R. R., and C. B. Truax. Concreteness or specificity of expression. In R. R. Carkhuff (Ed.), *The counselor's contribution to facilitative processes*. Urbana, Ill.: Parkinson, 1967, Chapter 6.

Carlton, S. Counselor empathy. In R. R. Carkhuff (Ed.) *The counselor's contribution to facilitative processes*. Urbana, Ill.: Parkinson, 1967.

Cartwright, Rosalind D., and Barbara Lerner. Empathy, need to change and improvement with psychotherapy. *J. consult. Psychol.*, 1963, *27*, 138–144.

Dickenson, W. A. Therapist self-disclosure in individual and group therapy. Unpublished dissertation, Univer. of Kentucky, 1965.

Eysenck, H. J. The effects of psychotherapy: An evaluation. *J. consult. Psychol.*, 1952, *16*, 319–324.

Eysenck, H. J. The effects of psychotherapy. In H. J. Eysenck (Ed.), *Handbook of abnormal psychology,* New York: Basic Books, 1960.

Eysenck, H. J. The effects of psychotherapy. *Int. J. Psychother.*, 1965, *1*, 99–178.

Fox, R. E., and P. C. Goldin. The empathic process in psychotherapy: A survey of theory and research. *J. nerv. ment. Dis.*, 1964, *138*, No. 4.

Jourard, S. *The transparent self.* New York: Van Nostrand, 1964.

Katz, R. L. *Empathy: Its nature and uses.* New York: Free Press, 1963.

Levitt, E. E. The results of psychotherapy with children. *J. consult. Psychol.*, 1957, *21*, 189–196.

Levitt, E. E. Psychotherapy with children: A further evaluation. *Behav. Res. Ther.*, 1963, *1*, 45–51.

Martin, J. C. The communication of genuineness: Counselor self-disclosure. In R. R. Carkhuff (Ed.), *The counselor's contribution to facilitative processes.* Urbana, Ill.: Parkinson, 1967, Chapter 3.

Murray, E. J. Learning theory and psychotherapy: Biotropic versus sociotropic approaches. *J. counsel. Psychol.*, 1963, *10*, 250–255.

Norvas, M., and A. Landfield. Improvement in psychotherapy and adoption of the therapist's meaning system. *Psychol. Rep.*, 1963, *13*, 97–98.

Piaget, G. Openness and flexibility. In R. R. Carkhuff (Ed.), *The counselor's contribution to facilitative processes.* Urbana, Ill.: Parkinson, 1967. Chapter 10.

Pierce, R. Counselor respect. In R. R. Carkhuff (Ed.), *The counselor's contribution to facilitative processes.* Urbana, Ill.: Parkinson, 1967.

Pope, B., and A. W. Siegman. Effect of therapist verbal activity level and specificity on patient productivity and speech disturbance in the initial interview. *J. consult. Psychol.*, 1962, *26*, 489.

Raush, H., and E. S. Bordin. Warmth in personality development and in psychotherapy. *Psychiat.*, 1957, *20*, 351–363.

Rogers, C. R. The interpersonal relationship: The core of guidance. *Harvard educ. Rev.*, 1962, *32*, 416–429.

Truax, C. B. The process of group psychotherapy. *Psychol. Monogr.*, 1961, *75*, No. 14 (Whole No. 511).

Truax, C. B., and R. R. Carkhuff. For better or for worse: The process of psychotherapeutic personality change. In *Recent advances in behavior change.* Montreal: McGill Univer. Press, 1963.

Truax, C. B., and R. R. Carkhuff. Significant developments in psychotherapy research. In *Progress in clinical psychology.* New York: Grune & Stratton, 1964. (a)

Truax, C. B., and R. R. Carkhuff. Concreteness: A neglected variable in research in psychotherapy. *J. clin. Psychol.,* 1964, *20,* 264–267. (b)

Truax, C. B., and R. R. Carkhuff. The experimental manipulation of therapeutic conditions. *J. consult. Psychol.,* 1965, *29,* 119–124.

Truax, C. B., and R. R. Carkhuff. *Introduction to counseling and psychotherapy: Training and practice.* Chicago: Aldine, 1966.

Truax, C. B., R. R. Carkhuff, and F. Kodman. Personality change in hospitalized mental patients during group psychotherapy as a function of the use of alternate sessions and vicarious therapy pretraining. *J. clin. Psychol.* 1965, *21,* 225–228.

Waskow, Irene E. Counselor attitudes and client behavior. *J. consult. Psychol.,* 1963, *27,* 405–412.

Wolberg, L. *The technique of psychotherapy.* New York: Grune & Stratton, 1954.

Chapter **3**

> . . . Our conception of the distressed
> client is analagous to our
> conception of the retarding parent,
> teacher, or counselor.

## A Model for Counseling

Traditional diagnostic categories and other dimensions of personality bear no relationship to current modes of therapeutic treatment. Experientially, as clinicians, we know that we often initiate acts characteristic of our own life style with all of our clients (and we may add, for those who expect the same generalization of effective living in therapy to real life which we expect from our clients, to people in general). Yet, to be sure, those among us who are successful are shaped in our continuing interactions by what is therapeutically effective, for ourselves as well as for our clients.

The development of the concepts involving a central core of facilitative conditions around which potential preferred modes of treatment are built forces us to expand our model to consider meaningful client and situational variables (Carkhuff, 1967b). We are suggesting, then, that client movement is, in large part, accounted for by the level of the therapist's functioning on the core conditions. What are the variables relevant to the client's level of functioning? We are suggesting that, given particular interaction patterns of relevant variables, a variety of counseling and psychotherapeutic approaches may constitute additional sources of effect in accounting for a separate and significant amount of the variability in the change indexes. What are the relevant client and situational variables which dictate the employment of one or the other of the available treatment approaches? In other words, we must ask, "With which clients and under what conditions do we employ a given treatment process as the best potential mode available to us?"

## A MULTIDIMENSIONAL MODEL

A comprehensive model of facilitative processes must take into consideration—first person variables (parents, teachers, counselors, and therapists), second person variables (children, students, and clients), and contextual variables, alone and in their various interactions. Thus, in counseling and psychotherapy:

> The therapist's personal characteristics, such as age, sex, and socio-economic status, as well as specialized techniques and other specific influences upon his role concept are relevant. The therapist variables, in turn, may be meaningful insofar as they interact with client characteristics, including especially population types in addition to other personal characteristics. Situation variables, such as the environmental setting and "atmosphere" in which therapy takes place as well as the "set" which the client has or has been given . . . might also become extremely potent considerations (Carkhuff, 1963).

Among these variables, we know that those related most extensively to a variety of second person change indexes employed to assess outcome involve those dimensions of the central core of facilitative conditions offered by the first person. Thus, those facilitators offering the highest levels of facilitative conditions tend to involve the persons to whom they are relating in a process leading to constructive behavior change or gain, both affective and cognitive, or intellective. At the highest levels, these facilitators communicate an accurately empathic understanding of the deeper as well as the superficial feelings of the second person(s); they are freely and deeply themselves in a nonexploitative relationship; they communicate a very deep respect for the second person's worth as a person and his rights as a free individual; and they are helpful in guiding the discussion to personally relevant feelings and experiences in specific and concrete terms. These facilitators, are, ideally, our parents, teachers, or counselors. We say "ideally," because many parents, teachers, and counselors offer very low levels of these conditions; others offer only some of these conditions at relatively high levels and other conditions at relatively low levels. Consider, for example, the typical harassed guidance counselor in many of our educational systems throughout the country.

Because of time and treatment limitations, his contribution may be tied to possibly high levels of concreteness and specificity at which he operates rather than to his accurate empathic understanding of the client.

Let us contrast, for the moment, our conception of the facilitator with a stereotype of the client in need of help. Not necessarily, but often, with varying degrees, the client brings a distorted frame of reference to most human encounters. Many of his verbalizations are unrelated to what he is feeling at the moment. When his responses are genuine, they are negative with regard to the second person, and he appears unable to employ them as a basis for further open-ended and meaningful inquiry. In general, he responds to other persons in such a way as to communicate little positive regard, and he deals with feelings and experiences in vague and abstract terms. It may by now have become apparent that we are describing the client on the same dimensions as we previously described our counselor; the client, however, is several levels below the facilitator. In short, our conception of the distressed client is analogous to our conception of the retarding parent, teacher, or counselor, and is contrasted with the facilitative parent, teacher, or counselor.

We have rewritten and modified extensively, earlier versions of scales specifically intended to assess the level of therapeutic functioning in order to apply them to all interpersonal processes. For our own purposes, we have incorporated five levels of functioning, with the lower levels being essentially commensurate with the description of the distressed client or retarding therapist, and the higher levels commensurate with the facilitative individual, whatever his label. On all of the scales, level 3 constitutes the minimal level of facilitative functioning. Thus, level 1 describes not only the retarding therapist, but also the severely disturbed client who is essentially immune to constructive human encounters. Level 2 describes the more moderately retarding therapist or distressed client who, unlike the level 1 person, lives in a world of distortion but does *live in the world* and is not oblivious to his world; level 3 describes the minimally facilitative therapist or the situationally distressed client who, for all other purposes, is functioning at a minimally effective level. Level 4 may characterize the more potent individual who relates effectively and "makes things happen," whatever his area of endeavor, but including in particular the facilitation of other persons. The level 5 person, in turn, is involved in a lifelong search for actualization for others as well as himself, and is readily amenable to the sharing of his search with others. In summary, then, whether he is client or therapist, student or teacher, child or parent, these (or similar) scales may be employed to assess the person's level of interpersonal functioning. The implications for a comprehensive model of facilitative processes are profound.

In Figure 2, we see that at each point of significant interactions in the

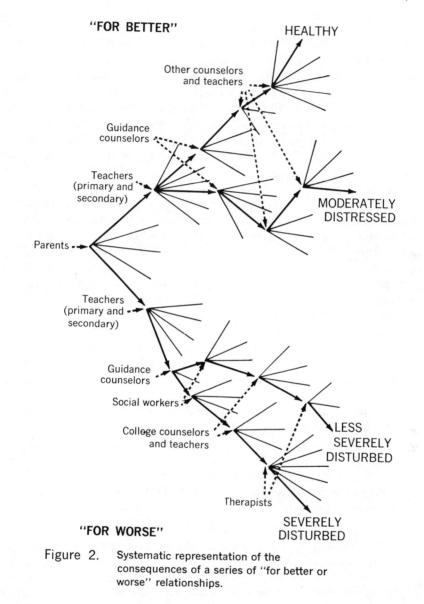

"FOR BETTER"   HEALTHY

Other counselors
and teachers

Guidance
counselors

Teachers
(primary and
secondary)

MODERATELY
DISTRESSED

Parents

Teachers
(primary and
secondary)

Guidance
counselors

Social workers

College counselors
and teachers

LESS
SEVERELY
DISTURBED

Therapists

"FOR WORSE"   SEVERELY
DISTURBED

Figure 2.   Systematic representation of the
consequences of a series of "for better or
worse" relationships.

individual's development, the consequences may be "for better or for worse"; that is, if we assume that the individual has the inherent capacity to be influenced in constructive or destructive directions, then each encounter with those significant persons designated by society as "more knowing" may have constructive or deteriorative consequences for the "less knowing" person. The assumption that the individual does not begin with a disposition toward either constructive growth or destructiveness is illustrated by a third-dimensional point of origin in the child's development. Only as the child grows outward does he move in a positive or negative direction. Thus, the dominance of high or low levels of facilitative dimensions in relationships with parents, teachers, and other significant figures will, in all likelihood, contribute to effective functioning or dysfunctioning in the individual. It makes sense to say that counselors offering a continuation of the same levels of facilitative dimensions will continue to produce further constructive change or deterioration in the individual.

In addition, a clear implication of the model is that individuals are growing constructively when they move toward higher levels of functioning on empathy, regard, genuineness, and concreteness, and are deteriorating when they move in the direction of lower levels of functioning on these dimensions. In this regard, on one of these dimensions—empathy—Blackman, Smith, Brockman, and Stern (1958) have described the absence of empathy as the most important feature in psychotics, and the improvement of their capacity for empathic understanding as the key development in their improvement.

Implicit in this theorizing is the assumption that the person in his relations with others shows the way he feels about himself. Again, only to the degree that he understands and respects a full range of experiences in himself, can he understand and respect a full range of experiences in others.

Let us look, then, at the individual at level 1, the severely distressed client. The evidence is firm. "He is the negative consequence of a succession of retarding relationships. . . . [The significant people] involved with him have been almost totally unconcerned or have lacked any real comprehensive understanding of him (Carkhuff and Truax, 1966)." His own personal development has been retarded by others, and he will retard the development of those with whom he comes in contact.

> There may, of course, be variations off the theme. While the evolution of the severely disturbed might include a series of failing relationships, the less severely disturbed or moderately distressed may be seen as the consequence of some relationships which have been facilitative and some which have been retarding. Thus, the less severely disturbed individual may be seen as the end product of a succession of deteriorative relationships interrupted by possibly one important facilitative relationship (Carkhuff and Truax, 1966, p. 9).

Here we find a description of the middle range of individuals, in particular, of level 2, a description which continues to level 3 and finally to levels 4 and 5:

Similarly, the moderately distressed case may be the result of a number of relationships of varying degrees of facilitation or retardation while the healthy case results from a succession of essentially successful relationships, which significantly outweigh the potentially negative direction which might otherwise be dictated by those important figures offering low condition relationships (Carkhuff and Truax, 1966, p. 10).

Thus, within limits, we can trace the development of individuals at any of the various levels. To be sure, we must acknowledge that the individual is not solely a result of a series of relationships or any other environmental factors. He is not simply "acted upon." Nevertheless, at this point in time, we can make a strong case for the critical and differential influences of the significant relationships in a given individual's evolution.

## THE MODEL IN OPERATION

We can stop for a moment and look again at our model. While we have not yet considered contextual or situational variables, it is a three-dimensional model involving first person, second person, and contextual variables (see Figure 3). For our present purposes, the first and second person variables may each involve five levels. The contextual variables serve to modify the effect of the interaction of the first and second person variables; that is, the contextual variables may operate to facilitate or retard the effect of the interaction of other variables. At this point we will consider the number of levels of the situational variables to be indeterminate, and we will simply consider the modifying effect of two global levels: (1) the duration of the treatment available and (2) the number of possible preferred modes of treatment available in any one setting. The effects of these modifying contextual variables will become readily apparent.

Let us consider again, in shorthand terms, the level 1 person, the person, who is a product of a succession of retarding relationships, and who is essentially immune to constructive human encounter. The model would dictate the need for a very long-term relationship with a facilitative person who is functioning at minimally high levels in order to compensate for the long-term effects of deleterious encounters (a long upward arrow would represent constructive growth for the disturbed client in Figure 2). Similarly, the level 2 person would require a moderately long-term relationship with a minimally facilitative person in order to correct the distorted perceptions which the level 2 person applies and which leads him into difficulties and, ultimately, to the deterioration of all of his significant relationships. On the other hand, the level 3 person and those above often require only the very briefest periods of time to work through their situa-

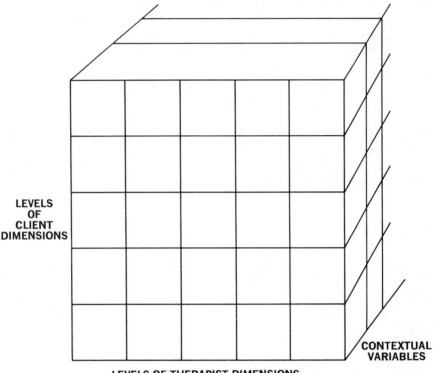

**LEVELS OF THERAPIST DIMENSIONS**

Figure 3.   A multidimensional model of the therapeutic
process variables leading to constructive
client change or gain.

tional difficulties. The availability or unavailability of long-term treatment
will have a modifying effect upon the potential gains available to clients
and others at the varying levels of development. Thus, the level 1 person
in need of long-term treatment will probably benefit very little from a
setting which offers only short-term contacts. In the same manner, the
availability or unavailability of necessary and appropriate techniques,
which might have a facilitative impact upon the client's development,
will have a modifying effect upon potential client gains.

In general, the model dictates that *persons at higher levels of
functioning can help persons at lower levels to achieve higher levels of
functioning.*

Briefly, we might acknowledge the three principal sources of
movement to higher levels: (1) the role-model which the higher level
person presents for more effective functioning; (2) the lower level
person's experience of the facilitative conditions; and (3) some direct

teaching or shaping of behavior involving the conditions of effective living. Thus, assuming the flexibility of time and setting, persons at level 1 may be brought to higher levels of functioning by persons at level 2 or above, and persons at level 2 may be helped by persons at level 3 and above. In turn, it is highly unlikely that persons at lower levels can have a significantly facilitative effect upon persons at higher levels of functioning. Rather, it would appear that extended contacts with severely retarding individuals who are the significant power sources in the relationships (that is, those designated by society as "more knowing" or as the agents of change) account for the deteriorative effects found in the "less knowing" persons in the different instances of all interpersonal processes. We might modify this last proposition with the recognition that the higher the level of development of the client, the less likely he is to become involved in, or be affected disastrously by, long-term encounters with persons in power who are functioning below his level.

Furthermore, below the minimal level of self-sustaining facilitation, that is, level 3, the level of the first person will have a limiting effect upon the level of the second person. The level 1 person will not achieve a level of functioning beyond his level 2 or 2.5 "helper." On the other hand, the level 3 person may enable a level 1 or 2 person to function at level 3, and the second person may, in turn, be able to achieve higher levels through his own continuing efforts. Indeed, once the second person has moved beyond a minimal level of facilitative functioning, we might generate predictions concerning the further development of the first person in a long-term relationship. It appears, then, that at some point in the individual's development, he has incorporated and integrated, at a minimally self-sustaining level, what is meaningful and effective for him in terms of his interpersonal functioning and his own personal fulfillment. Prior to this level of development, the quality of self-sustenance was not present to a sufficient degree. At lower levels, the individual was dependent, in large part, upon others to modify his communication problems and resolve the continuing problems which were a function of the varying degrees of distortion of his perception of the world. The attainment of self-sustenance allows the individual the possibility of moving to higher levels of development largely through his own efforts, with minimal assistance, and we might add, assistance of a very different character.

We can now set the model into operation in generating predictions of gain or change. For the present, we have fairly extensive evidence to suggest that on our five-point scale the maximum potential level of interpersonal functioning—that is, with persons given a mental set to be as helpful as they could with another person—is slightly lower than level 2 with the range between levels 1 and 3. We can make the assumption, then, that most client populations will be comprised of people functioning

## Table 2

Predicted Differential Levels of Client Gain Based
upon Initial Levels of Client and Therapist Functioning

### LEVELS OF FUNCTIONING

| Therapist | Client | Differences |
|-----------|--------|-------------|
| 1 | 1 | 0 |
| | 2 | −1 |
| | 3 | −2 |
| 2 | 1 | +1 |
| | 2 | 0 |
| | 3 | −1 |
| 3 | 1 | +2 |
| | 2 | +1 |
| | 3 | 0 |
| 4 | 1 | +3 |
| | 2 | +2 |
| | 3 | +1 |
| 5 | 1 | +4 |
| | 2 | +3 |
| | 3 | +2 |

between levels 1 and 3. In addition, there is tentative evidence to suggest that counselors and therapists range in their average level of functioning between levels 1 and 4 with a mean of approximately level 2. The average discrepancy, then, between the counselor and the client would appear to be minimal, with the main difference being the higher levels of functioning to which the counselors may range. Disallowing the midpoints, and operating strictly in terms of the nearest full levels, we can estimate the greatest potential gain, if we allow for the setting to provide the necessary and appropriate time and treatment approaches (see Table 2).

One can see readily that the counselor in the low ranges (levels 1 and 2) offers very little prospect for gain to his clients, and his longer term relationships with higher level clients promise some deterioration for the client. The higher level counselors (level 3 and 4) offer great prospect of constructive client change or gain and, at the minimum, offer little or no opportunity for deleterious effects. The predictions of Table 2 are consistent with much of the outcome literature concerning the significantly greater variability in the post-treatment change indexes of the treatment group when compared with the control group: the overall trend of the treatment group is slightly upward, with fewer members giving evidence of deleterious effects than those evidencing constructive effects, and approximately two thirds of those involved demonstrating varying degrees of improvement; the variability in the untreated control group remains approximately the same both before and after the treatment group receives therapy, again with an upward trend overall.

Thus, the predictions for both counseling and counseling training would be that therapists functioning at higher levels of facilitative dimensions would effect higher level gains in the functioning of their clients and trainees than would therapists functioning at lower levels. Pagell, Carkhuff, and Berenson (1967) cast both therapists and clients (who were subsequently randomly assigned to the therapists), in the helping role, and thereby obtained assessments of their maximum levels of interpersonal functioning. They generated differential predictions of gain or loss in client functioning according to the discrepancy between the therapist's and the client's levels of functioning, and found support for their predictions with both outpatient neuropsychiatric patients and counseling center clients. Pierce, Carkhuff, and Berenson (1967) set up a design in which two different trainer-therapists, one functioning at level 2 and one at level 3, were randomly assigned trainee-clients who were interested in becoming lay mental health counselors, and who were, in general, functioning midway between levels 1 and 2. The investigators found that the trainees assigned to the higher-level functioning trainer-therapist improved significantly more in their functioning on the core dimensions than did those of the lower-level functioning trainer-therapist. However, Kratchovil, Aspy, and Carkhuff (1967) suggest a very important qualification upon these hypotheses with their findings that the clients of those counselors who improved in their level of functioning from the beginning to the end of counseling demonstrate more improvement than the clients of those counselors who deteriorate in level of functioning over the course of counseling. Thus, not only the absolute level of the counselor's functioning, but the direction in which he is moving—that is, growing positively or negatively—in his level of functioning may be critical.

Again, the potential gain may be modified by the effect of contextual variables. To follow our example, the potential gain of two levels when a level 3 counselor sees a level 1 client may be qualified by the absence of long-term treatment possibilities and/or potential "preferred modes of treatment." For our present purposes, we might subtract arbitrarily one potential level for each or both of these situationally determined variables. Thus, where long-term treatment of a particular kind may be called for, but is unavailable, a client who might otherwise have gained two levels will gain only one level, if he has a minimally facilitative counselor.

## INTERACTIONAL EFFECTS

There is another, and perhaps more important, implication of the model. If we look again at Figures 2 and 3, we find that the ways in which we interact with a given individual may be determined by his level and by our level. Let us assume for the moment a minimally facilitative counselor. Spatially, we can easily see in Figure 3 that the interaction between a level 3 counselor and a level 1 client is a very different interaction than that between a level 3 counselor and a level 3 client. The spatial discrepancy points up the need to attend specifically to the particular level of the client's psychological development. We can no longer afford the luxury of designating a particular mode of communication in working with the client as appropriate for all levels of clients. The clinicians among us are all too aware of the not-so-subtle discriminations which most of the dominant approaches are unable to make. We have been dominated too long by approaches geared to a particular range of clients; that is, unhappy and highly anxious persons who, however distorted their perceptions and communications, are nevertheless functioning within their world—in other terms the level 2 client. In addition, these clients are often relatively bright, sophisticated, psychologically attuned members of the financially-able middle class or aspiring middle class. We have built up a body of dogma in the psychoanalytic and client-centered approaches which appears to respond, in large part, to the needs of the therapists rather than to the various levels of clients to whom they might attend. Indeed, there is great similarity between the demographic characteristics of both the therapist and their clients. It may well be that the shadowy figure of the analyst and the alter ego of the reflecting nondirectivist may be effective with the level 2 client in enabling him to articulate and modify the distorted perceptions and communications which continually lead him into difficulty. However, they may be totally ineffective or may even have a deleterious effect with other levels of clients. They give no recognition to their own evolution:

> All treatment and training "cults" or orientations and their techniques are the consequent of a particular interaction pattern of counselor, client and contextual variables. The very evolution of the variety of cults of counseling and psychotherapy is attributable for the most part to a more or less unique interaction of variables. A particular group of therapists, who, having many interests and beliefs in common, converge and linger in a given setting with all its implications and interact with a client population which is screened by themselves, the therapists or the setting to have many characteristics in common. Certain methods of approach soon come to connote more efficacious outcomes. A set of beliefs takes hold of the therapists and, shaped by what they believe to be effective practices, these therapists promulgate a theory of therapeutic practice. Unfortunately, it all-too-often ends there. The beliefs based upon generalizations from their own experience are passed on as doctrine and applied by their students in contexts involving a very different interaction of variables (Carkhuff, 1967a, p. 13).

It becomes incumbent, then, upon the clinical investigator to explore the realm of clinical experience in an attempt to articulate some dimensions of effective practice. Again we will assume a minimally facilitative practitioner in interaction with clients at various levels of functioning. As we noted in Table 2, both client and therapist are often functioning below level 3, with the client sometimes functioning above the level of the therapist. Furthermore, it may also be true that a given therapist functioning below level 3 may work more effectively with a particular client sub-population, when the therapists and clients have similar backgrounds, experiences, interests, identifications, and so forth. However, Hirshberg, Carkhuff, and Berenson (1967) found that with both inpatient schizophrenic and college counseling populations, the level of facilitative conditions was, for the most part, characteristic of the therapist, and not dependent upon the populations and settings with which the therapists had the most experience: some therapists functioned at high levels with both populations, while some functioned at low levels with both; others were differentially influenced by the different populations, in favor of relatively higher-level functioning with the population with which they had the most experience.

Let us attempt to articulate further the dimensions of interaction of the minimally facilitative counselor with the various levels of clients. The implications for the differential communication of facilitative conditions or the activities predicated upon these conditions are profound. Consider again the level 1 client. (The reader may note that we have carefully avoided some of the traditional diagnostic categorization in favor of a recognition of gross levels of dysfunctioning and functioning.) He is a severely disabled person who is out of contact with his world and is unable to engage in constructive human encounters. In short, the total communication process has broken down for him to a point where he may have to strike a ward attendant in order to establish contact. The goal of therapy, then, becomes one of re-establishing the communication process and of re-establishing contact with the world. In this process, the client is almost totally dependent upon the level of facilitative conditions offered by the counselor (Holder, Carkhuff, and Berenson, 1967; Piaget, Berenson, and Carkhuff, 1967); of necessity, this involves a long-term relationship. The process may have to be initiated at the most concrete level, the physical level of touch, and then gradually move toward varying levels of construct development. It is clear that the therapist must leave no gaping holes in his own communications. He must make every effort to make his communications as full as possible. He can assume nothing and, if necessary, he must be repetitious, so long as there is no basis for determining whether the client has perceived the communication. The therapist must employ all of his sensitivities, not simply reflect them. In summary, he must define and concretize himself, his messages, and the boundaries and extents of his interactions with the client as fully as possible, leaving no room for errors in the building of the client's assumptive world. Thus, at the lowest level of client functioning, the therapist communicates everything possible in order to re-establish a communication process. Interestingly enough, the chronic and regressed failure cases who comprise the back wards of our hospitals attest to the lack of attention which has been given this level of functioning in the therapeutic literature. It would appear most economical and beneficial, in the context of a relationship offering high levels of facilitative conditions, to conduct a systematic and concrete program to train level 1 persons to perceive and discriminate, and finally communicate relatively high levels of the conditions of effective functioning.

At level 2, the client is often functioning relatively well by societal standards. Nevertheless, he is dominated by errors (although he is not a living error, as is the level 1 client) in his assumptive world which lead him into continual difficulties, and keep him in constant disharmony with others. His distortions dictate the deterioration of those relationships which might be meaningful to him. As much as anything else, the therapist's goal is to help the client to clear up or modify the distortions in his communication. Obviously, there is some degree of validity to the client's assumptive world or he would not function at all. In a moderately long-term relationship, the therapist must enable the client to explore fully the client's expression of his distortions in order to assist in their modification. Both the psychoanalytic and the nondirective orientations are predicated in large part upon the size and sensitivity of the therapist's "ears." To hear and bring to bear the more appropriate frame of reference in interaction with the client's often inappropriate frame of reference is the preeminent task of therapy with the level 2 client.

The level 3 client is a different matter. Often, at this level, we speak of counseling rather than therapy. He is often a more than adequately adjusted individual who can, in general, be facilitative of the efforts of himself and others. However, he has reached a point where he feels pressed by a particular situation in which he finds himself. As a product of a number of facilitative relationships, he is not often in need of long-term assistance, and frequently requires only the briefest of assistance, such as information. He can become involved most effectively in the more cognitive pursuits of the decision-making and problem-solving processes. He rejects the reflections and interpretations of the traditionalist, and wants to know what you think and how you can help him in the present. A depth of understanding may be assumed, and the counselor may choose to act in terms of his understanding rather than to dwell on an already viable communication process. The effective counselor at this level may involve the client in a consideration of alternative courses of action, carefully weighing advantages and disadvantages. Typical of this level is the vocational and educational counseling approach, involving test interpretation and information-getting and -giving. In this regard, studies of the experimental manipulation of therapeutic conditions (Holder, Carkhuff, and Berenson, 1967; Piaget, Berenson, and Carkhuff, 1967) indicate that clients who function higher when cast in the helping role also explore themselves at significantly higher levels than do lower-functioning clients with high-level therapists. In addition, the intrapersonal exploration of high-functioning clients is not related to the level of conditions offered by the counselor, while the self-exploration of low-functioning clients is a direct function of the level of conditions offered by the counselor: the level 3 client, having established that the counselor is functioning at minimally facilitative levels, continues with his self-exploration and problem-expression independent of the counselor.

The levels 4 and 5 persons are only infrequently found in client populations and, indeed, in counselor populations. We can consider them for a moment if we believe any intimate relationship which elicits constructive change or gain to be therapeutic. The ingredients of movement are, however, vastly different from the lower levels; again, with a profound depth of understanding assumed, the dimensions seem to involve questioning, stimulating, agitating the other person and, at higher levels, sharing experiences with another person in a continuing attempt to make the communication process *most full.*

Thus, we move as agents of change or gain from the disabled person, with a total breakdown in his perceptive and communicative skills, to the person attempting to make the fullest possible communication, moving through various levels of distortion and situational distress. As can readily be seen, the implications for differential responding are pronounced; for example, the most empathic response to a level 1 person will be very different from that to a level 2 or 3 person. Again, and particularly in the interpersonal instances of counseling and psychotherapy, there are a variety of possible ancillary approaches which complement and supplement the primary gains in interpersonal functioning and communication.

Another view of Figure 1 might suggest some of the molar client dimensions involved; for example, the vocational and educational counseling approach may be appropriate for the client at a particular point in his life, when he does not have the necessary resources to make the decision but when he does feel pressure to reduce his percieved discordance. Other client dimensions require further exploration in order to relate them in some way to the preferred and appropriate treatment process. One example might involve some further exploration of the amenability of certain clients to the relaxation therapy approach of both the behaviorists and the hypnotists, in conjunction with some further illumination of the particular kinds of anxiety reactions which might be effectively and perhaps even differentially treated by these two approaches.

The ultimate equation for counseling and psychotherapy would involve an explication of client and counselor on both (1) the central core of facilitative conditions, and (2) the availability of, and amenability to, certain appropriate and preferred modes of treatment calculated to free the client to experience and communicate effectively.

The dimensions of effective living as communicated and learned in long-term therapeutic relationships may operate simultaneously with one or a variety of preferred modes of treatment. Thus, the therapist may conduct some systematic conditioning in order to bring the level 1 client back in contact with the world, or he may work in conjunction with a behavior therapist. In addition, and most important, any ultimate model for facilitative processes would be incomplete without attending to many more qualitative dimensions or horizontal dimensions of counselor and client (Hirshberg, Carkhuff, and Berenson, 1967). Thus, the model becomes a complex, multidimensional model. We have spelled the model out as fully as we understand it now.

## SUMMARY AND CONCLUSIONS

Both clients and counselors, as well as students and teachers, children and parents, and other persons designated as "less knowing" or "more knowing" by society may be assessed on the same central and relevant core ingredients of interpersonal functioning. Indeed, society's designations of "less knowing" and "more knowing" are often independent of the levels of interpersonal functioning or potential helpfulness of the individuals involved. The multidimensional model involving both first and second person variables, as well as contextual variables, does, however, allow us to make differential predictions concerning the potential value—ultimately perhaps for both parties involved—of a particular interaction or relationship. In addition to the constructive gains, the model also allows us to account for the all-too-frequently found deterioration in one of the parties of the relationship.

Perhaps most important, the multidimensional model enables us to consider the very different interaction patterns of first and second persons at different levels of development. The implications for counseling and psychotherapy, processes which often operate independently of the interactional patterns involved and in accordance with preconceived theoretical notions, are profound. The counselor or therapist who is shaped by what is effective both for himself and the client, must respond differentially to a severely disabled and deteriorated mental patient and to a situationally distressed normal. Concerning counseling and therapy in particular, secondary dimensions in the form of a variety of possible techniques or "preferred modes of treatment" built around the central core of facilitative conditions and appropriate to a particular interaction pattern of counselor, client, and contextual variables, may serve a rehabilitative function in enabling the client to experience and communicate the core of facilitative conditions after more natural and effective processes had broken down.

Further attempts to develop such a comprehensive model appear worthwhile. In addition to generating differential predictions and activities in practice, our model, unlike those of the psychoanalytic, nondirective, behavioristic, vocational counseling, and other dominant models, has implications for a meaningful developmental theory in terms of parent-child, teacher-student, and other significant relationships. The model does make assumptions concerning gradations of difference, or quantitative rather than qualitative differences, in both first and second persons. These assumptions appear warranted in terms of the growing body of evidence in other areas of interpersonal functioning concerning the evolution of difficulties in functioning (or in more traditional terms, psychopathology).

### References

Blackman, N., K. Smith, R. J. Brockman, and J. A. Stern. The development of empathy in male schizophrenics. *Psychiat. quart.*, 1958, *32*, 546–553.

Carkhuff, R. R. On the necessary conditions of therapeutic personality change. *Discussion papers, Wisconsin Psychiat. Institute*, Univer. of Wisconsin, 1963, *47*, 1–7.

Carkhuff, R. R. *The counselor's contribution to facilitative processes.* Urbana, Ill.: Parkinson, 1967. (a)

Carkhuff, R. R. Toward a comprehensive model of facilitative interpersonal processes. *J. Counsel. Psychol.*, 1967, *14*, 67–72. (b)

Carkhuff, R. R., and C. B. Truax. Toward explaining success and failure in interpersonal experiences. *Personnel guid. J.*, 1966, *46*, 723–728.

Hirshberg, F., R. R. Carkhuff, and B. G. Berenson. Differential levels of therapist-offered conditions with inpatient and outpatient populations. Unpublished research, Univer. of Massachusetts, 1967.

Holder, T., R. R. Carkhuff, and B. G. Berenson. The differential effects of the manipulation of therapeutic conditions upon high and low functioning clients. *J. counsel. Psychol.*, 1966, *14*, 63–66.

Kratchovil, D., D. Aspy, and R. R. Carkhuff. The differential effects of absolute level and direction of change in therapist functioning upon client functioning. *J. clin. Psychol.*, 1967, 23, 216–218.

Pagell, W., and R. R. Carkhuff. Client gain as a function of the initial level of functioning of client and therapist. *J. clin. Psychol.*, in press, 1967.

Piaget, G., B. G. Berenson, and R. R. Carkhuff. The differential effects of the manipulation of therapeutic conditions by high and low functioning counselors upon high and low functioning clients. *J. consult. Psychol.*, in press, 1967.

Pierce, R., R. R. Carkhuff, and B. G. Berenson. Trainee gain as a function of the initial level of functioning of trainee and trainer. *J. clin. Psychol.*, 1967, 23, 212–215.

# SECTION THREE

# Potential Preferred Modes of Treatment

The commitment of the whole counselor leads him to know all that is knowable so that he can fully discharge his responsibility to his client as well as to himself. He turns, then, to existing bodies of knowledge in order to determine for himself the contributions of each. Where appropriate, he employs the existing orientations. The previous section provided the base from which we can consider the dominant, current approaches to counseling and therapy. In each of the following five chapters, we consider the unique contributions to constructive client gain, over and above those accounted for by the central core of facilitative conditions, as well as the limitations of the major approaches to counseling and therapy. The client-centered approach (Chapter 4) is considered first because of its close relationship to the historical evolution of the core conditions, and the need to differentiate this approach from the role the core conditions play in the development of the systematic, eclectic stance of this book. Similarly, the existential approach (Chapter 5) is treated in the context of its relationship to the core conditions and the authors' focus upon the experiential base of therapy. In addition, the recent and vital challenge of the behavior modification approaches (Chapter 6) to all of the major systems necessitates their inclusion. Furthermore, the dominating role of the trait-and-factor approach (Chapter 7) in the areas of educational and vocational counseling demands an analysis of its contributions. The psychoanalytic approach (Chapter 8) is included, although aside from its enormous historical contributions, it appears to have the least to offer to constructive client change or gain.

Chapter **4**

 . . . . a highly verbal transaction,
emphasizing words about feelings,
rather than the more direct expression
of feelings themselves between
a self-denying, middle-class parental
surrogate and his initiate.

## Apparency in Search of a Person:
## The Unique Contributions of the Client-
## Centered Approach

*All therapists are client-centered in the sense that they serve for the benefit of their clients.* To the degree that any therapist is not client-centered, he is not doing therapy. However, the term, "client-centered," must be differentiated into those members of the client-centered school and those persons who are shaped by what is effective for their clients. In the hope that these groups might become one, we will attempt to discern and describe the potentially unique contributions of the client-centered system as it has evolved in its identification with Carl Rogers and his work (1951, 1954, 1967). By unique contributions, we mean those over and above the ones the client-centered approach shares with other interview-oriented therapeutic approaches.

Thus, we will attempt to discern where and under what conditions this approach accounts for practices more effective than those accounted for by a central core of facilitative conditions common to all therapies. This central core of conditions, involving the communication of counselor dimensions such as empathic understanding, positive regard, genuineness, and concreteness, or specificity of expression, is shared by almost all well-known counseling approaches, and evidence for the relationship of high levels of these dimensions to successful client process movement and outcome has been summarized elsewhere (Carkhuff, 1966, 1967a; Carkhuff and Truax, 1966a; Truax and Carkhuff, 1964).

Disclaimers notwithstanding, the greatest part of the unique identification of the client-centered approach must be attributed to the nondirective disposition. While outsiders may not be attuned to the subtle nuances in client-centered practice as, for example, the increasing emphasis upon the congruence of the counselor or therapist (Gendlin, 1962; Rogers, *et al.*, 1967), they continue to identify the client-centered process with many of the nondirective techniques, such as reflection (Carkhuff and Truax, 1967).

In order to explore the unique contributions of the "client-centered" approach, we might perhaps first view that approach in encapsulated form.

## THE CLIENT-CENTERED
## OR NONDIRECTIVE STANCE

The client-centered approach is built around two central theorems. First, inherent in the individual is the capacity to understand the factors in his life that cause him unhappiness and pain, and the capacity to reorganize his self-structure in such a way as to overcome those factors. Second, the individual's inherent powers will operate if a congruent therapist can establish with him a relationship involving a depth of warm acceptance and understanding. The process of therapy which follows is one by which the structure of the client's self is relaxed in the safety and security of the relationship with the therapist, previously denied experiences are perceived, and, by means of a verbal, symbolic analysis, integrated into an altered self (Rogers, 1951, pp. 66–74).

One of the effects which these theorems accomplish is an absolution of the therapist from the responsibility for effects other than the creation of a therapeutic atmosphere or relationship. In reaction to the distortions inherent in the other extreme, where the therapist is the sole focus of evaluation, the relationship is one where the therapist endeavors to keep himself out, as a separate person, and where his whole endeavor is to understand the other so completely that he becomes almost an alter ego of the client (Rogers, 1951, pp. 42–43). Rather than the interaction of two persons, each committed to experiencing and understanding himself in relation to the other and the other in relation to him, "the whole relationship is composed of the self of the client, the counselor being depersonalized for purposes of therapy into being 'the client's other self.'" It is precisely "this warm willingness on the part of the counselor to lay aside his own self temporarily, in order to enter into the experiences of the client, which makes the relationship a completely unique one, unlike anything in the client's previous experience" (Rogers, 1951, p. 208). Recent innovations in client-centered thinking have modified this typical middle-class self-sacrifice to allow for a kind of defensive congruence of the therapist (Rogers, 1957, Rogers, *et al.*, 1967), a genuineness which is employed at particular points in therapy, rather than for a full, open, and spontaneous emergence of the therapist's person. The second aspect of the relationship is the safety and security which the client experiences as a consequence of the therapist's consistent and deep acceptance. "It is this absolute assurance that there will be no evaluation, no interpretation, no probing, no personal reaction by the counselor, that gradually permits the client to experience the relationship as one in which all defenses can be dispensed with—a relationship in which the client feels, 'I can be the real me, no pretenses'" (Rogers, 1951, p. 208). We might add, "I can be the real me, no pretenses, while you, the therapist, are unreal, in all your pretenses." It is as if one person cannot be both real and constructive, as if another person cannot dispense with his defenses in interaction with a "real" person.

Rogers (1957), in a theoretical statement, organized what he termed "the necessary and sufficient conditions of therapeutic personality change." On the basis of his own clinical and research experiences as well as those of his colleagues, Rogers extrapolated six conditions which were "necessary to initiate constructive personality change, and which, taken together appear to be sufficient to inaugurate that process:

1. Two persons are in psychological contact.
2. The first . . . , the client, is in a state of incongruence, being vulnerable or anxious.
3. The second . . . , the therapist, is congruent or integrated in the relationship.
4. The therapist experiences unconditional positive regard for the client.
5. The therapist experiences an empathic understanding of the client's internal frame of reference and endeavors to communicate this experience to the client.
6. The communication to the client of the therapist's empathic understanding is to a minimall degree achieved"[11] (Rogers, 1957, pp. 95–96).

It should be noted that condition 6 was modified by Rogers (1959) to emphasize the client's perception of the communication, whether intended by the therapist or not. Nevertheless, Rogers (1957) emphasized that "No other conditions are necessary. If these six conditions exist and continue over a period of time, this is sufficient. The process of constructive personality change will follow" (p. 96). While evidence in support of these hypotheses has been presented (Rogers, 1962; Rogers, *et al.*, 1966; Truax and Carkhuff, 1963), the theoretical statement has not yet opened itself up to further and necessary refinements. For example, no provisions have been made for the differential weightings of the primary dimensions due to particular interaction units of relevant therapist, client, and contextual variables. Secondly, no provisions have been made for the possibility that additional or secondary dimensions may, for some therapists, clients, and situations, singularly or in their various interactions, operate to facilitate or even retard the effects of the hypothesized necessary conditions or simply account for an additional degree of effectiveness, themselves (Carkhuff, 1963). Furthermore, there are the studies such as Spotts (Rogers, 1962) which indicate that the variability of uncondition-ality is accounted for by the communication of positive regard alone, and suggest that the constructs involved must be open to further modification and delineation.

Concerning technique, says Rogers, "the sincere aim of getting 'within' the attitudes of the client, of entering the client's internal frame of reference, is the most complete implementation which has thus far been formulated, for the central hypothesis of respect for and reliance upon the capacity of the person" (Rogers, 1951, p. 36). In the therapist's reflections, clarifications, summarizations, and reformulations of the client's expressions, the client is able to see his own attitudes, confusions, ambivalences, and perceptions accurately (hopefully) expressed by another person ("who is only partly another person"), but with a new quality stripped of complications of emotion. The client can see himself objectively, and the way is paved for the integration of more clearly perceived aspects of the self. "In this attempt to struggle along with the client, to glimpse with him the half understood causes of behavior, to wrestle with feelings which emerge into awareness and slip away again, it is entirely possible that the simple concept of 'an accurate reflection of feeling' no longer fits the therapist's behavior. Rather than seeing as a mirror, the therapist becomes a companion to the client as the latter searches through a tangled forest the dead of night" (Rogers, 1951, pp. 112–113).

In recognizing that the techniques of the different approaches to counseling and therapy are relatively unimportant except insofar as they serve as channels for fulfilling one of the conditions, Rogers (1957) acknowledges that the therapist's technique of the reflection of the client's feelings (Rogers, 1954, pp. 26–36) is not per se an essential condition of therapy: "To the extent, however, that it provides a channel by which the therapist communicates a sensitive empathy and an unconditional positive regard then it may serve as a technical channel by which the essential conditions of therapy are fulfilled" (Rogers, 1957, p. 102).

The outcome of counseling and therapy, in turn, is highly related to the process of therapy in the sense that the therapist must be completely willing that any outcome, any direction, may be chosen by the client. Only then will the potentiality of the individual for constructive action be realized. "It is as if he is willing for death to be the choice that a healthy normality is chosen" (Rogers, 1951, p. 49). The client's self following therapy "functions smoothly in experience, rather than being an object of introspection" (Rogers, 1951, p. 129). Furthermore, ". . . there is a change in the valuing process during therapy, and one characteristic of this change is that the individual moves away from a state where his thinking, feeling and behavior are governed by the judgments and expectations of others, and toward a state in which he relies upon his own experience for his values and standards" (Rogers, 1951, p. 157).

## HISTORICAL CREDITS

The client-centered position must be considered a traditional one in the respect that its adherents follow and implement well-defined and prescribed modes of functioning in counseling and therapy, often independent of the ensuing process and outcome. We should note that a difficulty in assessing the contributions of traditional stances, in general, is the sense in which the position has made contributions which were once substantive and innovating but are no longer functionally related to the position of the original contributor (that is, many subsequent positions have incorporated those principles of the previous positions which have proved effective). These "historical contributions" deserve brief attention.

Perhaps the major historical contribution of the client-centered approach has been the impetus which it has given the growth of the idea of the central core of facilitative conditions. Rogers, following, in 1957, on the heels of Shaffer and Shoben in 1956 and others, attempted to discern and describe "the necessary and sufficient conditions of therapeutic personality change." Unfortunately, both positions, as well as many others which have followed them have been tied (in the perceptions of their audiences) to *the techniques* of the communication of attitudes and sensitivities.

In addition to the focus which it brought to the client's feelings, the client-centered approach, in general, provided more full attention to the whole person of the client, including in particular a fundamental belief in his constructive capacity. This position holds that something critical intervenes between the stimulus and the response, and this intervening variable really can only be understood in the present, subjective state of the individual involved. In so focusing upon the client's present feelings, the position has to a great degree rendered the past irrelevant.

In his emphasis upon freeing the individual's capacity for growth, the client-centered therapist often will institute the conditions of empathy and unconditionality quite independent of the client and his needs in any given instance for direction or dependency. The historical contributions have further limitations in the very respect that the conditions are often related to techniques. There is little proviso for the untrained teacher or ward attendant, whose students or patients improve on a variety of relevant indexes of constructive change. In addition, whereas client-centered therapy brought more complete attention to the whole person of the client, it has neglected the *whole person of the therapist* and the two-way flow of communication. Lastly, the position has emphasized the present and reality as the individual sees it to the exclusion of a very often relevant past and external world impinging upon the present functioning of the client.

In summary, seen for its stimulus value, the client-centered contribution is a most profound one: "If a theory could be seen for what it is—a fallible, changing attempt to construct a network of gossamer threads which will contain the solid facts—then a theory would serve, as it should, as a stimulus to further creative thinking" (Rogers, 1959, p. 191).

## THE UNIQUE CONTRIBUTIONS

Many of the unique contributions of the client-centered process must be tied to specific techniques such as the reflection of the client's feelings and attitudes by the therapist. Much of the remaining contribution can be accounted for by the facilitating effects of the central core of conditions of all effective human relations. To the following list of unique contributions we must add two important qualifications: (1) the client-centered mode is one of many possible modes or vehicles for making these contributions and, in some cases, it may be the most effective mode; (2) in most cases, we must add the expression "within limits" to qualify the effects of the approach in general. Given a desirable interaction of the relevant therapist, client, and contextual variables, the appropriate application of the "client-centered" approach would appear to make the following unique contributions:

### Process Contributions to the Client

1. The client-centered approach provides the client with an opportunity to find his own mode of expression.

The essential direction in the communication process comes from the client, and he has the opportunity to find his own words for his own feelings.

2.  The client-centered approach provides the client with immediate and concrete feedback of what he has just communicated.

The therapist's reflection offers the client an opportunity to hear a playback of what he has just communicated and allows him to judge the impact or adjust the communication.

3.  The client-centered approach provides the client with an opportunity to experience previously denied experiences.

In the client-centered atmosphere, the client may relax his defenses in the secure knowledge that no judgments or punitive action will follow.

4.  The client-centered approach draws the client's attention to many things to which he has not attended or which he has not communicated.

In expressing himself and in rehearing his own messages the client has the opportunity to attend to previously unattended areas.

5.  The client-centered approach provides the client with the opportunity for the discovery and correction of faulty generalizations.

In providing him with the opportunity for his own systematic construction of his communications, the client can discover the inadequacies of his reasoning and generalizations.

## Process Contributions to the Therapist

1.  The client-centered aproach provides one vehicle for the communication of the therapist's sensitivities and attitudes.

The atmosphere created by the client-centered approach offers the client the *promise* of full acceptance and the *apparency* of freedom.

2.  The client-centered approach allows the therapist an opportunity to gauge the client's level of affective expression or assertive behavior.

Simply because he is oriented to listening and hearing the client's expressions, the client-centered therapist, at least initially, has the most complete opportunity for understanding the level at which the client is functioning.

3.  The client-centered approach provides the therapist a means of knowing whether his perceptions and communications are congruent with those of the client.

The therapist is able to gauge whether his responses are related (and how highly related) to those of the client from the feedback which he gets from the client.

> 4. The client-centered approach provides an opportunity for therapist communications free from the professional jargon and interpretation which often is not understood by the client.

Since the therapist's messages are, in large part, restatements of feelings expressed by the client, he is constrained from employing many of the constructs which he might otherwise express.

> 5. The client-centered approach defines therapist reponsibilities within safe ranges.

The therapist who wishes to avoid responsibility for the condition or life of the client has fairly well-defined rules and regulations to guide him.

> 6. The client-centered approach keeps the unique and personal aspects of the therapist out of therapy.

This constitutes a contribution since it minimizes the potential destructive impact of some therapists while giving therapy the façade of being personal.


## THE LIMITATIONS
## OF THE CLIENT-CENTERED APPROACH

The limitations of the client-centered approach can be noted in a manner similar to the contributions. It may be seen readily that most of the limitations center around the therapist's inability to employ himself fully in the two-way communication of therapy.

### Process Limitations for the Client

> 1. The client-centered approach does not provide the client with real life conditions for functioning.

The apparent conditions are simply not lifelike and they make generalization to other areas of human functioning from a relationship with an alter ego difficult.

> 2. The client-centered approach provides no opportunity for the client to have an impact upon the therapist.

The therapist does not relate to communications which involve him as a person and thus communicates the following message to the client: "No matter what you do I will remain the same."

## Process Limitations for the Therapist

1.   The client-centered approach is unable to provide a vehicle for the therapist to give fully of himself.

In the highly personalized depersonalization process, the therapist is discouraged from a fully personal sharing, and relating to the client's very personal problems.

2.   The client-centered approach does not provide the therapist with an opportunity for the translation of his commitment to action.

Neither within therapy nor out of therapy can the therapist act upon the client or his environment in the manner which he feels will, in the end, be most effective for the client.

3.   The client-centered approach prescribes an apparency in the therapist's communication which elicits an apparency in the client's communications.

The client's responses will be as apparent as those of their elicitors and thus, nonfunctional in lifelike situations.

4.   The client-centered approach channels communication in a regression of expression toward a more socially acceptable mean or mode.

When the client's responses are superficial, the therapist responds at deeper levels, and when the client's responses are deep and inflammatory they are modulated by the therapist's words about feelings, whether or not the more socially acceptable response is helpful to the client.

5.   The client-centered approach does not leave the therapist free to explore feelings in a wide range of affect.

This is perhaps not so much the fault of client-centered theory as it is the mode of functioning of most client-centered therapists, that is, the emphasis is upon words reflecting depression and distress to the exclusion of all other feelings (depressing responses may be handled at level 3 of five-point scales assessing therapeutic functioning (Carkhuff, 1967b) and joyous, elated, excited, and hostile feelings at 1).

6.   The client-centered approach does not provide the therapist with an opportunity for the employment of other more directive techniques.

The client-centered therapist is denied the opportunity of employing more directive techniques, such as systematic counterconditioning, when these techniques appear appropriate to the conditions of the case.

## THE CONDITIONS OF SUCCESS
## AND FAILURE

The question, "where and under what conditions can the client-centered approach most effectively make these contributions?" leads us into several areas of inquiry. The condition that looms largest before us is that involving the initial or early stages of counseling or therapy. When the therapist does not know who and where the client is, and where he (the therapist) is in relation to the client, as is the case in initial encounters, it appears most facilitative to reflect the feelings of the client. When the therapist has not known the client long enough to really care about the client as an individual, and no basis of mutual concern has in fact been established, it might be most facilitative to employ techniques for communicating warm acceptance. When the therapist has been unable to establish communication or has lost communication with the client, then the client-centered approach appears efficacious, although even here a more direct and honest approach often appears most effective. However, as therapy continues, and the client has experienced freedom and acceptance and has explored his perceptual field, he seeks a more and more equalitarian relationship in which he has impact upon the therapist.

In general, there is some research evidence, and a great deal of experiential evidence to suggest that the client-centered approach is most effective with a population characterized as follows: depressed neurotic outpatient or level 2 individuals (Carkhuff, 1967b) who bring extremely distorted perceptions to bear in all of their human interactions, distorted perceptions which ultimately lead to the deterioration of all of these relationships; persons who nevertheless possess a sufficient degree of ego strength and other resources to function in many of the roles which society has prescribed for them; persons who supply their own motivation and are sophisticated, psychologically attuned and verbally facile; in sum, patients who have the potential for, and are indeed striving for, middle-class status. The client-centered approach appears to work best when the client's inner resources are really enough and when his greatest need is to understand and trust his own experience, and when the therapist's need is to understand the client's experience but he does not trust his own (the therapist's) experience. The client-centered approach works most effectively when the client's response is enough and the therapist's response is appropriate.

The client-centered approach would appear to be least effective in its more traditional form with low-level functioning or level 1 persons, such as hospitalized psychotics. An attempt has been made to employ the client-centered method with inpatient schizophrenics (Rogers, Gendlin, Kiessler, and Truax, 1967). The success of this application has been in large part contingent upon the therapist's ability to define himself, and the boundaries of his therapy in his interaction with the patient (Carkhuff, 1963). These success contingencies with psychotics have led to the growing emphasis within client-centered thinking upon therapist congruence.

Furthermore, for a variety of reasons, the client-centered method does not appear to be an effective mode of functioning with high-level functioning or level 3 persons. The constant emphasis upon the reflective mode of communication, for example, is unnecessary with higher-level functioning persons. Once the high-level functioning client is aware that his counselor is functioning at high levels and is genuinely sensitive and respectful, the client can continue on his own independently, whether or not the counselor continues to function at high levels (Holder, Carkhuff, and Berenson, 1967). The level 3 person is already functioning at effective levels of interpersonal dimensions: the distorted perceptions and communications, to the clarification of which the client-centered method is dedicated, are not dominant; his existence is not a miserable one aside from periodic episodes of situational stress.

It is interesting to note that when client-centered cases are viewed by theorists and therapists from differing orientations, the following generalities emerge:

> 1. The reflective method of communicating the therapist's empathic understanding is the ingredient most frequently pointed to as dominating the client-centered therapeutic process.

As seen by outsiders, reflection may dominate alone or in combination with other ingredients (Carkhuff and Truax, 1967). However, the expectation that the success or failure of the case be tied to the success or failure of reflection is not met.

> 2. The success or failure attributed to the client-centered cases appears independent of the effectiveness or ineffectiveness of the method of reflection.

Reflection succeeds as often as it fails in client-centered cases designated as success cases by outsiders; reflection fails only slightly more than it succeeds in cases which are seen as failures. The suggestion, then, is that the success or failure of client-centered cases is not (or only minimally) related to the success or failure of its principal method.

> 3. The ingredient most highly related to success in client-centered cases involves the therapist's active, personal reaching out and involvement with the client.

It is significant that, while these acts of caring appear only infrequently, and do indeed go beyond the prescribed role, this ingredient was seen as the principal source of effect in several successful cases. Only in one case, in which no improvement was discerned, did the therapist successfully communicate a giving of himself.

> 4. In relatively few client-centered cases, the effectiveness of dimensions such as structuring the client's comments has been related to successful outcome, and the ineffectiveness of these dimensions has been related to unsuccessful outcomes.

Thus, it appears that successful client-centered outcomes can be attributed to techniques quite antithetical to the client-centered stance, although it should be noted that just as many failure cases as success cases may be attributed to structuring (Carkhuff and Truax, 1967). The effective employment of structuring, however, would seem to suggest that the therapist must break free of his nondirective orientation in order to function effectively.

Thus, it appears that the success or failure of client-centered therapy is independent of its principal mode of communication, but is in large part related to the communication of the therapist's personal involvement and giving of himself—a communication certainly unintended and, at the minimum, limited by the position. If the acts of personal involvement account largely for the effectiveness of client-centered therapy, then we might consider how much more successful these therapists might be if they had a more open and spontaneous vehicle for communication—themselves.

Alternate theories of the effectiveness of client-centered process and outcome have, of course, been postulated. Frequently, however, the sources of effect would seem to function in spite of the avowed intention of the client-centered therapist. Among the most creative of these are those posited by Whitaker (Carkhuff and Truax, 1967) who suggests two principal dynamic sources of change: (1) the therapist by his impersonal, dispassionate, self-denying example teaches the client to become uninvolved and detached from life's exigencies and mischances; (2) the client finally must "break free" of an unreal relationship with his "alter ego," and, in breaking free affirms his own identity and existence.

## SUMMARY AND CONCLUSIONS

*Beyond the initial phases of therapeutic encounters, the technique of client-centered therapy appears to make no significant contribution to constructive change over and above that change accounted for by the central core of facilitative conditions. To be sure, its philosophy is not only* in keeping with but also gave great impetus to the development of thought concerning a central core of conditions. Perhaps most importantly, its founder, Carl Rogers, found the client-centered mode of functioning most effective for himself. The central message, then, is that others must find a mode appropriate for themselves. Today we have the opportunity to learn to use our own personalities most effectively, in part because Rogers dared to break free of the psychoanalytic tradition in finding the method by which he, personally, could be most effective.

The major limitation, then, would appear to be in those phases beyond the introductory, exploratory experience. At some point along the line in therapy the therapist must move from technique to person. Since by its nature all therapy is client-centered, it is more than understandable that the therapist starts out client-centered. However, we would hypothesize that it is also understandable and indeed necessary that therapy become relationship-centered, and finally, in truly therapeutic cases, become a kind of existential sharing in an equalitarian relationship.

To the extent all therapeutic processes are inherently client-centered in the sense that they occur for the benefit of the client, none are truly client-centered in the sense that the conditions which they institute are often independent of the client's needs and attitudes. However active or passive the client-centered therapist, there are many not-so-subtle indications that the process is a rather precise reflection of a polite middle class, and will function most effectively with persons who share the attitudes, the values, and the potentials of this polite middle class.

In summary, *the client-centered approach is a highly verbal transaction, emphasizing words about feelings, rather than the more direct expression of the feelings themselves; (that is, "I am angry," rather than angry expressions) between a self-denying, middle-class, parental surrogate and his initiate.* The approach suffers not so much because of the clarification of communication which it is able to achieve during initial phases, as because of what it excludes: the full personalities of all parties to a relationship; persons who do not share in the same tradition and values; persons, both client and therapist, who cannot be defined by any set of techniques and cannot relate role to role; persons, to each of whom benefits can only accrue in a full communication process between full humans.

### References

Carkhuff, R. R. On the necessary and sufficient conditions of therapeutic personality change. Discussion papers, *Wisconsin Psychiatric Institute,* Univer. of Wisconsin, 1963, *47,* 1–7.

Carkhuff, R. R. Training and practice in counseling and psychotherapy: Requiem or revielle? *J. Counsel. Psychol.*, 1966, *13*, 360–367.

Carkhuff, R. R. Toward failure or fulfillment. In *The counselor's contribution to facilitative processes*. Urbana, Ill.: Parkinson, 1967. (a)

Carkhuff, R. R. Toward a comprehensive model of counseling and psychotherapy. *J. Counsel. Psychol.*, 1967, *14*, 67–72 (b).

Carkhuff, R. R., and C. B. Truax. Toward explaining success or failure in interpersonal learning experiences. *Personnel guid. J.*, 1966, *46*, 723–728.

Carkhuff, R. R., and C. B. Truax. The client-centered process as viewed by other therapists. In C. R. Rogers, E. T. Gendlin, D. Kiessler, and C. B. Truax (Eds.), *The therapeutic relationship and its impact*. Univer. of Wisconsin Press, in press, 1967.

Gendlin, E. T. Client-centered developments and work with schizophrenics. *J. counsel. Psychol.*, 1962, *9*, 205–211.

Holder, T., R. R. Carkhuff, and B. G. Berenson. The differential effects of the manipulation of therapeutic conditions upon high-and-low functioning clients. *J. counsel. Psychol.*, 1966, *14*, 63–66.

Rogers, C. R. *Client-centered therapy*. Boston: Houghton Mifflin., 1951.

Rogers, C. R. The necessary and sufficient conditions of therapeutic personality change. *J. consult. Psychol.*, 1957, *22*, 95–103.

Rogers, C. R. A theory of therapy, personality and interpersonal relationships, as developed in the client-centered framework. In S. Koch (Ed.), *Psychology: A study of a science*, vol. III. New York: McGraw-Hill, 1959.

Rogers, C. R., and Rosalind F. Dyamond. *Psychotherapy and personality change*. Chicago: Univer. of Chicago Press, 1954.

Rogers, C. R., E. T. Gendlin, D. Kiessler, and C. B. Truax. *The therapeutic relationship and its impact: A study of psychotherapy with schizophrenics*. Madison, Wisc.: Univer. of Wisconsin Press, 1967.

Truax, C. B., and R. R. Carkhuff. For better or for worse: The process of psychotherapeutic personality change. In *Recent advances in the study of behavior change*. Montreal: McGill Univer. Press, 1963.

Truax, C. B., and R. R. Carkhuff. Significant developments in psychotherapy research. In L. E. Abt and B. F. Riess (Eds.), *Progress in clinical Psychology*, New York: Grune & Stratton, 1964.

# Chapter 5

. . . . Those who fear death must face
death before they can live life;
those who do not fear death live life.

## Man for Each Other: The Unique
## Contributions of the Existential Approach

*The essential task of all therapy is to enable man to act and to accept the awesome freedom and responsibility for action.* Although in its origins, existentialism described the condition of modern man rather than his therapy, it alone addresses itself directly to the feelings of loneliness and alienation, which incapacitate man and disallow his action. Even in its application in therapy, the existential approach concentrates upon the philosophical assumptions underlying therapy, rather than upon "the technique of therapy." In this sense, the existential approach to therapy deserves a unique treatise: it does not involve "unique contributions to treatment," as much as it involves a philosophical base for man in his human relationships, some of the dimensions of which we have attempted to specify. Of all the major therapeutic approaches, the existential approach alone focuses exclusively upon the crucial questions concerning the nature of man; its answers are sometimes poetic, often confusing, but always stimulating.

## THE EXISTENTIAL APPROACH
## IN ITS RELATION TO THERAPY

The currently popularized existential approach to therapy (May, *et al.*, 1958, 1961; Ruitenbeck, 1962) has its origin in European existential philosophy (Jaspers, 1913; Kierkegaard, 1954; Sartre, 1947), in the phenomenological method (Husserl, 1928; Straus, 1955, 1956), and in integrative efforts to make application of both approaches to therapy (Binswanger, 1956; Boss, 1958, 1963; Heidegger, 1962; Minkowski, 1926; Sartre, 1953). Perhaps of greatest significance historically, in attending to the depersonalization and isolation of modern man in his human relationships, existentialism fills a very real treatment void left behind by the Freudian, behavioristic, and trait-and-factor-centered approaches to counseling and psychotherapy. It asks basic questions—questions which are not asked elsewhere—concerning the nature of man, and develops in response a core of basic human values which are not developed in other therapeutic orientations. In addition, it posits, for the first time, a unique combination of both the subjective and objective world in man's phenomenological existence.

An overview of five common, although not unqualified, dimensions of the existential approach in relation to therapy can be stated and commented upon as follows:

1. Man, whose sense of self is developed through his relatedness to others, doesn't know himself except in relation to others.

Man is so concerned with "knowing" others, and knowing himself *only* in relation to them, that he does not know himself. He cannot be creative since he does not have his own experience with which to create. Although we think that man, as the existentialists suggest, is dependent upon others for self-definition, we must qualify this attitude with the suggestion that the healthy environment produces a self-sustaining person (level 3 or above) who, having incorporated in his identity significant persons from his past, has an identity independent of immediate relationships.

2. Man's principal source of anxiety is his fear of losing others and being alone.

With the breakdown in communication with his fellow man, the threat of being alone elicits high levels of anxiety which preclude man's engagement in creative processes. In addition, man experiences guilt in relation to others. He is in debt to everyone around him for his existence. He flays himself for never living up to the possibilities which others offer him, but he can never expiate this guilt and he is, therefore, never relieved.

3. Man's real guilt is that he cannot act.

Because of his "other-directed" development, man cannot become an autonomous, acting being. Man is entitled by action to creative processes which he is now unable to achieve. But he has lost his ability to act. In not fulfilling himself as a constantly changing, creative creature, man has let himself, not others, down.

4. Man must face the fact that he is alone, for only he has the responsibilities for acting upon his choices.

This is, perhaps, the key existential proposition with implications for therapy. Since man has an awareness, he can question his existence. By bringing the unconscious into awareness, he is more conscious of his choices and their implications for himself and others. Thus, he has a mastery which he has denied and been denied. Because man can choose and because he, alone, is ultimately responsible for his choice, he is ultimately alone.

5. The task of therapy is to enable man to act and to accept the freedom and responsibility for acting.

*Although man's life in its very nature has intrinsic meaning, man's tragic burden is his compulsive search for meaning in a meaningless world.* In the context of an intimate therapist-to-client relationship, man's experience of freedom will emerge with his recognition of the meaninglessness of his existence. Only in a full confrontation with the ultimate in "aloneness" or death can man choose life.

The therapeutic process begins with the formation of a significant one-to-one relationship, in which both therapist and client "act" as if they were the only persons existing at this point in time. Through his fulfilled need for intimacy, the patient experiences his own existence as "real"; his false sense of guilt is relieved, and he achieves a continuity within himself, finally assuming responsibility for his behavior with active decision-making. A further goal, that of preventing a split between the patient's artificial world and his real life, is not consistent with the other aims and appears superfluous since man must, of necessity, stand independently (in a statistical sense) of the artificial world, sometimes functioning without regard to it. Sometimes a split between the real and the artificial is necessary.

Consistent with our descriptions of the core dimensions, the therapist, in the context of an assumedly genuine relationship, communicates his understanding and full regard for the human dignity of the patient. Most often, the communication process involves analyzing the existential meaning of human experience rather than the direct expression of experience. Infrequently, the therapist shares his experience of the patient with the patient. Nowhere to be found, however, is the ultimate in regard for a fellow human, acting upon his experience of another. Thus, the process is, as in client-centered therapy, a highly verbal transaction emphasizing words about feelings. *It is as if the therapist analyzes as the client acts.* Yet, only in acting does the therapist expose his own "being." Instead, regard for human dignity is communicated in verbiage. It is not that we can act upon our experience with everyone. Rather, it is the naïve way in which most existentialists treat the notion of respect for the dignity of another. With those for whom we have the most respect, we act in terms of our experience of them. With those for whom we have the least respect, we concentrate upon the communication, especially verbal, of respect. Thus, we must, on the one hand, recognize fully the necessity for the low-level functioning person's experiencing and his therapist's communicating respect for his dignity and worth and, on the other hand, accept the implicit superiority of the therapist's power role in communicating this respect. The existentialists must acknowledge fully the highly cognitive therapeutic process which moves from experience to awareness to technique, particularly with lower-level functioning patients. Again, however, *the ultimate goal of any successful therapeutic process must be action on the part of both therapist and patient.*

Constructive action for both therapist and client involves each, ultimately, acting to (1) find himself, and (2) find others in relation or in reaction to him. It is precisely a continuation of the destructive experiences in the artificial world for either party simply to react to (1) find others, and (2) find himself in relation or reaction to others. Most often we are talking about the latter process in existential therapy, *a process of inter-reaction rather than interaction.* Only two actors can interact. The system most often described, heard, or experienced involves reactors, not actors. It is as if the therapist is saying, "Do something I can be spontaneous with." In essence, they imply, "we validate each other by reacting to each other."

## THE CONTRIBUTIONS AND LIMITATIONS
## FOR THERAPIST AND CLIENT

Since the existential stance deals primarily with the dimensions related to our development of the core conditions, it is difficult to discern the unique contributions; that is, those over and above the ones accounted for by the central core of facilitative conditions. Nevertheless, we can benefit from some specificity of description of the contributions and limitations. In doing so, however, we often find it difficult to separate the contributions to the client from those to the therapist. In addition, sometimes potential contributions may constitute limitations under different circumstances.

1. The existential approach offers both client and therapist an opportunity for an honest human encounter.

The existential approach, in spite of its highly intellectual orientation, offers at least the potential for a fully honest communication process. Indeed, of all the major therapeutic orientations, the existential approach offers the greatest possibility for both therapist and client to employ themselves fully.

Again, this potential contribution is not without qualification and, under some circumstances, the honesty of communication may actually constitute a limitation for the progress of therapy. Thus, with patients functioning at significantly lower levels than the therapist, the therapist may attend cautiously to the client's condition. He will not share with the client that which would make the client's condition the more desperate. Cognitive processes do provide the transition between the therapist's experience and his communication techniques.

Ultimately, however, *all therapy must offer the prospect of an open and honest exchange.*

2. The existential approach offers both client and therapist a well-developed cosmology for his existence.

The client who has no direction or meaning in his life may accept and incorporate an existential philosophy. However ready made the cosmology, it may be a more constructive one than that with which the client was previously functioning or than no direction at all. The same holds for the therapist, although he has the additional benefit of confidence in his therapeutic endeavors. Nevertheless, the existential orientation is limited by its own thinking and by what its own thinking excludes.

*The existential approach emphasizes a cosmology which might ultimately limit the development of both client and therapist.* Any well-developed cosmology can be, at best, transitory; that is, useful until more fundamental and more functional approaches are available. A system of basic "truths" can limit as well as enrich the growth of its adherent, whether client or therapist, and deprive him of other enriching possibilities.

3. The existential approach makes explicit values which are left implicit in other approaches while disregarding potentially useful techniques dictated by other approaches.

The therapist is aware of, and the client becomes aware of, an explicit value system. Most systems do not define the value systems which underly them, and thus, in a very real sense, do not define the implicit goals of the then therapy. One of the very critical values of existentialism, for example, is the emphasis upon the ultimate responsibility of the client for active decision-making. While the therapist takes responsibility for making the therapy process happen, the client takes the responsibility in action for giving his life direction.

On the other hand, *many of the explicit values of existentialism deny the possibility of the effective employment of many potentially useful techniques.* Although it may be argued that techniques are most useful when more human and natural processes have broken down, nevertheless, it is evident that they are useful under just those circumstances. Thus, techniques such as the counterconditioning of isolated symptomatology and the vocational counseling involved in realistic decision-making, both dictated from a deterministic base, are excluded by the value system of existentialism. A fearful thought strikes us that the therapist is both restrained from intervention and freed to intervene out of his deep awareness that life as he and the client both live it is ridiculous: his intervention does not, after all, matter.

4.   The existential approach minimizes the definition of roles for both therapist and client.

The existential approach allows for a more free and spontaneous interaction. Role definitions exclude many important functional characteristics of each party to the relationship and insofar as this constitutes a delimiting factor, the lack of role definition is a contribution. However, the necessity for going beyond the absence of roles is clear. In a logical extension of existential thinking, the therapist, and ultimately each party to the relationship, can be guided by what is effective for the other. Thus, if the absence of role definition can be extended to *the free selection of any appropriate role definition,* an existential therapeutic encounter might incorporate any of a number of potentially useful contributions from any of a number of potentially useful orientations.

5.   The existential approach assumes a most healthy therapist—something which it cannot always do.

As in all psychotherapy, the process is as effective as the therapist is whole. However, in existential therapy, the therapist is the living embodiment of the values which the system makes so explicit. It must be underscored that insufficient attention is given this logical extension of existential thinking: *the therapist must teach by the example of his person, not his analysis. In acting, the therapist exposes his existence—and it had better be a good one!*

## THE CONDITIONS OF SUCCESS
## AND FAILURE

The conditions under which the existential approach would appear to be most efficacious are those involving a creative therapist who communicates in his "being," the secret of health, an intelligent but lost and confused client seeking the meaning which he has lost in his "lonely crowd," and a free environment in which a process which is open in the sense that experiences which are not defined can take place in the context of explicit abstract values that have been defined. Of all the major therapeutic systems, the existential approach defines most clearly the second half of the necessary movement in therapy, from technique to person. At the same time it inadvertently allows for the necessary utilization of technique with the lower level functioning patient.

Thus, the existential approach is most effective with the level 3 client, where the therapist may employ his experience, awareness, and technique simultaneously in an open-ended interaction with a person who is capable of choosing but has not yet acted upon any of his choices. Indeed, the existential approach is the only approach, aside from the trait-and-factor orientation, which seeks primarily to clear away the obstacles to decision-making with higher level functioning clients, and which offers high-level functioning clients the opportunity for moving to higher levels of creative processes.

On the other hand, the existential approach could be effective with level 1 patients, where the healthy therapist's conscious awareness of his experience of the patient dictates the utilization of one set of techniques or another in restoring the integrity of the communication process for this individual. Unfortunately, the existential therapist's techniques are confined mostly to the communication of attitudinal conditions related to the dignity and worth of the patient as a human being. Valuable techniques such as the operant conditioning of patients to interact meaningfully with other patients are precluded.

The existential approach is, however, least likely to be effective with patients functioning at the lower levels, simply because they will be unable to employ the cosmology and the value system in other than a rigid, dogmatic way. Most therapies fail because they are insight therapies geared to clear the distortions of the level 2 neurotics. They fail because *neurotics cannot constructively utilize insights simply because they are neurotic.* Neurotics cannot effectively employ a useful cosmology because they must distort even the most effective one.

The existential approach is most subtly dangerous for the high-level functioning person who is closest to autonomy in choice and action. It provides him with a most lucid rationalization for lingering at level 3, and not proceeding to higher levels of relating to himself and others. The consequence is a desperate juggling act by the person who sees the artificial world clearly but cannot act to choose life for himself—or for another. In the client's crisis, the existential therapist observes but does not intervene.

## SUMMARY AND CONCLUSIONS

Again, protestations to the contrary, the existential approach is not merely an adjective but rather a position of relatively well-defined propositions. However, its assumptions concerning the nature of man address themselves primarily to the existence and effect of the core conditions to which we have attended and, thus, it makes few unique contributions over and above those accounted for by the core conditions. Concerning the core conditions, many of the existential assumptions must be modified, many must be extended. The core conditions are most compatible with (1) the existential spelling out of the goals of therapy, and (2) the existential emphasis upon the necessary movement within therapy toward the full persons of both therapist and client.

The existential approach would appear to be the highest form of psychotherapy within the artificial world. Its adherents see the artificial world most clearly while at the same time being within the tolerance limits of that world. The existential approach comes closest to the point of defining free man. It is handicapped only by its need for a system and its value for a consistent one. *Free man,* whether therapist or client, *needs no one system;* rather if he is to live effectively, he draws upon many systems, utilizing those, or the aspects of those, which are most effective in a given instance.

In general, we could summarize our experience in listening to tapes of existential therapy by saying that the existentialists write at level 4, but live at level 3 or less: they formulate precise definitions of man's condition and necessary direction without acting in therapy upon this knowledge. The existentialists write, they do not act. To define yourself is not to live; to act to define yourself is to live. In a sense, then, in its clarity of perception, existentialism is most painful for those who cannot act upon what they see and fear most clearly.

The existential approach, ironically enough, in some ways offers the most potential for an open-ended eclectic stance. It is particularly compatible with an eclectic position if therapy is viewed as a two phase process, the first phase of which the goal is client self-exploration and the second phase of which is a period during which a variety of potential approaches or techniques might be brought to bear. Of the existing approaches, the existential might offer the most during the initial phase. In its extension, existentialism need not be incompatible with a free eclectic position where the therapist is shaped by what is effective for both parties to the relationship. In its loose role definitions, both therapist and client could be open to a variety of meaningful and effective experiences and techniques which would allow each, in turn, to move to higher levels of functioning. *The dogmatic stance of precluding the techniques of more deterministic positions is unnecessary.*

Man's ultimate fear is not, as the existentialists suggest, to be alone. Man's ultimate fear is to be alone with himself. The existentialists have developed man in their thinking from an empty, dependent person through an awareness of his alienation to a stage of effective interaction with others. They have not gone far enough. They have moved from "man for himself" to "man for each other." They must move to where man can live alone with himself—to where he is not, as in therapy, accompanied by others in his voyage into the unknown—for the unknown is in him. He must come to love what is in him before he can return to the world to love and care for what is in others. Initial relations with fellow man is only a phase along the way, to be left to return to oneself. At best, the existential position is a transitory phase; at worst, a tomb.

In its focus upon the necessity for man's facing death before choosing life, the existential stance does not attend to the man who has moved to the phase beyond. It suggests, further, that man must face that there is nothing before and nothing after, before he can choose life. It leaves no room for the healthy product of the healthy environment. It leaves no room for the healthy man who alone can implement this stance. Those who fear death must face death before they can live life; those who do not fear death, live life.

### References

Binswanger, L. Existential analysis and psychotherapy. In Frieda Fromm-Reichmann, and J. L. Moreno (Eds.), *Progress in psychotherapy.* New York: Grune & Stratton, 1956.

Boss, M. *The analysis of dreams.* New York: Philosophical Library, 1958.

Boss, M. *Daseinanalyse and psychoanalysis.* New York: Basic Books, 1963.

Heidegger, M. *Being and time.* London: SCM Press, 1962.

Husserl, E. Phenomenology. In *Encyclopaedia Britannica* (14th Ed.), 1929, 17, 699–702.

Jaspers, K. On my philosophy. In W. A. Kaufmann (Ed.), *Existentialism from Dostoevsky to Sartre.* New York: Meridian, 1956, pp. 131–158.

Kierkegaard, S. *The sickness unto death*. New York: Doubleday, 1954.

May, R. (Ed.) *Existential psychology*. New York: Random House, 1961.

May, R., E. Angel, and H. F. Ellenberger (Eds.) *Existence: A new dimension in psychiatry and psychology*. New York: Basic Books, 1958.

Minkowski, E. Bergson's conceptions as applied to psychopathology. *J. nerv. ment. Dis.*, 1926, *63*, 553–568.

Ruitenbeck, H. M. *Psychoanalysis and existential philosophy*. New York: Dutton, 1962.

Sartre, J. P. *Existentialism*. New York: Philosophical Library, 1947. (Sartre is a pioneer in phenomonological psychiatry.)

Sartre, J. P. *Existential psychoanalysis*. New York: Philosophical Library, 1953.

Straus, E. The upright posture. *Psychiat. quart.*, 1952, *26*, 529–561.

Straus, E. *Von sinn der sinne* (On the meaning of the senses) (2d ed.) Berlin: Springer, 1956.

Chapter **6**

> . . . there is no significant
> learning without action.

## To Act or Not to Act:
## The Unique Contributions
## of Behavior Modification Approaches

*To the extent that therapy does not translate itself into action in life, it is not therapeutic.* All counselors and therapists should serve to alter the overt real-life behavior of their client. However, most counselors do not, in fact, focus upon manifest behavior.

Counselors and clinicians have, for too long, settled for apparent insight as the criterion for success, with little or no concern for the behavior of the patient outside of, or following therapy. Perhaps most significant, the complexity of our abstractions, and their vague implications for therapeutic treatment are so far removed from behavior and life that assessing efficacy takes the form of crude judgments based upon modification of hypothetical dynamics. The dynamic, living, behaving person is lost in the labels.

It is ironic that the behaviorists, those who lay no direct claim to a cohesive therapy, or complete therapy program, focus our attention upon the patient's real life behavior, and they do so without the need or the concern for the "inner person"! *Behavior modification for the benefit of the patient is the primary goal.*

Since Watson (1916), it has only been a matter of time before learning principles would be applied to therapy problems. Learning theory and research has, for some time now, dominated the academic scene in general and psychology specifically. Since World War II the prominence of the applied clinician at the university has been on the decline. The teaching of behavior modification techniques insures the clinical professor of academic respectability even though he may not employ them in his work with patients or may not even work with patients at all. Applicants with scientific talent and inclinations are more and more favored for admission into graduate counseling and clinical programs. *There is no doubt that therapeutic techniques first formulated in the experimental laboratory will be more acceptable to this future generation of therapists.*

## BEHAVIOR MODIFICATION

Since the principles of learning and the field of learning theory, itself, are attempts to account for the acquisition, performance, and extinction of behavior, and since psychotherapy, itself, is truly a process of inducing behavioral change, it is natural enough that these principles of learning be applied to the explication of the therapeutic process. The behavioristic approach, in general, holds that psychotherapy is a learning process or a complex of learning processes. Stripped to its essentials, this "tough-minded" stance assumes (1) that psychotherapy is a lawful and directive process which can be investigated most economically in a learning theory framework, and (2) that the variables which effect psychotherapy are essentially the same as those in other interpersonal situations, involving reinforcement, extinction, acquisition, and other constructs. In addition, the behaviorists insist upon the application of empirical procedures to theory building.

The behaviorists have split into two schools of thought on the issue of behavior control. There are those who advocate certain techniques "derived" from learning theory and emphasizing conditioning procedures based upon classical (Eysenck, 1960; Salter, 1961; Wolpe, 1958) or instrumental (Bandura, 1961; Frank, 1961; Krasner and Ullmann, 1965; Salzinger, 1959; Shaw, 1961; Ullmann and Krasner, 1965) learning. These theorists, as well as others employing directive forms of control and impersonal manipulations of primary drives, have put the therapist back in therapy, by focusing upon the therapist as the manipulator and controller of the therapy situation. The therapist is thus seen as a programmed therapy machine or computer which administers specified reinforcement schedules to the response system of a machine-like patient.

Murray's (1963) "biotropic" designation (as contrasted with his "sociotropic" stance) has been appropriately applied to this group of theorists who emphasize constitutional and genetic factors as relevant variables in psychotherapeutic personality change. They focus upon considerations such as innate differences in client "conditionability" as ultimate causal factors in psychopathology. Also, there is a tendency for the biotropic group to view pathology with an implicit disease orientation, where symptoms are characterized as "bad" things which, therefore, must be extinguished or eliminated. They reject the more "tender-minded" view of symptoms as motivated responses serving some life function of the client.

At no point are the "biotropes" further apart from their "sociotropic" brethren than in their rejection of the basic views and evolutionary tendencies of dynamic psychology, and in their concomitant de-emphasis of the therapeutic relationship itself as the "something more" of the psychotherapy process.

Miller (1959) and Murray (1963), with their historical antecedents in Dollard and Miller (1950), Mowrer (1953), and Shaffer and Lazarus (1952), have attempted to incorporate the more "tender-minded" view of psychotherapy within the framework of learning or social reinforcement theory. Their attempts, however, have been theoristically limited since they tend only to translate therapy as we know it today into learning theory terminology without really offering anything new. They have been accused of simply translating the form without in any way altering the substance. They have attempted to fit the process of psychotherapy into traditional learning theory, by liberalizing the stimulus-response (S-R) concepts to include more functional definitions of S and of R (Miller, 1959).

Only the behavior therapists, among learning theorists, have been concerned with exactly *how the patient learns*. Most often, these approaches make operational only a few principles to the exclusion of others. While the "sociotropes" focus upon the translation of the more traditional, psychoanalytically-oriented therapy into the terms of (1) the extinction of inappropriate affective responses and (2) discrimination learning due to the distinctive verbal cues of traditional interpretations which label behavior, the other behavior approaches directly emphasize techniques derived from learning theory and focus upon overt or public behavior. Thus, the Wolpe-Eysenck school makes extensive use of counterconditioning with the assumption that neurosis consists of systems of maladaptive, learned habits which can be ameliorated only by a reverse learning process involving the active induction of antagonistic responses usually of an assertive, relaxing, or sexual nature. The instrumental school is oriented toward the acquisition of new behavior, and emphasizes systematic, simple, primary, and secondary reinforcement in a variety of forms to teach or "shape" new responses to situations and cues.

Krasner and Ullmann (1965) spell out three major, initial questions for the behavior therapist: (1) "What behavior is maladaptive and with what frequency does it occur?", a question which enables the therapist to distinguish between behaviors which need to be enhanced and those which need to be extinguished; (2) "What aspects of the situation or environment are supporting and maintaining the symptom?" That is, what events in the life of the client may reduce the chance that normal or healthy responses can be elicited by the client?; and (3) "What situational or environmental events are amenable to manipulation?" Again, it is important to note that there is no assumption concerning pathological processes in the client and no employment of the usual diagnostic categories and techniques. Indeed, and to the consternation of the psychoanalysts, the ignorance of inner dynamics did not lead to symptom substitution (Wolpe, Salter, and Reyna, 1964)!

The means of understanding maladaptive or pathological behavior depart sharply with the more traditional clinical systems. The behavior modification approach classifies abnormal behavior into four major categories (Krasner and Ullmann, 1965): (1) *behavior deficits,* as characterized by the catatonic or autistic child; (2) *surplus or inappropriate behaviors,* such as repetitive behaviors which require no apparent reinforcement and which describe many acute psychotics; (3) *improper stimulus control,* illustrated by psychosomatic illnesses and enuresis; (4) *inadequate reinforcing systems,* where normal reinforcers are lacking or have been replaced by a damaging reinforcer such as drugs.

Obviously, the manner in which the behavior therapist explains behavior dictates the way he treats it. Whatever the specific technique employed, the behavior therapist attempts to effect change by manipulating conditions systematically in the therapy hour and/or in the social-physical environment between therapy sessions. Thus, Bachrach, Erwin, and Mohr (1963) successfully treated anoxeria by "shaping" patient behavior so that appropriate responses were made to food employed as a secondary reinforcer. Using the same basic approach, but employing physical rewards, Lovaas (1964) treated autistic children. Ayllon and Haughton (1962) treated a fastidious female patient by spilling food on the patient whenever she did not eat. The patient could avoid this aversive stimulus only when she ate. Other clinical problems have been handled by the use of negative practice (Yates, 1958) and various other extinction (Williams, 1959) and counterconditioning procedures (Lazovik and Lang, 1960).

The behavior therapist has at his disposal a wide variety of learning principles upon which he can draw. The creative therapist of any stance has, to some degree, employed behavior modification techniques without identifying them as such. More than likely, his use of the procedures are not very systematic, and he may very well miss many opportunities for their effective employment.

As a preferred mode of treatment (for clinicians of any system) behavior therapy offers the following sample of modification principles derived from classical conditioning: (1) counterconditioning; (2) direct conditioning; (3) reciprocal inhibition; (4) extinction. Instrumental conditioning yields procedures based upon (1) shaping of the successive reinforcement of small segments of desired behavior; (2) direct manipulation of the social-physical environment; (3) punishment; and (4) omission learning.

The behavior therapist must be willing to dictate the procedures and direction of therapy. The client influences the process only with his responses to treatment. Client feedback enables the therapist to assess the efficacy of what he is professing to do. The client is not a thinking, feeling, valuing person; he is, however, a behaving, acting organism, subject to the influence and impact of his interaction with his environment. The therapist can act upon the client only from the outside with the use of rewards, punishments, and the various other behavior modification techniques offering the possible alleviation of symptoms.

As the research literature related to learning grows so will the boundaries of behavior therapy. The direct linkage to a basic area of psychology is perhaps the most distinct advantage of the behavior modification stance (Wolpe, Salter, and Reyna, 1965).

## HISTORICAL CREDITS

The scientific respectability of the application of learning theory principles to problems of behavior modification dates back to the beginning of the twentieth century, and, in this sense, behavior therapy may indeed be considered a traditional approach. Unlike psychoanalytic theory and client-centered counseling, however, the learning approach is not dependent upon other disciplines and does not deal with philosophical issues such as whether or not man is basically good or evil. The turning away from the mysteries of the "inner" man and the focus on overt, public behavior freed the behavior therapist from the necessity for abstract speculation. Thus, a concentration of effort bringing together explanations of behavior and the means of changing that behavior became possible. In other systems, it is difficult, and often not possible, to see the relationship between the theory and the technique. The behaviorists' direct translation from theory to technique has forced other orientations to re-examine their stances, attempt operational definitions of constructs, assess outcomes, and consider giving up the vestigial appendages of assumption and practice.

These efforts, on both sides, may lead to statements of theory and practice which are more direct, simple, and more easily incorporated by the trainee-therapist and better understood by the client. Learning theory translations to therapy practice may provide, at long last, society with a language about adaptive and maladaptive behavior it can understand and use and verify.

By bridging the gap between clinical practice and the experimental laboratory, behavior modification techniques have accomplished more than encouraging communication between the hitherto separate camps in psychology. This growing alliance has, for the first time, built into therapy checks on the utility of the techniques employed at all critical stages and clearly defined goals and outcome. The commitment to do what works, to innovate, to assess efficacy, and to re-examine assumptions directly are indeed major contributions. There is less chance of explaining away failures in terms of client resistance, or a lack of readiness for treatment. When the data do not fit the theory, the behavior therapist is more apt to re-examine his assumptions, while others summarily dismiss or broaden their theory to explain away the phenomena.

The observation that the role and responsibilities of the therapist are well-defined, at least within the limits of the theory and data, is compelling. In addition, for the first time, the role of the client is well-defined. Although often a passive recipient of the techniques, he is well-informed about the procedures and goals. There is no burden of introspections, free associations, or learning an obtuse abstract language. He need only share with his therapist that material which allows for an understanding of symptoms and the formulation of manipulative techniques. While the therapist has principal responsibility, the client is the major focus of attention, with little regard for social values, parental influence, and unconscious processes. To their credit, *the behavior modification therapists are the first to share with their patients a detailed explanation of what is, and will be done, at each stage of the treatment process.*

The apparent simplicity and directness of the behaviorists challenged therapists of other orientations to focus on the measurable and observable. In other systems, it is really quite impossible for the client to "win," in that all or any aspect of his behavior can be explained or explained away in terms of his dynamics. *With behavior modification techniques, either the symptom dissipates or it does not.*

The supporters of the behavior approach, quite unlike their clinical counterparts, make no broad claim to being able to manipulate or change all maladaptive behavior. However, they accept the challenge to extend their treatment boundaries—often with clinical problems others would not and have not touched.

The specificity of procedures and the direct statement of the rationale lend a strong base, hitherto unknown, for therapist confidence. The therapist is not "on the line" as a person, and he needs no personal treatment prior to implementing these techniques. He is, during the course of treatment, a technician. Although there is recognition of the fact that the behavior therapist must become in some way a potent reinforcer, it is believed that he need not be functioning at high levels himself, nor must he necessarily be deeply involved personally with the client. However, here there is a growing recognition by some, that the therapist's emergence as a potent reinforcer is a function of his interacting at high levels of interpersonal dimensions.

In most systems of counseling and psychotherapy, understanding and communication among clinicians and modifications of theory rely heavily upon constructs used to describe the psychodynamic life of the patient. In turn, psychodynamic structure depends upon, or relates to, the un-coverings of psychodiagnostics. The behavior modification approach has no need for either, and has demonstrated effective behavior change without deep or detailed knowledge of psychodynamics or diagnostic categories. Related to this are the relatively large number of apparently dramatic cures within a short time span of treatment; demonstrations which are lacking in other systems.

From another vantage point, this approach has opened a rather basic and usable means for exploring and implementing social engineering by the use of systematic alteration and manipulation of the physical and social environment.

*The most unique historical credits, however, center around the promise of a timely, systematic approach to behavior change, and the use of a minimum number of constructs to describe behavior change.*

In summary, the historical contributions of behavior modification techniques are many. In addition to tapping the roots and contributions of learning theory, the explicit searching for translations to life, freed of excess theoretical and mystical baggage, is among the most valued. The commitment to implementing and incorporating what works, puts a system "on the line" without employing client defenses as an explanation for failure.

Finally, perhaps the most vital message is that *there is no significant learning without action.*

## THE UNIQUE CONTRIBUTIONS

The unique contributions of the behavior modification approach center around (1) the clear and relatively systematic direction it gives to treatment, (2) the well-defined criteria for outcome, and (3) the capacity for offering real hope for some of the most neglected patient populations.

When the behavior therapist provides appropriate levels of facilitative conditions this approach appears to make the following unique contributions, above and beyond contributions accounted for by high levels of those conditions.

### Process Contributions to the Client

1. The behavior modification approach provides the client with an understanding of the treatment process and his role.

The direction and implementation of techniques and roles are shared with the patient and, to that extent, the patient is a part of the process.

2. The behavior modification approach provides the client with concrete awareness of his level of progress in therapy.

The client, at every stage, is aware of the extent to which his symptoms have been extinguished. It is, therefore, possible that the client is also aware of the duration of treatment, which most often is relatively short.

3. The behavior modification approach provides the client with a useful knowledge of the history of the reinforcements which have created and sustained his symptoms.

The use of learning theory constructs to explain the development of a symptom is likely to be more easily understood and accepted by the patient than are explanations rooted in dynamic theory. Most people have some rudimentary knowledge or intuitive understanding of learning principles which simplifies the complexity of mental illness.

4. The behavior modification approach provides the client with knowledge that the therapist is guided by client feedback insofar as it fits the therapist's system.

The client in this sense has an awareness that his response to treatment does have an influence on the processes and the use of techniques. That is, what is happening to him influences the therapeutic process.

5. The behavior modification approach provides the client with an opportunity to actively accelerate the treatment process.

By translating therapy gains into life between sessions and practicing (relaxation, assertion, and so on), the client may materially contribute to the symptom amelioration. In addition, the client is forced to try out new modes of functioning with some minimal level of confidence.

6. The behavior modification approach provides the client with an opportunity to deal with maladaptive autonomic functions.

Behavior therapy is the only psychotherapeutic system, other than hypnosis, which deals directly with autonomic dysfunction.

> 7. The behavior modification approach provides the client with the assurance that the treatment process is geared to "curing" what it sets out to "cure."

In expressing the goals of therapy clearly, the client is assured that the procedures will not get sidetracked or uncover some conditions the client deems private or adaptive.

### Process Contributions to the Therapist

> 1. The behavior modification approach provides the therapist with a system of well-defined procedures.

Well-defined procedures enable the therapist to exhaust less energy and time in trial and error behavior.

> 2. The behavior modification approach provides the therapist with a well-defined role.

The therapist's role is explicit, his goals clear and well understood. Role definition further provides the therapist with a direct relationship between diagnosis and differential treatment, and a full and less ambiguous awareness of his responsibility to the client.

> 3. The behavior modification approach provides the therapist with a high and extremely useful level of confidence.

The specificity of techniques and the focus on symptoms rather than dynamics provides the therapist with a knowledge of what he is doing, unmatched in other systems, and undoubtedly reflected in client benefits.

> 4. The behavior modification approach provides the therapist with the opportunity to become meaningfully involved beyond the therapy hour.

The therapist is free and encouraged to act between sessions. He may, for example, manipulate the social and/or physical environment, rework therapeutic techniques, and the sequence of treatment.

> 5. The behavior modification approach provides the therapist with an opportunity to look for translations from therapy to life.

The therapist searches out and explicitly encourages meaningful and direct actions to be taken by the client in his real life situation.

> 6. The behavior modification approach may be implemented by a reasonably well-functioning person.

The implementation of many of the techniques do not require a high level of knowledge or talent and, thus, lay practitioners may be trained to employ them effectively.

    7. The behavior modification approach eliminates the transference/countertransference neurosis.

The therapist not functioning effectively himself need not fear that his neurotic needs will damage the treatment process.

    8. The behavior modification approach encourages the therapist to attend fully to nonverbal cues.

By focusing on all public and overt behavior, the therapist has a larger and broader base of client behavior to observe, discriminate, and evaluate. He is not limited to the complex meaning of client verbal expressions.

    9. The behavior modification approach provides the therapist a specific (behavioral) base for understanding behavior after the fact (post hoc), thus increasing his level of confidence for the next encounter with the patient and other patients with similar symptomatology.

The specificity of learning theory encourages direct modification of techniques toward a higher level of efficacy, thus providing a high level of learning and communication. As such, the orientation taps a ready source for data for the growth and expansion of the therapeutic system.

    10. The behavior modification approach gives the therapist an opportunity to fill the behavior vacuum with adaptive behavior.

The therapist can, if creative enough and willing to assume the responsibility, enhance the client's chances to realize a more full life by conditioning or suggesting behaviors to take the place of extinguished symptoms.

## THE LIMITATIONS
## OF THE BEHAVIOR MODIFICATION APPROACH

    Any broad statement about the limitations of the behavior modification approach surprisingly resembles that made about the client-centered approach; that is, most of the limitations center around the therapist's inability to employ himself fully and the inability of the client to do the same.

### Process Limitations for the Client

    1. The behavior modification approach cannot effectively work with clients who are unable to emit public cues.

With the absence of the overt behaviors necessary to identify treatable symptoms, an appropriate and economical set of procedures and the frequent evaluations of the efficacy which typify the behavioral approach will be difficult.

>   2.  The behavior modification approach limits the extent of client gain whenever the client's feedback goes beyond the scope of the rigorous system.

The therapist in reality is not influenced by the client's responses that carry the therapist away from his specific orientation and techniques.

>   3.  The behavior modification approach is geared to a minimal coping with the world.

The approach is not geared to go beyond the fundamental relief of symptomatology. In many instances it brings the client to the point where he can maintain a marginal tolerance for life.

>   4.  The behavior modification approach drains the therapy experience of all creativity for the client.

The experience of *creatively* participating in opening new experiential frontiers is denied so that the probability of the client meeting the demands of living more creatively is likely to be very little greater than it was before therapy.

>   5.  The behavior modification approach can set the stage for aversive conditioning.

The danger of aversive conditioning is always present. Without adequate client feedback the danger is very likely to become a reality.

>   6.  The behavior modification approach does not provide the client with the experience and conditions for self-fulfillment or self-actualization.

The basic and only aim is rehabilitative. The basic conditioning techniques alleviate some degree of suffering, but a rich awareness, discriminations, and a full life are not products of these techniques. If a cosmology is developed, it has its roots in a deterministic stance and a predictable future. There is reason to believe that those functioning at levels 3 and 4 would not be subject to the same rewards and punishments, and are likely not to be predictable. Left with only the devices of conditioning procedures, the client can only reach level 2 or 2.5.

>   7.  The behavior modification approach may promote client complacency with problems, once symptoms have been successfully controlled or extinguished.

The willful control of anxious feelings, or the capacity to relax selected parts of the body when inappropriately employed by the client may be more maladaptive than the effect of the treated symptom.

8. The behavior modification approach encourages the client to externalize or depersonalize his psychopathology.

Rather than reaching some level of functioning when he can assume some responsibility for his actions, the client is free to live life passively, ready to be conditioned to a new fear or take on psychopathic and manipulative modes of social interaction. With treatment, the client's concomitant learning leads him, in his crisis moments, to be repetitiously dependent upon men and means that are often highly impersonal and mechanistic.

### Process Limitations for the Therapist

1. The behavior modification approach rests its success on the assumption that the therapist can become a potent reinforcer for the client.

The individual therapist's ability to acquire reinforcing value to clients varies widely. To have maximum impact, this approach must train or select potent reinforcers.

2. The behavior modification approach does not control for the faulty model or faulty schedule which a poor clinician might develop.

In the end, the employment of any system or system of techniques is dependent upon the skill and sensitivity of the clinician. A poor clinician might develop inappropriate goals and schedules for behavior modification.

3. The behavior modification approach sets up the danger of the therapist becoming aversively conditioned to behavior therapy itself.

Once the hierachy and schedules are worked out, there is little or no challenge and considerable boredom. In its emphasis upon the present and the concrete, it limits the creative process of therapy.

4. The behavior modification approach limits the number of clients with whom the therapist can work.

It is very doubtful if any therapist could for any length of time work with even three or four desensitization cases per day.

5. The behavior modification aproach does not allow the therapist to learn more about who he is.

With this approach, the theory and techniques, not the therapist, are "on the line." The degree of personal involvement is minimal beyond the initial contacts used to establish the therapist as a potent reinforcer. The system creates distance and exploits closeness only for potency in reinforcement.

6. The behavior modification approach may be destructively employed by a sick society.

Based on the studies cited in Chapter 1, and recalling that behavior modification techniques are most effective with level 1 and level 2 clients, a "1984" is possible.

## THE CONDITIONS OF SUCCESS AND FAILURE

The behavior modification approach focuses upon several conditions where it can be employed most effectively. These conditions or problem areas are largely those avoided or inadequately understood by other systems. The specificity and emphasis on overt behavior, and the knowledge that behavior can be modified with disregard for "inner" processes enabled the behavior modification therapist to extend the boundaries of treatment efforts.

*There is extensive evidence that behavior modification techniques are effective with level 1 patient populations.* In order to make a minimal or self-sustaining adjustment, the patient, for whom the communication process has broken down (Carkhuff, 1967a) must eat, sleep, and attend to fundamental hygienic tasks. Verbal communication is frequently of no avail. Basic schedules designed to shape these behaviors have (1) relieved some custodial burdens, and (2) readied the patient to regain contact with his body and immediate environment. At this later stage, verbal efforts or more traditional therapies can be employed or attempted.

*In addition, there is evidence, both clinical and research, to indicate that behavior modification techniques are effective with level 2 or higher level clients exhibiting relatively isolated anxiety reactions.* An acutely neurotic population may have the potential for more adequate levels of adjustment but for some obvious and restricting behavior (Carkhuff, 1967a). These patients, in addition to having distorted perceptions of themselves in relation to their environment, are often led to deeper degrees of deterioration as a function of inappropriate physical or social behavior or behaviors. In addition and with less frequency, behavioral approaches may alleviate the distress of higher-level functioning clients who have vestigial or isolated symptomatology which is no longer functional, but which causes the person some degree of distress.

There are three additional conditions with more broad implications:

(1) *behavior modification techniques are particularly well-suited for use in experimental settings:* the techniques and constructs are easily operationally defined in the laboratory, and inter and intratherapist variability can be reduced to a minimum; (2) *behavior modification techniques are well-suited for efforts to engineer social and physical environmental manipulations directly:* the system may point to specific aspects of the environment to change, often resulting in social and/or psychological changes in areas such as human engineering, communication, attitude change, social perception, judgments, and beliefs; (3) *the behavior modification approach may be most useful when there is an acute press for time:* we may simply not be able to attend to the therapy as a leisurely effort involving an indefinite long-term period.

In summary, the behavior modification approach appears most effective in shaping behavior essential to basic living in the most severely disabled populations or in less severely disabled populations with relatively isolated anxiety reactions. The behavior modification approach is most effective when the therapist can provide the necessary level of facilitative conditions establishing him as a potent reinforcer.

We can now examine the success and failure of behavior modification techniques by pulling together selected points made in other parts of this chapter. Several general statements can be presented.

1. Man is at the beginning an unwritten slate.

The behavior technique is not tied to any assumption about the basic nature of man. From this view man has equal potential for good and evil; once shaped by society, however, there is no possibility for individual action. Even creative acts are explained in terms of the creator being shaped, with no data to support or fit the learning model.

2. The behavior modification technique applied to therapy is enriching for learning theory.

Although the most dramatic success is obtained with level 1 patients or level 2 clients with isolated symptomatology, there is no evidence or claim from this approach that the client can go on to take his own steps toward high levels of self-actualization. This therapy, however, affords the behaviorist a wide field in which to extend his constructs and to reformulate techniques for manipulating behavior and theoretical assumptions.

3. Behavior modification techniques aim at behavior change.

This provides the therapist operating within this system, specific and concrete criteria with which to evaluate the progress of therapy. It also frees him of mystical or ambiguous assumptions about the "inner" man typically used by other systems to support their successes or explain away their failures.

> 4. The behavior modification system puts the therapist back into the therapy process with great emphasis.

The behavior modification therapist assumes considerable apparent responsibility for the success or failure of his therapy. The theory or techniques, however, are more basically the cause of success or failure. The therapist as a person is absolved of *total* responsibility.

> 5. There is a behavior vacuum left by the extinguished symptom.

True success or long term success of this system may depend upon the therapist taking the responsibility to fill this vacuum with constructive behaviors.

> 6. The specificity and systematic base of behavior therapy reduces ambiguity.

The reduction of anxiety is greatly dependent upon the reduction of ambiguity, and this may be the major source of variability accounting for the large number of success cases.

> 7. Clients functioning at relatively high levels are left wanting.

The very deterministic base of this system allows for only a narrow view of creative living. The client seeking substantive meaning to his life, a cosmology, or a deeper experiential base cannot rely on another "determined" man.

## SUMMARY AND CONCLUSIONS

The success or failure of the behavior modification approach to therapy may depend largely upon therapist confidence and the selection of patients functioning at level 1, or level 2 clients with isolated symptomatology. Beyond this we need to raise a number of questions not as yet fully researched or explored.

> 1. The behavior therapist assumes that he can become a potent reinforcer with the use of some stereotyped procedures, often resembling client-centered techniques.

Basically, this assumption states that the impersonal acting out of a role can be more effective in establishing the therapist as a potent reinforcer than a personal and genuine caring and understanding. We would strongly suggest that a genuinely warm, empathic counselor, not fixed with a calculating, impersonal mask of understanding, would establish himself as a more significantly potent reinforcer.

2. The deterministic position of the behavior modification approach to therapy can be reduced to an existential stance.

As the behavior therapist looks out upon the world, he sees both himself and the client as having been determined. However, *his very act of viewing the world is existential in nature since it describes the viewer's immediate phenomenology.* Just as the existentialist views himself as a free and creative person who chooses "systems," so is it inconceivable to the behaviorist that he could choose. He views himself as having to be fit to a system (Carkhuff, 1967b).

3. The deterministic stance leaves room for only apparent responsibility on the part of the therapist as well as the client.

The lives of level 1 and level 2 clients and behavior therapists are determined and, within this framework, avoid all real life responsibility. In behavior therapy the therapist starts with this basic stance: "His life and my life are both determined." It follows that it is difficult to understand who is on who's schedule of reinforcements. Both client and therapist are stimulus bound. A man who accepts that his life is determined cannot hold himself to be responsible and cannot meet real responsibility. Those functioning at the highest levels live lives that are not predictable. Those people functioning at high levels are both free and responsible.

4. The question remains as to whether or not behavior modification techniques can be employed to widen rather than narrow choices.

Shaping behavior connotes a smaller and smaller number of behavioral choices in the repertoire of the clients. Creative living requires a large pool of responses, not all of which are predictable.

5. Does systematic reinforcement lead to symptomatology? Do we need rigorous schedules to eliminate symptoms?

The client may be conditioned so that he is cut off from experiencing body tension when it's appropriate. This has far reaching implications. The therapist, for example, may be aversively conditioned to the therapy situation itself, as a function of boredom and the movement of the client's "pinky." Without appropriate bodily feedback, the client, like the therapist, is forced to fake spontaneity, even anger and fear.

6. Within this system random schedules allow the person the experience of freedom.

Random schedules at best create apparent freedom. They have nothing to do with the reality of freedom. The experience of freedom can be used to justify the use and abuse of conditioning techniques beyond the therapy setting. It is interesting to contemplate the implications this question has for child-rearing practices.

7.   How much of the outcome variance can be accounted for by change and attention factors?

The full focus of attention is on the client. The Hawthorne effect or the effect of change or attention is especially likely since each client presently being seen is seen as an experimental case.

It can readily be seen that not all the data fits the model. But the efficacy of behavior modification techniques has been demonstrated to a level where we are forced to consider social as well as individual goals. The hope for society is, however, in the nurturance of creative, free people, rather than those so cut off from their bodily experience that they must feign even the most fundamental emotional experiences. In this regard, the reliance on verbal conditioning reinforcers such as "hmmm" seems now to be absurd.

The behavior modification approach is an outgrowth of our time and a technical society. *If it is successful to the point of being the new "wave of the future" for therapists and social engineers, it will become the next major social problem of our time.* Unless it is geared or coupled with other systems, it cannot hope to free low-level obstacles in order to enable the client (or society) to function at higher levels.

We will live in a land where there are only narrow choices and no real choices with regard to interpersonal functioning, creativity, spontaneity, love, and friendship. We will perform our roles and experience apparent freedom and apparent satisfaction in an apparent world.

## References

Ayllon, T., and E. Haughton. Control of the behavior of schizophrenic patients by food. *J. exp. Analysis Behav.*, 1962, 5, 343–352.

Bachrach, A. J., W. Erwin, and J. P. Mohr. The control of eating behavior in an anorexic by operant conditioning techniques. Unpublished manuscript, 1963.

Bandura, A. Psychotherapy as a learning process. *Psychol. Bull.*, 1961, 58, 143–157.

Carkhuff, R. R. Toward a comprehensive model of facilitative interpersonal processes. *J. counsel. Psychol.*, 1967, 14, 67–72. (a)

Carkhuff, R. R. The contributions of a phenomenological approach to deterministic approaches to counseling and psychotherapy. *J. counsel. Psychol.*, in press, 1967. (b)

Dollard, J., and N. E. Miller. *Personality and Psychotherapy*. New York: McGraw-Hill, 1950.

Eysenck, H. J. (Ed.) *Behavior therapy and the neuroses*. New York: Pergamon, 1960.

Frank, J. D. *Persuasion and healing*. Baltimore: The Johns Hopkins Press, 1961.

Krasner, L., and L. Ullmann. *Research in Behavior Modification*. New York: Holt, Rinehart and Winston, 1965.

Lazovik, A. D., and P. J. Lang. A laboratory demonstration of systematic desensitization psychotherapy. *J. Psychol. Stud.*, 1960, *11*, 238–247.

Lovaas, O. Clinical implications of relationships between verbal and nonverbal operant behavior. In H. J. Eysenck (Ed.), *Experiments in Behavior Therapy*. New York: MacMillan, 1964.

Miller, N. E. Liberalization of Basic S-R Concepts: Extensions to Conflict Behavior, Motivation and Social Learning. In S. Koch (Ed.), *Psychology: A Study of a Science*, Vol. II. New York: McGraw-Hill, 1959.

Mowrer, O. H. *Psychotherapy: theory and research*. New York: Ronald, 1953.

Murray, E. J. Sociotropic-learning approach to psychotherapy. In P. Worshell and D. Burns (Eds.), *Personality Change*. New York: Wiley, 1963.

Salter, A. *Conditional Reflex Therapy*. New York: Capricorn, 1961.

Salzinger, K. Experimental manipulation of verbal behavior: a review. *J. gen. Psychol.*, 1959, *61*, 65–95.

Shaffer, G. W., and R. S. Lazarus. *Fundamental Concepts in Clinical Psychology*. New York: McGraw-Hill, 1952.

Shaw, F. J. (Ed.) *Behavioristic approaches to counseling and psychotherapy*. University of Alabama Studies, 1961, No. 13.

Ullmann, I., and L. Krasner. *Case studies in behavior modification*. New York: Holt, Rinehart and Winston, 1965.

Watson, J. B. Behaviorism and the concept of mental disease. *J. Phil. Psychol.*, 1916, *13*, 589–597.

Williams, C. D. The elimination of tantrum behavior by extinction procedures. *J. abnorm. soc. Psychol.*, 1959, 59, 269.

Wolpe, J. *Psychotherapy by reciprocal inhibition*. Stanford: Stanford Univer. Press, 1958.

Wolpe, J., A. Salter, and L. Renya. *The conditioning therapies*. New York: Holt, Rinehart and Winston, 1964.

Yates, A. J. The application of learning theory to the treatment of tics. *J. abnorm. soc. Psychol.*, 1958, *56*, 175–182.

# Chapter 7

. . . an effort to systematize
man's efforts to systematize
man's life . . .

## Chance, Not Choice or Change:
## The Unique Contributions of the Trait-
## and-Factor Vocational Counseling Approach

Man spends the greater part of his life attempting to bring order and reason into the major decisions of his life. The trait-and-factor approach addresses itself to this end. It is neither stance nor theory but rather an immense effort to bring order and reason into the major decisions of life. Although its efforts to reduce the contributions of chance factors confounding vocational and educational choice have created a large and useful pool of information about man's attributes, the socioeconomic world, and their complex interactions, the utility of these findings has been limited, largely because trait-and-factor adherents have not gone beyond the early concept of matching men and jobs (Parsons, 1909). When, for example, a client is determined to make a choice in opposition to the predictions of tests, the trait-and-factor counselor then helps the client to upset the unfavorable prediction. The implication here is simple: the counselor stands for nothing; a viable theory and practice is not possible. Indeed, *there is more hope for the client than there is for the counselor.*

**105**

## THE TRAIT-AND-FACTOR APPROACH
## AND ITS HISTORICAL CONTRIBUTIONS

At its core the trait-and-factor approach to counseling focuses on an effort to match men to their occupational environments (Parsons, 1909). The assumptions posited to justify this effort are simple and direct: (1) *men differ along measurable but relatively stable dimensions;* (2) *jobs differ along measurable but relatively stable dimensions.*

The task has been to identify important variables upon which people vary and jobs vary, develop reliable and valid measuring instruments, and apply these tools along with occupational information, to the problem of matching. Ideally, the resolution is accompanied by a statement reflecting the probability that a good or a bad choice has been made, within the limits of available data. The counselor is aware of the fact that he and his client will never have all the data. They attempt only to reach an apparently reasonable choice.

What begins based upon two simple assumptions becomes very tenuous and arbitrary along the route. The very determination of what constitutes an important variable is often influenced by theories of vocational choice, if indeed there are "theories" of vocational choice (Carkhuff, Alexik, and Anderson, 1967).

Methods used to study occupational choice have varied from pure speculation to attempts at rigorous experimentation. Even though the trait-and-factor counselor lays claim to an empirical base, the tools of his research vary, and are often found to be unreliable and/or interdependent. Questions which center around fitting men to jobs (Hoppock, 1957; Shartle, 1946), appropriateness of choice (Strong, 1943, 1955; Super, 1949, 1957), interest development (Ginzberg, Ginsberg, Axelrad, and Herma, 1951; Holland, 1962; Roe, 1956; Super, 1949, 1957; Tiedman, O'Hara, and Baruch, 1963), personality (Darley and Hagenah, 1955; Roe, 1956; Tyler, 1953), heredity, environmental and other socioeconomic factors (Caplow, 1954), and basic learning processes in general, include an overwhelming number of considerations and likely variables for investigation. The most pressing task to be met is an integrative one. Yet the complexity of the material cannot be rendered more coherent without a stance capable of going beyond the use and abuse of empirical methodology and philosophy.

With the goal which the trait-and-factor adherents have set for themselves, helping clients to make appropriate choices, empiricism is not enough. The tenacious clinging to objectivity has led to a rigidity, culminating in a collector's role for the counselor based on self-neutralizing research and practice. For example, there is a strong deterministic base to the trait-and-factor approach, yet it searches ways and means to supply clients with data relevant to critical choices. This is something of a paradox! *Perhaps underlying this effort is the implicit awareness or assumption, that with adequate data, the client will make his inevitable choice more quickly and with less trial and error groping.* The implication is that most men are suited for rather specific work roles, and discordance in life can be greatly reduced by matching men to appropriate work situations.

Perhaps the trait-and-factor approach is the most heroic of all the major systems. Its adherents have unfortunately been seduced by the apparent logic of the basic assumptions, the simplicity of the tools and the reverence for objective data that is not objective. A close examination of the large volume of literature and consequent impact of trait-and-factor efforts strongly suggests that *the system has either attempted to stabilize modern social-vocational movements or, at another level, to render reasonable, a great portion of man's behavior which has been, historically, unreasonable.* Even the historians, by using creatively artistic methods, have managed to weave only some semblance of reason into human history.

If the trait-and-factor theorist is making an effort to systematize man's effort to systematize man's life, in essence he is fighting two formidable and basic sets of events which he needs to recognize: (1) man was and continues to be a biological accident and (2) man's history reads like a chronology of interactions of social, economic, and political accidents, complicated and contaminated by periodic and violent physical accidents. On rare occasions violent change was brought about by some atypical and unpredictable personality, functioning independently of the conditions around him, further upsetting the web of assumed predictions about the interaction among the basic components of society, culture, and the individual's situation.

Nevertheless, there are a number of rather specific historical contributions which the trait-and-factor approach makes to counseling and psychotherapy.

1. The trait-and-factor counselor attempts to move the client within the environment, with a minimum change or no change in either the client or the environment.

Most therapies attempt to change the person to fit the environment or adjust to it. The behavior therapist may change the environment to fit the client. Environmental manipulation may be considered by the trait-and-factor counselor only when human limits are reached. In general, there is minimal upheaval of what exists.

2. The trait-and-factor approach emphasizes information assumed to be useful to the client in his effort to make a choice.

An effective counselor does not need a trait-and-factor orientation to justify providing the client with selected and useful information; however, the trait-and-factor adherents build the counseling sessions around information-giving and receiving.

3. The trait-and-factor approach provides descriptive information about a variety of relevant aspects of life as it is.

From this base of descriptive data, large numbers of people can be placed with a success rate better than chance. These data have served to identify levels of available human and environmental resources.

4. The trait-and-factor approach offers reason for believing that, for most men, life is predictable.

The level of satisfaction for the great majority can be anticipated and influenced by appropriate and inappropriate choices. Accident theories of occupational choice offer more excitement and surprise for those who are not predictable.

5. The trait-and-factor approach provides the client a base from which he can act.

Once a choice is made, the client is encouraged to act on it, thus providing him with the most important sources of learning about himself in relation to his world.

6. The trait-and-factor approach has provided a large number of useful comparisons.

The search for basic dimensions via factor analysis and comparisons among a wide variety of human attributes has led to the development of occupational ability patterns, occupational reinforcement patterns, expectancy tables, and social-educational characteristics scales.

The total impression of the trait-and-factor approach is one of a shotgun effort, using overlapping data to fit a set of overlapping assumptions. The integration needed for a dynamic theory is lacking; the inability to go beyond the basic tenet of its founder is obvious; the adherents' devaluation of its essential contributions dominates. The emphasis in all cases is upon "choice, not change."

## COUNSELOR AND CLIENT CONTRIBUTIONS

It is very difficult to separate the unique contributions and limitations of the trait-and-factor approach because the system neutralizes itself for the following reasons: (1) it attempts to deal reasonably with what is often an unreasonable life situation; (2) it is not able to incorporate or to interpret extremes meaningfully; (3) it cannot deal with affect; (4) it relies on summary information about the world and on modal or normative data; (5) its values are rooted firmly in the middle class.

The effort to take the extremes out of life, ignore affect, and make decisions on the basis of objective data shapes the whole system as a product of middle-class values. *Life is rendered perfectly reasonable on the surface.*

1. The trait-and-factor approach focuses upon one of the two most important choices in life.

Vocational choice and marital choice are two of the most important and basic choices influencing the life of the individual in our society. Information about the foundations for such choices, alternative choices, and implications of each, provides a considerable mass of useful data.

2. The trait-and-factor counselor can reduce anxiety significantly for the client by focusing on information, and making concrete the decision-making process.

The specific reliance on test data and occupational information reduces ambiguity, not only for the client but for the counselor as well. There is little need, if any, for the trait-and-factor counselor to probe or venture into the "unknown" areas, such as the many and varied aspects of interpersonal relationships. The counselor does not go beyond his level of confidence in the data he has available to him.

3. The trait-and-factor emphasis upon the reality aspects of choice and the maximum use of available data often aids in the consideration of factors not previously considered by the client and counselor.

Discussion of information often points out what is not known, and what kinds of additional information or clinical treatment is needed. It may also lead to a feeling that there are too many factors to take into account, and a reasonable choice is not really possible.

4. The trait-and-factor approach is particularly useful in situations where prospects for change are minimal.

When the environment is determined and/or characteristics of the client offer no hope for change, the trait-and-factor counselor may be in the best position to create an optimum solution or adjustment. This contribution also holds for situations where there is not enough time to change either the person or his life situation. Such conditions often occur when dealing with the geriatric, the handicapped, the culturally deprived, and with people attempting a second career. Of all major systems, the trait-and-factor approach offers the most promise for making such choices with the creative use of electronic computer facilities.

5. The trait-and-factor approach serves a growing technologically-oriented society.

When dealing with large numbers of people, the trait-and-factor counselor can employ an expedient and practical system based upon objective public criteria. The results can be evaluated in terms of change in the rate of productivity and other variables reflecting satisfaction. For the good clinician, however, objective data serves as a contributory appendage. Creative acts at the highest levels are not predictable.

6. The trait-and-factor counselor often leads the client to a better definition of the client's values.

The determination of a choice point, accompanied by useful information, is greatly influenced by the degree to which the client is aware of what is important to him as a human being living in a complex society; that is, a good decision, from the trait-and-factor point of view, is a consequence of what the client is willing to accept. The client is not seen as a black box. Values come from the client. But to respond and to realize fully the constructive potential of what is in the client, the counselor must be something more than a black box filled with information.

7. The trait-and-factor practitioner-counselor requires the least amount of training.

From this stance, a modestly endowed lay person can be trained to use and dispense information in a very short period of time and, indeed, many guidance counselors who employ this orientation are untrained or minimally trained.

8. The trait-and-factor approach provides a didactic role for the counselor.

The trait-and-factor counselor is allowed, even encouraged, to become involved in the life of his clients to the extent that he can teach them something useful; that is, to bring the client directly to the level where he, the client, can improve the quality of his experiences.

9. The trait-and-factor approach is often most useful in short term consulting roles.

The clinical versus statistical approaches to prediction have been resolved: *The actuarial approach is a more successful base from which to operate than the average counselor.* The alive issue before the field involves, however, the discrimination and development of the potent counselor.

## COUNSELOR AND CLIENT LIMITATIONS

The limitations of the trait-and-factor approach reflect, for the most part, the problems inherent in attempts to apply normative data to the individual and his unique and often extreme situations. In addition, the role of the counselor, when structured primarily as a source of information, does not fully attend to the subtle and complex aspects of a one-to-one interaction.

1. The trait-and-factor literature has not as yet reported the critical test of the stance.

Clients could be randomly assigned to one of two groups, one group counseled to enter fields of work based on test data, and the other group counseled to enter the "wrong" field. A follow-up study employing a variety of appropriate indexes could serve as a useful test. Choices of a less critical nature may be employed for experimental purposes.

2. The trait-and-factor approach has been largely limited to initial choice and career patterns to maturity.

Early developmental trends offer conflicting impressions. The study of vocational patterns of late maturity, the relationship between the major work role, and the movement to other jobs has not been extensively studied. The use of data reflecting the decision-making process at crisis points in life may yield a pool of variables more critical than those traditionally employed.

3. The trait-and-factor approach has emphasized the analysis of worker attributes with a tendency to exclude systematic patterns of job changes over time.

Little is offered in the way of systematic patterns of job changes over time. If there is any hope for relatively lasting and satisfying matching, such data is essential. This is especially true in a time when entire industries are in the process of radical change in production systems. At a more simple level, more information is needed in any specific case, reflecting situational factors such as the personality of the supervisor and status of the job on the local scene, and whether it is a family business, corporation, or governmental agency.

4. The trait-and-factor approach does not give sufficient attention to the counseling relationship, related attitudes, and motives.

The ability of the client to accept and use information maximally may be directly related to how the client perceives the counselor. The willingness of the client to share aspects of his life which interfere with his optimum functioning is related to the level of therapeutic conditions offered by the counselor. It is absurd to treat personal choices in an objective, impersonal manner. Clients may be more in tune with this absurdity than the average trait-and-factor counselor. The counselor trained to deal directly with counselor-client differences is at a distinct advantage (Banks, Berenson and Carkhuff, 1967).

    5.   The trait-and-factor approach appears to be limited in effectiveness to the upwardly mobile.

The nature of the normative data employed renders it minimally useful to those clients representing the extremes of socioeconomic status.

    6.   The trait-and-factor approach gives little recognition to the fact that decisions vary in significance.

The implications of major and minor decisions are not systematically and differentially weighted. There is an implicit set that the goal in counseling is to help the client to become settled in life, thus discouraging further explorations. A decision to study engineering at age fifteen is or should be more reversible than the same decision at age twenty-four. Some decisions require more data, reflecting higher levels of reliability and validity, than do other decisions.

    7.   The trait-and-factor approach is basically dependent upon only three main sources of information, and often the major determinants of choice are never uncovered.

The counselor attempts to integrate information gleaned from tests, occupational information, and the client. Some test results are of questionable reliability and validity, and occupational information is often scant and dated. Information offered by the client is often reduced to efforts on the part of the client to be objective about his history and future. The deeper feelings of the client are often the major determinants of choices and may never come to light. Too little attention has been given to building, by way of discriminating useful from useless sources of information.

    8.   The trait-and-factor approach emphasizes a reasonable consideration of choice to the exclusion of the crises which constitute the fabric of life.

The most compelling moments in life are made up of crises points. These moments of stress or heightened activity constitute the fabric of the life style of the client and his spurts of growth. Crises rarely occur in trait-and-factor counseling. A calm, careful, and reasoned consideration of a personal choice offers little that constitutes significant learning or growth.

9. The trait-and-factor approach implies that choice = information + client values + probability of success.

This raises the question about the efficacy of training counselors (1) to compartmentalize life experiences and (2) to render all subjective experiences objective.

10. The trait-and-factor reliance on data seemingly excuses the counselor from functioning at high levels of interpersonal skills.

The utility of the information is likely to be directly related to the level of functioning of both the counselor and client. A counselor functioning at low levels might not communicate the full value of the data. A level 4 counselor contributes over and above the value of the information alone.

11. In a trait-and-factor counseling situation there is often not enough information to act on.

This system frequently forces choices in the name of norms. When action is taken, it is done only on the basis of what information is available. This somehow makes critical life choices analogous to a bridge game.

12. The trait-and-factor approach gives little attention to client energy levels, motivation, and neuroticism.

The ability to act is directly dependent upon the energy level of the individual. High energy levels, coupled with the motivation to break free of one's own history and measured limitations, are the behavioral components necessary to upset actuarial predictions. However, if these components are subject to a high level of neurotic drainage, inaction or inappropriate action is the rule.

## THE CONDITIONS OF SUCCESS AND FAILURE

The trait-and-factor approach appears to have the greatest contribution to make in the counseling and/or assigning of those who could not otherwise make necessary choices. *Thus, with mentally or emotionally disabled (level 1) or physically disabled persons, vocational assessment and assignment would appear to be most efficacious.* The relevant dimensions of the person and the job may be assessed, and the man may be matched to the job or the job to the man. Assignments making maximum use of human and vocational resources can be made accordingly.

Similarly, *vocational and educational counseling, in turn, would appear to be most effective with the level 2 individual who is hampered by obstacles and is unable to make necessary life choices.* Counseling can clear away the obstacles or, at a minimum, give the client a clear perspective on the obstacles involved and a probability statement on his success or failure in action. Hopefully, appropriate choices will free the individual to function at higher levels.

However, although it may free the individual to function at higher levels, *the trait-and-factor approach appears to be the least effective in the assigning or counseling of higher-level functioning persons.* Thus, persons functioning above level 3 are already self-sustaining and facilitative of the efforts of others as well as their own. They are capable of making their own choices, vocational as well as marital. The choices which they make are appropriate for them and independent of actuarial tables. Often their choices can be made only, and directionality can be found only by denying most of their previous experiences in life.

There are more broad implications in the use of the trait-and-factor approach:

1. The reliance on normative data encourages passivity on the part of the client and the counselor.

There is an implicit and often explicit distrust of impulses and feelings. Decisions based on the best available facts, without a deep level of personal involvement, absolve both the client and counselor of some vital level of responsibility. Both learn to trust outside sources of information more than they trust their own experiencing of the world. With this set, only minimum personal change is possible.

2. The trait-and-factor approach reinforces the client's identity as an object or commodity.

The client is related to as a potential source of productivity valued by society, and his worth weighted in terms of occupational, economic, and educational levels. In order to depersonalize counseling to this degree, the counselor must see himself as a commodity.

3. Measuring job satisfaction in terms of norms is absurd.

This leaves little or no room for the possibility that the average is miserable; the extremes often serve as the impetus for change. But to rely on a norm table to determine something as personal and unique as satisfaction is even more absurd.

4. The extended hope is a regulated world with data on everyone and every job.

Where does new data come from? One often does not creatively understand the game while playing it.

## SUMMARY

Any system geared to operating in terms of norms tends, over time, to neutralize itself to such an extent that real change is extremely difficult. Creating within these limits is not possible. It does, however, lead to results which are socially acceptable at the moment simply because they upset nothing. The fact that the system restricts certain behaviors (affective and physical) is perfectly consistent with the dominant middle-class values.

In addition to assuming a deterministic-empirical base, the trait-and-factor approach to counseling places great emphasis on factors of heredity. This further reduces the possibility for change, and justifies ignoring motivation, energy levels, and dominating neurotic needs. *If nothing else changes, man does change, not only within his life span, but over the span of modern history.* Man's day-to-day behaviors have been increasingly more moderate, or at least more subtle. In time of crises his behaviors are more indirectly violent (war, nuclear arms). The polite, quiet, conforming child is often the one who shocks his community with some violent act.

The assumed causes of behavior naturally lead to what is to be done to change behavior. Thus, we find the trait-and-factor counselor creating and collecting more and more descriptive knowledge. He shares his knowledge and can do so at a great personal distance from his clients. His clients, like himself, can change only very little beyond the natural influences of hereditary factors in their life span.

If employed with great success on a large scale, trait-and-factor counseling would produce, in each generation, an army of determined people who follow or live in reaction to free people. The free person, in turn, is able to disregard his total life history and live life independently of norms.

*Confirmation of existence can be obtained only from a physical and affective base, not at a distance through a complex web of knowledge.*

### References

Banks, G., B. G. Berenson, and R. R. Carkhuff. The effects of counselor race and training upon Negro clients in initial interviews. *J. clin. Psychol.*, 1967, *23*, 70–72.

Caplow, T. *The sociology of work.* Minneapolis: Univer. of Minnesota Press, 1954.

Carkhuff, R. R., Mae Alexik, and Susan Anderson. Do we have a theory of vocational choice? *Personnel guid. J.*, in press, 1967.

Darley, J. G., and Theda Hagenah. *Vocational interest measurement: Theory and practice*. Minneapolis: Univer. of Minnesota Press, 1955.

Ginzberg, E., S. W. Ginsburg, S. Axelrad, and J. L. Herma. *Occupational choice*. New York: Columbia Univer. Press, 1951.

Holland, J. L. Some explorations of a theory of vocational choice: I. One- and two-year longitudinal studies. *Psychol. Monogr.*, 1962, Vol. 76, No. 26 (whole No. 545).

Hoppock, R. *Occupational information*. New York: McGraw-Hill, 1957.

Parsons, F. *Choosing a vocation*. Boston: Hughton Mifflin, 1909.

Roe, Anne. *The psychology of occupations*. New York: Wiley, 1956.

Shartle, C. L. *Occupational information*. New York: Prentice-Hall, 1946.

Strong, E. K., Jr. *Vocational interests 18 years after college*. Minneapolis: Univer. of Minnesota Press, 1955.

Strong, E. K., Jr. *Vocational interests of men and women*. Stanford Univer. Press, 1943.

Super, D. E. *Appraising vocational fitness*. New York: Harper & Row, 1949.

Super, D. E. *The psychology of careers*. New York: Harper & Row, 1957.

Tiedeman, D. V., R. P. O'Hara, and R. W. Baruch. *Career development: Choice and adjustment*. Princeton, N. J.: College Entrance Examination Board, 1963.

Tyler, Leona. *The work of the counselor*. New York: Appleton, 1953.

Chapter **8**

> . . . a passive acceptance of life as a
> series of painful episodes with
> infrequent periods of balance
> and no real joy.

## The Illusive Suicide: The Unique
## Contributions of the Psychoanalytic Approach

*Freud was keenly aware of the tragedy in human history and its repetitive compulsion to record crimes on larger and grander scales.* Freud understood that the average man is truly an impotent victim who can only hope to tolerate the pain of living (Freud, 1924b, 1927, 1933, 1943; Jones, 1953; Brill, 1938). The raw data for any theory of personality and therapy arises out of stressful situations (Freud, 1924a, 1935, 1938, 1943). It is precisely these crises periods that are focused upon in life and therapy; the rest of the patient's life stands summary dismissal. From the psychoanalytic point of view, crises involve periods of acute pain only, without the possibility of high levels of pleasure, joy, or creativity upon "breaking through" the crisis experience. Perhaps this, in part, explains why psychoanalytic theory and practice has been unable to cope fully with the free man while, at the same time, it has offered the most comprehensive insights into the psychodynamics of the sick man. *To understand and accept fully the validity of the psychoanalytic stance promotes a passive acceptance of life as a series of painful episodes with infrequent periods of balance and no real joy.*

The dismal state of man is depicted vividly in the psychoanalytic postulate stating that pleasure is sought only to reduce tension (Freud,

[1]Those readers who wish for a converging perspective from within psychoanalysis should refer to Appendix B, where one of our students, Raphael Vitalo, establishes a somewhat similar position.

1938). Furthermore, tension is likely to become pain, for there are few, if any, opportunities for direct discharge. When discharge of tension is accomplished, it is done through a highly complex system of energy changes and compromises which, once again, leave the individual prey to the conflict between internal and external pressures.

The implications of facing this cycle again and again without the gain of *constructive* learnings can only lead to the development of a defeated and empty man. Freud's insight into the victim's benign subjugation to these destructive forces in society was profound. His stance, woven out of this neurotic fabric, filled a need at a time when there was an accelerated growth in the great middle class. It supplied the empty man with some considerable substance, and conceptually emptied the whole man.

The major contributions of psychoanalytic theory are historical and center largely around man's effort to maintain some minimal or tolerable level of survival (Freud, 1920, 1933, 1936). In addition, from our view, Freud identified and described that from which persons functioning above level 3 must escape. *In its essence, psychoanalytic theory supplies a highly complex and all-encompassing intellectual justification for a substantive but essentially impotent stance toward life.*

## THE PSYCHOANALYTIC STANCE

It is our purpose here only to present the briefest of outlines of essential psychoanalytic constructs or assumptions. The focus will center on Freud's view of psychodynamics and their implications for therapy. With the notable exception of Adler (1917, 1927), we view the neo-Freudians (Fromm, 1941, 1947; Horney, 1939, 1942, 1945; Jung, 1927, 1928, 1939; Rank, 1929; Sullivan, 1938, 1948) as having lived largely in qualification of Freud rather than emerging as vitally new and original contributors. The credits are due Freud, the limitations may be charged to his socially acceptable followers.

### Some Basic Assumptions

1.  Man is basically evil and is governed by rudimentary instincts, yet he is destined to become a victim of the interaction and conflict between these instincts and social forces.

2.  Man's only real hope is to achieve, and, then diligently maintain a tolerable balance between internal impulses and external demands and restrictions. In this way he may be able to tolerate life and living.

3.  Man can accomplish this delicate balance through a deep understanding of what makes him weak. He achieves this understanding and learns to employ it in an effort to live more rationally by analysis.

4. A basically evil person who has achieved some reasonable level of balance between inner and outer forces can help another basically evil person.

Psychoanalysis is firmly based on a theory of instincts. In addition to a reflex reaction to external stimuli, the organism is subject to the forces of powerful and incessant inner stimuli. The internal stimuli are said to be instinctual. For Freud, the energy expended to relieve the tension brought on by an instinct is directly related to the strength of the inner stimuli (Mullahy, 1948). The major objective for the individual is to overcome or control the stimuli. Thus, the individual lives in continual fear of being overwhelmed by internal and external forces. The basic organism, however, seeks some kind of equilibrium, an equilibrium that is difficult to achieve because of the limited opportunities in society for direct discharge of tension. The individual is often caught between the possibility of being severely punished from the outside and of being overcome by the intensity of his instinctual tensions and impulses. In order to maintain some minimal level of ego integrity and tolerable survival, he is forced to create and employ mechanisms which serve to mediate and compromise these demands. The defense mechanisms are a "mixed blessing." On the one hand they allow the person to come to some adjustment with the outside world, yet on the other hand, they can come to dominate the psychic life to such an extent that the basic energies which have to be diverted, changed, or repressed can build up to a point where the individual is living a basically sick life. When stored up or repressed energies govern behavior without the awareness of the individual, he is in need of understanding how the defense mechanisms work and what they are keeping from consciousness. To the acculturated person, the internal impulses are mainly unacceptable wishes. The aim in therapy is to attempt to make possible an awareness of this core of buried fears and anxieties.

Simplified, the aim of the instinct is activity, and the aim of the superego (internalized social restrictions on behavior) is to curb behavior directed by instincts (of the id). Activity is then most often moderated or entirely neutralized, pressing behavior into some kind of golden social mean. The discrepancy between what the organism wishes to do and what his acquired psychic system allows him to do is often immense. The successful resolution of the ensuing frustration may constitute moments of growth toward a more balanced adjustment. Therapy supplies the patient with painful frustration and resolution of the frustration, such as that involved in the working through of the transference. Since a weakened ego constitutes the conditions for the development of neurosis, the therapist is committed to ally himself with the ego against the id and superego.

The role of the therapist is largely a didactic one in which he uncovers and integrates unconscious material. He is also involved in making judgments as to whether or not a defense is appropriate or inappropriate.

The question here rests on the influence of the defense. If it weakens the ego, denies reality, or threatens to change the structure of the entire psychic system, it is maladaptive. In a real sense, the therapist judges a defense helpful or not in accordance with the difficulty or ease in making psychoanalytic interpretations. The patient most difficult to analyze is the most sick. Although Freud did not extend his thinking explicitly this far, the implications are clear: *The free man or the artist would be seen as the most acutely ill individual in society because he cannot be readily analyzed.*

The therapist is a somewhat distant but understanding, all-knowing authority. His theory and manner communicate to the patient that he (the therapist) is truly a superior person. The therapist not only understands the patient's unconscious processes, but also is able to render irrational material rational. There is an implicit assumption that therapy cannot work if the patient insists on questioning the therapist's knowledge and authority. In such cases the patient may be judged to be too resistant to be amenable to treatment. The level of intensity of any denial is a reflection of the validity of the interpretation.

The entire course of therapy is enhanced by the skillful handling of the transference; that is, the patient grows to view the therapist as a reincarnation of important figures of the patient's past. In the case of a positive transference, the patient gets well out of a love for the therapist. Negative transference encourages high levels of resistance as well as the operation of a cruel superego and the blockage of the affect associated with the original trauma.

It is obvious that the patient who has a great deal of intellectual curiosity about himself enjoys a distinct, if not questionable, advantage in psychoanalytic therapy.

The patient is considered well to the extent that he is aware of the workings of his psychic life in psychoanalytic terminology, free of the intensity of original affect as well as intense direct discharge of impulses and feelings.

## HISTORICAL AND OTHER CONTRIBUTIONS

The major historical contributions of psychoanalytic theory and practice center around several broad and major possibilities: (1) the real possibility that mental life and the nature of man cannot only be understood, but that these insights can be applied to alleviate, to some degree, human suffering (Freud, 1943); (2) the great majority of man's behavior is irrational, and is governed by unconscious forces and processes

(Freud, 1920, 1935); (3) the findings of the therapist can be applied to areas of life beyond therapy (Sullivan, 1938); (4) the uncovering and systematic depiction of the development and maintenance of destructive forces in man and society (Fromm, 1941, 1947; Sullivan, 1948).

*From our viewpoint, there are no major contributions of psycho-analytic theory, (above and beyond the limited concentration upon the central core of facilitative therapeutic conditions) when applied to therapy and counseling.*

If there are contributions beyond the historical, they are infrequent and limited to the rather unique experiences of a small number of people amenable to this kind of therapy: (1) persons functioning at level 2; (2) psychologically attuned, affluent, intelligent, sophisticated, and intellectually curious persons who are functioning adequately at a concrete level; and (3) future analysts.

> 1.  Psychoanalytic theory has provided a base for interpretation to fields of study beyond the helping professions.

Psychoanalytic theory has been directly applied in anthropology, sociology, literature, economics, politics, the arts, history, and religion.

> 2.  Psychoanalytic theory has provided a systematic focus for interpreting the symbolic in behavior and interpersonal relationships.

By going beyond the myths and the obvious, psychoanalytic theory rendered the more subtle aspects of behavior and the therapist-patient relationship not only comprehensible but therapeutically useful.

> 3.  Psychoanalytic theory has offered the most comprehensive view of the interpersonal relationships in the family and their implications for psychological development.

In essence, the child learns to be acted upon and not to become an actor. He then carries into life a mental set which allows him to relate to others as a sibling or parental surrogate. The sequence and nature of psychosexual stages and development has its roots in the family complex.

> 4.  Psychoanalytic theory has provided a stance emphasizing the common attributes of the sexes.

Freud's concept of bisexuality has led to a deeper understanding of the overlay between the sexes along a number of critical dimensions, with particular focus on active-passive impulses and behavior. This has allowed others, as well as Freud, to devote their energies to the basic human situation.

5.  Psychoanalytic theory was the first system to deal with and begin to comprehend the importance of affect.

The central role of catharsis in successful therapy is now almost fully accepted: emotional discharge is a prerequisite to understanding.

6.  The psychoanalytic stance was the first to set up and implement standards for training and practice.

The trainee and novice practitioner is not only provided with intense and ongoing supervision, but, in addition, the supervisor is charged with making judgments about the trainee's level of functioning and personal adjustment. This brings into full view the notion that a therapist must be in touch with the nature of his own motives before claiming the right and ability to help others.

7.  Psychoanalytic theory and practice has given focus and meaning to the polarities of feeling and behavior.

Such constructs as ambivalence, pleasure-pain, subject-object, and active-passive came into full maturity within the psychoanalytic system (Mullahy, 1948).

8.  Psychoanalytic theory has provided a meaningful framework from which to understand the means by which the individual attempts to maintain a sense of uniqueness and ward off annihilation.

The postulation of defense mechanisms and the growth of the ego through psychosexual development depicts the possibility and means by which the individual avoids drowning in a flood of anxiety.

9.  Psychoanalytic theory has provided an explanation of the implications and durable effects of trauma.

While repetitious retarding is essential for severe deterioration, both clinical experience and research attest to the validity of the lasting impact of some kinds of one trial learning situations.

10.  Psychoanalytic theory has provided an explanation of the durable influence of early childhood experiences for those functioning below level 3.

The nature and function of the entire symptom process, as well as the structure of personality, may well have its roots in the early years of childhood.

Most of what has followed Freud as positive contributions to personality theory and psychotherapeutic practice can be credited to these major historical contributions. His attempts at theoretical breakthroughs made possible the development of other systems.

## THERAPIST AND PATIENT PROCESS LIMITATIONS

Most of the limitations are tied to the observation that psychoanalytic theory and practice applies only to those functioning below level 3. In addition, patients functioning below level 3 are least able to use constructively the insights and interpretations offered by their therapists. If there is any gain for these patients at all, it is most likely due to the extent to which the therapist communicates relatively high levels of facilitative conditions and confidence in interaction with the client's neurotic dependency on authority.

1.  Psychoanalytic theory explains away everything but the negative and destructive aspects of the human situation.

Freedom from one's own history, and creative acts that are not merely sublimations, but full expressions of a whole person, are beyond the scope of psychoanalytic theory. The person functioning below level 3 *is* dominated by destructive forces, and only psychoanalytic theory interprets his psychic life comprehensively: *the overall impression is that life is hardly worth living or ending.*

2.  Neither the patient nor the therapist can win anything of value.

The patient or the critic who persists in questioning the authority of the theory is seen as operating to defend against the exposure of his deeper motives. Psychoanalytic theory is too often used as a weapon to fend off its critics and explain away its own failures.

3.  Psychoanalytic practice often defines success in terms of the patient's degree of acceptance of the therapist's view of life.

This is not only a limitation for the patient, but also closes the therapist off from significant new learnings from the patient.

4.  Psychoanalytic theory assumes that man is basically evil and he must learn to live with his irrational impulses.

It seems to us that more of man's behavior, history, and society can be better understood by assuming that man is born with the potential for both good and evil. He is largely shaped by what society rewards. Those functioning below level 3 cannot or have not broken free of such schedules of reinforcement. In another sense, there seems to be an implicit assumption that if there is any hope for gaining strength, it comes from knowing how really weak one is.

5. Psychoanalytic theory and practice leave room for creative interpretations and synthesis on the part of both the therapist and patient only within the limits of the theory.

Any suggestion that the person can view the world in some way other than through the theory is unacceptable. A personalized interpretation of experience is less likely and most often filtered through a highly intellectual process. The persons of the therapist and patient become encapsulated in the theory. This relegates the therapist to the role of an intellectual "Peeping Tom," peering at life but never participating fully. The patient who adopts this stance must come to the same fate.

6. Psychoanalytic theory and practice do not leave room for environmental manipulations in any systematic way.

Behavioral approaches have demonstrated the efficacy of environmental manipulations for those functioning at low levels. The analyst is likely to interpret a crisis situation, leaving the patient with an intellectual understanding but without the energy to face it fully, or to act and grow. Instead of selectively altering the patient's world, the therapist again offers insights to the person functioning below level 3, the patient least able to use them.

7. Psychoanalytic theory and practice tend to explain away affect before destroying it completely.

Affect (catharsis), when it is encouraged therapeutically, is seen as something the patient must get out of his system. Genuine or strong affect from the therapist is rare and inappropriate, reflecting the incomplete nature of his own analysis. At a deeper level, psychoanalytic theory seems to be saying that its goal is to break the meaningful tie to life: the life one can only tolerate and the life one must eventually lose. An intellectual framework replaces direct expression of affect. Like the client-centered process the perfect product of psychoanalytic therapy only *talks* about feelings; he does not act on them.

8. Psychoanalytic theory and practice offer little or no outlet for direct discharge.

Any direct or full discharge of affect is seen as potentially self-destructive and/or destructive to society. This assumption, like so many of the others in psychoanalytic theory, does apply to those functioning below level 3. Again, the theory's inability to bring the individual to level 3 and above constitutes its major limitations. Along with the understanding psychoanalytic theory offers of the artificial world, its comprehensive description of the psychic experience and behavior of those functioning below level 3 constitutes its major contribution.

9.  Psychoanalytic theory promotes a basic distrust in one's self and others.

There is no room for a direct, honest, and accepting experiencing of one's self or others. Relationships can only develop through a screen of multiple interpretations and, hence, at a great distance. This point, however, is also appropriate for those functioning below level 3.

10.  Psychoanalytic theory and practice encourage the belief that the ritualistic aspects of therapy contribute significantly to positive outcome.

Again, this holds only for those functioning at lower levels. Beyond this, the compulsive following of stages of therapy by the therapist dissipates much of his potentially creative energy into a kind of masturbatory behavior. Psychoanalytic therapy leaves no room for the patient or the therapist to enter openly any significant life experience. Psychoanalytic theory and practice tend to destroy spontaneity and creativity.

11.  Psychoanalytic therapy offers nothing but a retarding experience to the patient functioning above level 3.

A psychoanalytic stance toward life is largely unacceptable for a healthy and whole person. He needs no such complex apology for his motives, impulses, and behavior. The whole person trusts his impulses and acts on them with responsibility. He does not experience an inner evil, and the analyst cannot therefore confirm it. He may, as mentioned earlier in this chapter, experience the psychoanalytic interpretations as something he has gone through. To be fully conscious of weaknesses allows one to choose tragedy, a notion alien to the whole person.

12.  Psychoanalytic theory does not deal fully or reasonably with the area of female sexuality.

Although psychoanalytic theory exposes much of what a Victorian society has done to shape the superficial aspects of female sexual behavior and response, it still describes the average woman as either something more or less than human: more than human in the sense she allegedly is not distracted by a strong libido; less than human because her identity revolves around not possessing a penis.

## SUCCESS AND FAILURE

Psychoanalytic theory had its most significant insights during the period of its initial marginal struggle; since then it has striven to make its most significant contributions acceptable. Society has now moved to incorporate the stance in such a way that psychoanalytic theorists now function well within the limits of social acceptability and, indeed, in many quarters, constitute the mainstream of thinking. Contributions in the form of additions and reinterpretations can now take the form of modifications of, and reactions to, earlier writings. Operating within tolerable social limits denies the very possibility of the emergence of a truly creative contribution. Yet, most theorists strive for social acceptance, which once achieved, assures their own impotence. Freud's followers and critics offered innovations to his theory which led to its stagnation, and limited its therapeutic potential largely to those who aspire to be psychoanalysts. History moves slowly but insidiously to engulf the giant talent and by so doing neutralizes any potentially creative impact. To seek society's support and approval places the most powerful limitations on creativity. *Only sustained and creative existence, responsibly independent of society, can creatively endure.* Acting to accept society's rewards, as did the adherents of psychoanalytic theory, leaves no room for further breakthroughs. In this way, we can account for psychoanalytic success and failure in the short span of something over fifty years.

Furthermore, Freud's inability to account for, or accept the possibility of those functioning at levels above 3, explains why his insights are only half true. To apply his notions to the person functioning at level 4 or 5 is to render beauty, ugly.

The perfect product of psychoanalytic therapy can, at most, be an empty person functioning at level 3—the full embodiment of the aspirations of middle-class society. Psychoanalytic treatment is now doomed to failure because it provides the middle-class patient with what he experiences in everyday life—the treatment can only confirm his emptiness. Psychoanalytic treatment serves as a model of interpersonal relationships in which each person can experience only human deprivation.


## SUMMARY AND CONCLUSIONS

Although the psychoanalytic movement began with efforts to borrow from biological and physiological systems, it now appears to deny that life has a physical base in several important ways: first, in the assumption that psychoanalytic insights and the proper use of intellect can dominate affect; second, in the implication that all intense feelings, impulses, and behavior are pathological. It has been our experience that often the success or failure of therapy depends largely on the therapist's and the client's energy level, in addition to the therapist's and client's direct and intense expression of feeling, in such a way that the experience is primarily a physical one. *If, at the most intense moments of therapy, the therapist acts to render the moment anything less than fully honest, he acts to abuse the physical base of life.*

The final summary points can be listed without additional comment:

1. *Psychoanalytic theory has become a widespread game rarely effectively applied to therapy.*

2. *The perfect product is at best a person functioning at level 3.*

3. *In its essence, life, from a psychoanalytic point of view may not even be worth ending; on the other hand, the fully analyzed person is too impotent to undertake a perfectly reasonable suicide.*

4. *The psychoanalytic therapist can really only hope to treat patients successfully if he breaks free of his role.*

5. *Some of the therapy outcomes judged to be poor by the psychoanalytic therapist may, in fact, be among his success cases in that the patient escaped.*

The future of theory and practice in counseling and psychotherapy, whatever shape it assumes, rests on Freud's shoulders. Psychoanalytic theory and practice spent its creative energies because those who followed Freud did not seek their own direction, a fate perhaps inevitable for every school or system, but most dramatically illustrated by the rise and fall of psychoanalytic theory.

The implications of a society's acceptance of psychoanalytic theory are chilling. The world and the people in it are doomed to be victims of the neurotic and destructive motives of those functioning below level 3. It offers no hope either for realizing or using the potential of those functioning at higher levels, or for bringing those at lower levels to higher levels. Psychoanalytic treatment at best appears to fix acceptable growth satisfaction and tolerable creativity at level 3.

Life below level 3 becomes a battle to fend off tragedy and pain with frequent periods of acute fear, anxiety, and even panic. The rare moments of balance only prepare the individual for the series of tragedies and complete loss of love of life that will enable him to accept death. The person below level 3 strives to cope with, and measure out, his energies with earnest effort, knowing he must in the end capitulate to overwhelming forces. Even his apparent success is a hollow experience; deep inside himself he is aware that he has not stood for anything real, attested to by the fact that his former critics now give him his due. *He has lived life as if it were real.*

In the end there is a complete submission of both the therapist and the patient to the theory. This degree of depersonalization of both parties must culminate in an immense mutual disgust or hate, but each is now too impotent and resigned to act on that hate. They have come to view one another in the same way the therapist has viewed the rest of humanity—with a mixture of pity and contempt. Each now can justify how the other has lived.

What follows in life must, however subtle, include the full experiencing of not only impotence but the growth of cruelty. It is in this sense a blessing that reviewers dealing with the efficacy of psychoanalytic therapy report a low percentage of success. In the light of those who followed Freud, and society's now eager effort to include their theories, psychoanalysis has become a gross perversion for the empty middle-class man. By withholding affect, the therapist allows this man to seek a personage with only the outer attributes of humanity.

In summary, while Freud's unique contribution may have been his accurate perception of the world in all of its destructiveness, it is destructive for any individual to accept the implications which Freud uncovered. After peeling back the trappings and exposing the undergarments of an ugly world, Freud found no alternatives. The process of psychoanalysis is a triumph of the death instinct. The irony is that in spite of his own creative output, he, himself, did not understand creativity without agony. The irony is that in spite of his comprehensive description of the world and its victims, he became one of the victims. Even allowing for his deep understanding of the arbitrariness of institutional structures, he did not understand the possibility for a man to live freely and creatively within the world—or, perhaps, independently of it. The final irony is that only the free man, the person whom psychoanalysis does not comprehend, can make the discriminations necessary to put psychoanalysis in perspective, and to make appropriate application of the stance.

### References

Adler, A. *The neurotic constitution,* trans. by Glueck and Lind. New York: Moffat, Yard and Company, 1917.

Adler, A. *Understanding human nature,* trans. by Beran. New York: Wolfe & Greenberg Publishers, 1927.

Brill, A. A. *The basic writings of Sigmund Freud.* A. A. Brill, ed. New York: Random House, 1938.

Freud, S. *Selected papers on hysteria and other psychoneuroses,* trans. by A. A. Brill. Nervous and Mental Disease Monograph Series, No. 4, 1920.

Freud, S. *Beyond the pleasure principle.* London: Hogarth and The Institute of Psycho-analysis, 1924. (a)

Freud, S. *Collected papers.* London: Hogarth and The Institute of Psycho-analysis, 1924. (b)

Freud, S. *Totem and taboo,* trans. by A. A. Brill. New York: New Republic, Inc., 1927.

Freud, S. *New introductory lectures,* trans. by H. Spott. New York: Norton, 1933.

Freud, S. *The ego and the id.* London: Hogarth and The Institute of Psycho-analysis, 1935.

Freud, S. *The problem of anxiety.* New York: The Psycho-analytic Quarterly Press and Norton, 1936.

Freud, S. *The future of an illusion.* New York: The International Psycho-analytic Library, No. 15, 1943.

Fromm, E. *Escape from freedom.* New York: Holt, Rinehart & Winston, 1941.

Fromm, E. *Man for himself.* New York: Holt, Rinehart and Winston, 1947.

Horney, Karen. *New ways in psychoanalysis.* New York: Norton, 1939.

Horney, Karen. *Self-analysis.* New York: Norton, 1942.

Horney, Karen. *Our inner conflicts.* New York: Norton, 1945.

Jones, E. *The life and work of Sigmund Freud.* New York: Basic Books, 1953.

Jung, C. G. *The psychology of the unconscious,* trans. and intro. by Beatrice M. Hinkle. New York: Dodd, Mead, 1927.

Jung, C. G. *Contributions to analytical psychology,* trans. by H. G. and Cary F. Baynes. New York: Harcourt, 1928.

Jung, C. G. *The integration of the personality,* trans. by Stanley M. Dell. New York: Holt, Rinehart and Winston, 1939.

Mullahy, P. *Oedipus myth and complex:* A review of psychoanalytic theory. New York: Grove, 1948.

Rank, O. *The trauma of birth.* New York: Harcourt and London: Routledge, 1929.

Sullivan, H. S. Introduction to the study of interpersonal relations. *Psychiatry.* Vol. 1, 1938.

Sullivan, H. S. The meaning of anxiety in psychiatry and life. *Psychiatry.* Vol. XI, No. 1, 1948.

SECTION FOUR

# Life, Death,
# and Touching:
# Clinical Applications

The movement from construct to clinic is not an easy
one. The inevitable discrepancy between neat theoretical modes and sticky, clinical cases is fully confronted. The necessity to go beyond what is known and
even what is knowable in both (1) the downward or
inward phase or period of the formation of the relationship and the exploration of personal problems and
experiences, and (2) the upward or outward phase or
period of emergent directionality of counseling and
therapy is covered in Chapter 9. In Chapter 10, crises
in and out of therapy are treated as the only truly
relevant moments in clinical practice, and in Chapter
11 the necessity for honesty in the confrontation of
client by therapist is underscored in a collaborative
chapter under the leadership of John Douds. The frequently replicated experience of not knowing what to do
following the client's full exploration of problem areas
and experiences, and attempts to seek effective directions, is treated in Chapter 12. Finally, in Chapter 13,
there is a full realization of the impossibility of pro-
gramming the less-than-whole person to cope with the
multitude of clinical situations, and the necessity for
delegating such immense therapeutic responsibilities
to the whole person, alone.

Chapter **9**

. . . the whole person trusts
the unknown, perhaps more
than the known.

**Beyond the Known:**
**The Phases of Therapy**

After nearly one-half century of monumental effort, educators, psychologists, sociologists, and statisticians have been able to account for approximately one fourth of the movement in their indexes of academic achievement. To be sure, over the past decade their prediction curves have flattened out; that is, no matter how many or what variables these researchers add to their equation predicting academic achievement, they do not increase their predictability.

Meaningful research in counseling and therapy is in its infancy compared to the sophisticated efforts of research in academic achievement. If we are fortunate in our search of counseling and psychotherapy, within the not-too-distant future, we will be able to account for one fourth of the movement in our indexes of client change or gain before our own prediction curve flattens out. That is, if we develop sufficiently appropriate instruments, methodologies, and statistical analyses, we may be able to produce a regression equation to account for one quarter or one third of the variability in our change indexes.

That is not to say that we have resolved all of our problems in outcome criteria (Truax and Carkhuff, 1964). It is not, on the other hand, to say that we have not made reasonable progress in predicting quasi-outcome criteria such as indexes of insight (Truax, 1961; Carkhuff, 1966), which, however, as in the case of academic achievement, may or may not be related to indexes of real life achievement or change (Holland and Richards, 1965). It is to say that in counseling and psychotherapy, as in the area of academic achievement, we will face our own inability to account for motivational and other emotional factors, such as perseveration; physical factors, such as energy level and stamina, and the multitude of environmental variables which impinge upon our functioning. Beyond these, there are many variables for which we may never be able to assign global categorizations such as motivation and environment. We speak of what is unknown to us now and may always remain unknown in terms of our ability to articulate clearly, operationalize in research, and produce empirical evidence. Yet, we continue our practice of counseling and psychotherapy, somehow trusting that the 70 or 80 percent of what is presently unknown to us will operate in either the therapist's or the client's favor. *We continue to live and relate in spite of the fact that the greatest part of man's functioning remains unknown to us. This is as it must be.*

We have spent the greatest part of this book focusing upon what is known or knowable to us. In spelling out our open eclectic model, we have described core conditions which, themselves, move from relatively well-known and defined constructs for which we can produce a great deal of empirical evidence, to many core variables which are ill-defined and for which we have little evidence, and, finally, to core variables which are presently unknown to us. Beyond the core conditions, we have attempted to discern the unique contributions of many of the now dominant approaches to counseling and psychotherapy. We have not gone far enough in these efforts, for each of the potential preferred modes of treatment which we have considered may, upon reflection and research, have additional contributions to make. In addition, there are many other approaches (Harper [1959] suggests fully thirty-six systems of counseling and therapy), the unique contributions of which we have not considered. There are many qualifications and many extensions of the model for counseling and therapy which we have not contemplated sufficiently. There is much that takes us from the known to the unknown in the actual operation of counseling and therapy.

Related to the concept of core conditions around which preferred modes of treatment are built is our concept of the major phases of therapy. *There are two major phases of all truly therapeutic processes (1) the "downward" or "inward" phase, or the establishment of the relationship and client self-exploration; and (2) the "upward" or "outward" phase, or the period of emergent directionality.* Very simply, during the initial phase, the therapist takes the client "down" or moves "down" with the client into the depths of the structure of the client's "self" and his situation.

In the latter phase of therapy, the therapist attempts to facilitate movement "up" toward more effective functioning. During the establishment of the relationship, the main therapeutic goal is client engagement in self-exploration involving intense self-experiencing and extensive problem expression. During the latter phase of therapy, the main therapeutic goal involves a change in those behaviors which have led to difficulty in the client's functioning.

## THE "DOWNWARD" PHASE OF THERAPY

In the initial phase, the main therapeutic vehicle to effective client self-exploration involves the therapist's communication of high levels of facilitative conditions, the theoretical rationale for which we presented in Chapters 2 and 3. In practice, there will be many modifications in the operation of these conditions. We have already, for example, acquainted ourselves with the necessity for the therapist to understand the more naturalistic and humanistic base of the core of facilitative conditions. In addition, there are other important qualifications.

Most important, the core conditions account for what is known concerning the efficacy of therapeutic processes *as they are currently practiced in their more traditional forms.* However limited to their current orientation and form of practice, the core conditions account for a great part of their effectiveness. The dominant modes of practice, the client-centered and the psychoanalytic, and, to a large extent, the existential, focus primarily upon what we consider to be the initial phase of therapy: self-exploration culminating in emotional insights. All of our findings, then, are qualified by this consideration. The whole notion of emotional insights has made for a great deal of confusion in theorizing.

When we consider, for example, that it is the therapist's final, and not his initial, level of understanding that is critical to positive movement, we are concerning ourselves with the final level of understanding within the initial phase of therapy where the focus is upon the communication of sensitivities and attitudinal conditions. Again, we must underscore that *most therapists conclude therapy where we conclude the first phase.* Within the initial phase, then, the emphasis in training should be upon the therapist's final level of understanding the client, which must in large part be dependent upon how whole the therapist is. Instead, the focus of training, as it is replicated throughout the country, is upon the clichés involved in the initial introduction to the client. They are only too well known to us: "It must have been very difficult for you to come here"; "You feel that there are lots of things that you wish to say but it is very hard to say them." It is similar with other conditions.

We know that, even within the first phase of therapy, a point must come where we move from the communication of unconditionality to the communication of positive regard per se, yet we emphasize in our training the communication of unconditionality ("This is your hour and you may do with it as you wish."). Again, our assessment of the dimension of concreteness is limited by its application in the initial phase. Even here, however, we focus upon specificity of expression ("Tell me more about it"), when much of the really significant material during the latter part of the initial phase involves more abstract communications to and from the unconscious. In general, we underscore cautiousness and professionalism ("It is not for me to say what is important but rather for you to explore your problems fully, here, together with me, so that we may resolve your problems.") in our training rather than the cautious movement toward honesty of communication, even during the initial phase. Again, the honesty is not in the service of the therapist but in the service of the client, or, in the service of both parties to the relationship.

There are many more cogent examples of qualifications in practice. Whereas, a level 3 response in empathy may be considered minimally facilitative, in actuality the therapist's response may be considered one that is interchangeable with that of the client. The following brief example may serve to illustrate this point:

CLIENT: I'm just so under it all. I don't know if I've got the strength or the will to get up again.
THERAPIST: You're just so far down you don't know if you can make it anymore.
CLIENT: Yes, I don't know if I can do it.

The therapist is communicating that he is with, but not beyond the client. He is tuned in on the client's wavelength but he adds nothing more. He does not provide the level of empathic communication in which one person anticipates another. He does not facilitate the client's movement to a deeper level except insofar as he has understood the previous level. It can readily be seen that in spite of the fact that level 3 is defined operationally as the minimum level of facilitative interpersonal functioning, it is in practice not always adequate to give any kind of direction to the process. In order for the therapy process to move effectively, the therapist must add something to the client's response, and we might add, something which the client at his present level of development can use constructively. This brings us into the area of what we term depth reflections or moderate interpretations all of which, if accurate, enable the client to go a level deeper in his explorations. Thus, the following example:

CLIENT: I'm so overwhelmed. I can't say whether I can make it—now or ever. I don't even know if it's worth saying anymore, to anyone.
THERAPIST: Life's not worth struggling for anymore, not even with me.
CLIENT: I am alone and I'm terribly frightened.
THERAPIST: I am *with* you.

The therapist anticipates the client and shares something of himself to make it possible for the client to move to deeper levels of exploration and experiencing.

The level 3 empathic response may be considered a reflection of what is known or knowable. That is, it is the best response of an interchangeable nature which the therapist can relate to the client's response. Again, in spite of the fact that most therapists do not function at level 3, it is easily attainable with a minimum amount of communication training (Berenson, Carkhuff, and Myrus, 1966; Carkhuff and Truax, 1965a, 1965b; Martin and Carkhuff, 1967; Pierce, Carkhuff, and Berenson, 1967). The fact is that a therapist can easily learn to "technique" level 3 responses essentially independent of the client's needs. In this manner, the level 3 therapist may neutralize what might otherwise have been effective outcome. If the therapist is not functioning at sufficiently effective levels of living himself, and continues only to "fake" understanding with the client, he can effect no constructive change. However, *if the therapist is going to enable a distressed client to move to deeper levels of self-exploration, the therapist must be functioning above level 3. If the therapist is going to involve the client in a process leading to change toward more effective ways of living, then he, himself, must be functioning at effective levels.* In this respect, the therapist adds as much to the client's response as he is whole in relation to the client. In order to perceive the client's troubled world accurately, the therapist must be able to experience his own accurately and fully. Thus, even during the initial phase, in addition to communication training, *the therapist must himself be functioning effectively either because of constructive therapeutic personality change or through his emergence from his own healthy environment.*

The implications of the therapist's ability to add to or subtract from the client's response suggests an important qualification of the model described in Chapters 2 and 3, in terms of the absolute levels of the therapist's and the client's functioning. It has been suggested that even if a level 2 therapist is functioning at higher levels than his level 1.5 client, he may be subtracting from the client's essential message and thus, in a very real sense, contributing to the deterioration of a client who is functioning at a level lower than he is. Tentative evidence is consistent with this qualification suggesting that a level 2 therapist has very little ability to effect constructive change in the functioning of the lower level client (Berenson and Mitchell, 1967; Pagell, Carkhuff, and Berenson, 1967; Pierce, Carkhuff, and Berenson, 1967).

In actual practice the communication of highly facilitative conditions will vary with the individual client. Thus, as described in Chapter 3, in very broad terms, the communication process between a given therapist and level 1, 2, and 3 clients will vary with the levels of the populations. With the level 1 client the integrity of the communication process must be restored or constructed in the first place from the most basic level, whereas the concentration with the level 2 client is on clarifying the distortions in communication which lead the level 2 persons into continuous difficulty. Given the establishment of an initial level of effective communication with his therapist, the level 3 client will go on to work effectively on his own. The differential communications may be highlighted with the example of client silence. During a difficult period with a distraught level 1 patient, the therapist might respond to silence by reaching out and touching or holding the client's hand. On the other hand, with a level 2 client under similar circumstances the therapist might respond with an empathic reflection as follows: "It's very hard to say all that you need to say." Finally, with a distressed but high-level functioning client, the therapist might simply respond by not responding, assuming that the client can effectively use this period for constructive work. Each response can be considered to be a facilitative one, enabling each client to become more deeply involved in the process than he might otherwise have been. It can readily be seen that most of our treatment programs are oriented toward the kind of verbalization which we have illustrated with the level 2 client. Differential treatment is necessary with clients functioning at different levels of effectiveness. Differential communication is necessary with clients communicating at differentially effective levels.

Thus, the effectiveness of the level at which the therapist is functioning will vary with the client's level of functioning. It will also vary, within cases, with the client's readiness to use the therapist's communications effectively. In general, except with clients who are immediately known to us from our own past experiences, the therapist will initially establish an effective base for therapy; that is, he will attempt to make level 3 responses or responses of a character essentially interchangeable with the responses of the client. When he has an accurate grasp of the client's frame of reference, the therapist will attempt to take the communication process to deeper levels as the client is able to employ his resources constructively in relation to the therapist's responses. If the client cannot take the lead to deeper levels, the therapist may do so. The initial phase of therapy may last as long as it takes the client to feel secure enough to share as much as he is capable of concerning his difficult life experiences. During later phases of therapy, *the therapist may give the process directionality, for the client looks to the therapist for the directionality which he cannot find in himself.*

Unfortunately, the first phase of therapy is precisely the phase where most practitioners, theoretical orientations, and training programs leave off. The best practitioners work to establish an effective, working therapeutic relationship of one kind or another. The most effective practitioners enable the clients to explore themselves fully, to experience themselves with intensity and emotional proximity, and to express a full range of personal problems. They end here and, as a result, the client frequently achieves no direction in his life; he does not act upon his environment. Thus, in the following case, the client-centered practitioner continues session after session to reflect the feelings and expressed experiences of the young female client functioning between levels 2 and 3:

CLIENT: Well, maybe my homosexual behavior isn't the cause of all my problems.
THERAPIST: You're wondering whether you can tie everything to a single problem.
CLIENT: Maybe the homosexuality is big only because of how other people see it.
THERAPIST: How others see it influences you.
CLIENT: Yes, but maybe there's something else. . . .
THERAPIST: Something bigger.
CLIENT: Right, maybe there's some bigger problem I'm avoiding.

The therapist works very effectively with the client. Together they are always discovering something really new, or at least from a new perspective, about the client. However, the client never really has anything from the therapist to sink her teeth into, react to, or act upon. The client does not change constructively. The goals for which she came to therapy have not been met. She has not been served. In addition, sometimes, the implications of self-exploration involve actions which the therapist cannot allow himself to experience, let alone tolerate. Thus, the analytically oriented practitioner spends much of his time and the client's money in making many interpretations which enable the client to get "insight" into his problem area. When the client has sufficient insight, that is, when he has caught onto and is in agreement with the therapist's frame of reference, he is assumed to have successfully handled the area of difficulty. Often though, the therapist, as in the following series of excerpts, is unable to allow the client to "go all the way" to wherever he is going. Initially, the therapist enables a very highly intellectual young male client functioning below level 2 to move to deeper levels of meaningful self-exploration and self-awareness via his moderate interpretations and confrontations.

CLIENT: I have not been able to actualize any potential. In addition, I am acutely aware of my lack of masculinity in contacts with my fiancée.
THERAPIST: You sort of feel there may be latent homosexuality.
CLIENT: Perhaps there are some feelings of this sort but they are, to be sure, latent.
THERAPIST: At an interpersonal level things are quite confusing.
CLIENT: To be sure.

Finally, after several months of intensive psychotherapy, the client explores himself very deeply and with great immediacy and intensity in his experiencing.

CLIENT: If it hadn't have been for sex, this wouldn't have happened.
THERAPIST: Why does one have to follow the other?
CLIENT: I don't know. It's not just guilt. I just feel responsible for her now. I have to protect her now.
THERAPIST: Like a father.
CLIENT: Like a husband, only I can't make it. I can't do it.

The client continues to deeper and deeper levels.

CLIENT: I'm so sad—separated from everyone—by everything—things don't change.
THERAPIST: Even by talking about it?
CLIENT: I don't change.
THERAPIST: You don't feel it will change by talking about it?
CLIENT: I don't know.
THERAPIST: Isn't there some part of you that wants to change by talking about it?
CLIENT: Why? Oh, why? I guess it's not my habit.
THERAPIST: Habit? Habits are learned—and can be unlearned.
CLIENT: Maybe I'm just protecting myself.
THERAPIST: That's it! People make you anxious. You can see it that way, can't you? You remember when I was talking about. . . .

As can be readily seen, the therapist is unable to allow the client to go beyond the therapist's tolerance limits. Having enabled the client to confront himself effectively, the therapist does not appear equipped to go all of the way with the client. Indeed, there is good reason to believe from this excerpt that the therapist does not believe in the possibility of the client's constructive change. The client-centered and psychoanalytic orientations concentrate exclusively upon the initial phase of therapy; via different routes, they emphasize the client's attainment of insight into his areas of dysfunctioning. *Insight is not enough.* In a direct way, *insight must translate into action, exploration into tangible client benefits.*

Some therapists move into phase 2 prior to phase 1. Another way of putting this might be to say "they shift their mouths into second before they shift their minds into first." In the following excerpt, a directive therapist working with a young male client at level 2 makes extraordinary generalizations from the briefest of material during an early interview:

CLIENT: He acts like he's doing it for me but I don't know.
THERAPIST: There are no "shoulds" or "shouldn'ts" with parents. You don't have to kowtow to them. You don't owe them a thing. Your birth was an accident.
CLIENT: But I feel bad about not going along with them.
THERAPIST: You go ahead and do it, whether they like it or not.
CLIENT: But I don't know if *I* want to do it.
THERAPIST: Do it anyway.

The direction, imposed openly by the therapist, seems premature. The therapist's activities act to stimulate the client's reactions. We cannot help but wonder if such premature direction does not come more out of the therapist's needs than of serving the benefit of the client.

## THE "UPWARD" PHASE OF THERAPY

During the latter phase of therapy, the period of emergent directionality, the main therapeutic vehicle to client change involves the therapist's full employment of all his resources, intellectual as well as emotional, physical as well as moral, trained as well as innate. During the second phase, the therapist does not concentrate upon the communication of conditions except insofar as there is an honest sharing by each with the other concerning where the process is leading, and how effective the direction is. It would be difficult indeed to assess the facilitative dimensions during the second phase if the therapist were employing conditioning techniques or analyzing the results of a Strong Vocational Interest Blank.

The period of emerging directionality involves the therapist in interaction with the client, bringing all that he is and all that he has to bear upon the client's area of difficulty. During this period, the therapist again must be guided by what is effective for the client—to the degree that he is able to discriminate who and where the client is; indeed, he may discern the client's readiness and ability to determine his own direction. To sum, the therapist will discriminate effectively to the degree that he is whole.

In addition, the whole person must be complemented by a working knowledge of all possible ways of helping the client. *The whole therapist is much more than the whole person.* He is equipped with all that is knowable from theory and technique so that with any given client, at any given point in time, he may institute those techniques which are appropriate to the client's condition. If the therapist himself is not expert enough to employ the techniques, he knows at least enough to call for the employment of a particular technique. Furthermore, in instituting the technique, as well as in calling in a consultant, he shares with the client, as honestly as is possible, what he intends to do and what his goals are.

Whereas during the initial phase the concentration is upon the core conditions with all of their noted qualifications, the emphasis during the latter phase is, in a genuine and sharing relationship, upon the dimension of concreteness: concrete and specific direction and goals implemented by concrete steps. Again, although the dimension of specificity may move during the initial phase from the concrete to the abstract, during the latter phase the movement involves again specific consideration by both therapist and client of the advantages and disadvantages of alternative courses of action with the intention of developing the one best direction and translating this into action by the client.

In the initial phase of therapy, then, the therapist communicates empathy and positive regard, as well as genuineness to an initially more limited degree, in order to establish a genuine, fully sharing relationship in which the client can feel himself freely and deeply. During the latter phase, the emphasis is upon concrete considerations of problems and their possible solutions within the context of this genuine relationship. The necessity to communicate empathy and positive regard is less critical and may well be implicit. Indeed, in many effective processes the therapist, having established himself as a potent reinforcer, may be conditional, depending upon how constructively the client is or is not acting. Thus, *the whole therapist has available to him both his own effective way of living and relating which enables the clients to explore themselves deeply, and a working knowledge of a variety of potential "preferred modes of treatment" which may enable the client to live and relate effectively.* The therapeutic process flows accordingly: (1) the therapist institutes high levels of facilitative conditions which (2) enable the client to explore himself meaningfully and (3) sets the therapist up as a potent reinforcing agent who helps to give directionality to the client's struggle, and finally (4) translates to constructive action on the client's part. We are describing a system totally based upon an interaction between a "more knowing" therapist and a "less knowing" client and involving a fully sharing moment-to-moment encounter complemented by anything that will work.

During the period of developing direction, the therapist relies heavily on his own experience of the client, an experience which is filtered through his active intellect and working knowledge of available treatment approaches. Again, his ultimate choice of approaches will be as effective as he is a fully integrated and creative person.

*In a very real sense, the effective practitioner, although equipped with the basics of many theoretical orientations, begins therapy atheoretically.* Through his experience of the client, he develops and acts upon the implications of his own individual theory, personalized for each individual client. He is not bound by conceptualizations which are elaborated upon before contact with the client. At the same time he allows for the employment of appropriate approaches and techniques if the generalizations from his experience with client so dictate.

Concurrent with both the initial and the latter phases of therapy are a series of crises involving client and therapist, individually and in interaction with each other. In operation, however, it appears as if the superstructure of the crisis may be imposed upon the phases of therapy rather than vice versa: both phases of therapy appear encapsulated within the crisis; that is, the crisis period incorporates both phases of exploration and emergent directionality.

*The techniques and approaches which the therapist employs during the latter phase must add to the directionality of the process.* Again, training can accomplish familiarity and effectiveness in the utilization of technique, whereas constructive therapist change alone enables the therapist to discern clearly the appropriateness of the technique and the unique contributions which it makes to the client's constructive change.

The therapist must ultimately trust his own experience, for all he really has to offer another person is his experience and those approaches which his experience dictates utilizing. To the degree that he himself is open and full, can he be shaped by the feedback from others and, thus, enable others to be open and shaped by the feedback of still others. The process in which the therapist is both model and agent continues indefinitely. *Psychotherapy, then, has direction only insofar as the therapist is whole and can communicate his sensitive perceptions and experience of another.*

In summary, then, in our embryonic existence, we act as if the 21 or 22 percent of what we know accounts for most of the therapeutic process. Indeed, most individual orientations have not accounted for this much, yet act as if they have accounted for the entire process. We are working in a strange "science art." Science may ultimately account for 25 to 30 percent of what happens. Presently, however, what we can account for takes place largely during the initial phase of therapy. Most of the potential preferred modes of treatment have yet to establish their unique contributions, even given a relevant interaction of therapist, client, and contextual variables. The art part of the science art involves a great deal more. It involves a whole person for whom the science part is very real, but not, at least presently, enough; a whole person, who at crisis points pushes out his own boundaries in order to make the unknown more and more knowable but who in doing so trusts the unknown as he trusts himself or because he trusts himself. *The whole person trusts the unknown, perhaps more than the known: it may always be greater than the known and he is bound to act upon it.*

## References

Berenson, B. G., R. R. Carkhuff, and Pamela Myrus. The interpersonal functioning and training of college students. *J. counsel. Psychol.,* 1966, *13,* 441–446.

Berenson, B. G. and K. Mitchell. *Confrontation in psychotherapy.* Book in preparation, State University of New York at Buffalo, 1967.

Carkhuff, R. R. Training in counseling and psychotherapy: Requiem or reveille? *J. counsel. Psychol.,* 1966, *13,* 360–367.

Carkhuff, R. R., and C. B. Truax. Training in counseling and psychotherapy: An evaluation of an integrated didactic and experiential approach. *J. consult. Psychol.,* 1965, *29,* 333–336. (a)

Carkhuff, R. R., and C. B. Truax. Lay mental health counseling: The effects of lay group counseling. *J. consult. Psychol.,* 1965, *29,* 426–431. (b)

Harper, R. *Psychoanalysis and psychotherapy.* Englewood Cliffs, N. J.: Prentice-Hall, 1959.

Holland, J. L., and J. M. Richards. Academic and nonacademic accomplishment: Correlated or uncorrelated? *J. educ. Psychol.,* 1965, *56,* 165–174.

Martin, J. C., and R. R. Carkhuff. The effects upon personality and interpersonal functioning in counseling training. *J. clin. Psychol.,* in press, 1967.

Pagell, W., R. R. Carkhuff, and B. G. Berenson. Therapist offered conditions and patient development. *J. clin. Psychol.,* in press, 1967.

Pierce, R., R. R. Carkhuff, and B. G. Berenson. The differential effects of therapist level of functioning upon counselors in training. *J. clin. Psychol.,* 1967, *23,* 212–215.

Truax, C. B. The process of group psychotherapy. *Psychol. Monogr.,* 1961, *75,* No. 14 (Whole No. 511).

Truax, C. B., and R. R. Carkhuff. Significant developments in psychotherapy research. (L. E. Abt and B. F. Reiss, (Eds.) ) *Progress in clinical psychology.* New York: Grune & Stratton, 1964, Chapter 70.

> . . . the therapist handles the
> crisis or not as he is a
> whole human or not.

## Crisis Therapy:
## The Crossroads
## for Client and Therapist

The pattern of psychotherapy, as of life, is comprised of a series of interrelated crises. We benefit or not as we act constructively or not. Put another way, each crisis encapsulates a process leading to constructive change. In a very real sense, the rest of psychotherapy and, indeed, the rest of life is at a maximum, supportive, and, at a minimum, irrelevant.

Today it is in vogue to talk about "crisis therapy." Talking is precisely what most therapists do. When they talk about crisis therapy, they talk about the therapist in some way intervening at a crisis point in the client's life. They consider this intervention, and the talk about it to be a bold, new step in counseling and therapy. To be sure, for many it is a bold, new step, but as always it does not go far enough.

When we write about crises, we are not simply concerned with the crises in the past or the present of the client. We are writing about crises which occur for the therapist as well as the client, and between client and therapist, both in and out of therapy.

The obvious example of crisis therapy involves some critical moment in the life of the client where what he does or does not do will lead him toward more full emergence or deterioration. Thus, in the following excerpt the male client, who is an executive in his forties functioning at approximately level 2, presents the very real and immediate crisis of his life:

CLIENT: I just can't go on anymore. Oh, no! I just can't go in each day.
THERAPIST: The way things are going now, you know you can't make it the same way anymore.
CLIENT: I've had it. I think it's going to end each day. I live in fear of not making it through each day. The pressure is unbearable. I think I am going to have another breakdown.
THERAPIST: You're going to have to consider alternatives.
CLIENT: Yes, but what can I do, what about my wife, my family?
THERAPIST: Jim, you have no real alternatives to quitting.
CLIENT: Yes, but what do I do?
THERAPIST: We can work out something.

In this case, when the therapist realizes that his client is "at the end of his rope," he moves in, softly and firmly, to emphasize that there are no real alternatives to quitting. The immediate crisis of work and other pressures is met with the full realization of the implication of continuing. Future crises to be encountered might involve the reorientation of the client's life, including his different relationships as well as exploring occupational areas presently unknown to the client.

What constitutes a crisis for some may not for others. The external crises for the client may range from something as apparently innocuous as concern for an impending classroom presentation to the moment of contemplating suicide. For some the most innocuous may merge with the most serious. Thus, for example, the severe stutterer, who has had a traumatic experience in a previous presentation, and who in some way sees his career resting upon his next performance, may consider the very serious consequences of a disastrous classroom experience. Thus, we can see most clearly the essential character of the crisis: whether physical or psychological, it is of life and death urgency.

In addition, there may be crises which occur during the therapy process itself. Thus, during the initial phase of therapy, the client's growing feeling that the therapist cannot understand him may constitute a crisis of minor or major proportions, depending upon the desperateness of the client's situation and the ability of the therapist to handle the crisis. For the deteriorated schizophrenic, who is a consequent of a series of severely retarding relationships (Carkhuff and Truax, 1966), the therapeutic encounter may offer the last promise of hope. He may make a feeble attempt to reach out for help. Whether or not the therapist can understand him is indeed of life and death urgency.

An example of a potentially critical moment during the second phase of therapy might involve the therapist's inability to enable the client to find direction; that is, having probed inward intensely and extensively as far as he could go, the client in his relationship with the therapist is not able to establish a meaningful direction for his life's activities. Again, depending upon both the client's and the therapist's level of development, the consequences may be constructive or deteriorative.

Also neglected are the crises which occur both in and out of therapy for the therapist, alone, and in his interaction with the client. Thus, occurrences in the therapist's own life situation and experiences in his relationships may constitute crises for the therapist. For example, marital difficulties or a lack of sexual fulfillment might have a critical effect upon the therapist interacting with a sexually attractive client and create a crisis in therapy. Within the therapy process itself, the moment when the therapist has "lost" the client, when he is no longer in communication with the client, perhaps at a difficult moment for the client, may constitute a severe crisis point for the therapist.

## AN HOURLY INTENSIFICATION OF LIFE

The only real psychotherapy takes place at the crisis point, most often with the focus initially upon external crises for the client, but eventually crises involving both client and therapist, in and out of therapy. At the crisis point, both client and therapist are stripped of all facade, which is indicated by what they do or do not do. This communication is the most intimate person-to-person communication that there can be. There are no rules for responding at the crisis, no techniques, no rituals. The therapist simply has to "be" to experience the moment and stand the tests. The effective therapist responds most honestly from the deepest wells within him. His response reflects his recognition of the life and death urgency of the situation. *He responds the way he lives his life and he chooses life in his response.* In his "being" and acting he discloses the meaning and efficacy of his approach to life.

The first stage in crisis therapy is an acknowledgment of the crisis by the therapist. He cannot turn away from the crisis. Yet, many therapists do turn away from the crisis point. Those therapists functioning below level 3 cannot clearly see the life and death urgency through the client's eyes. They cannot experience his desperateness. They cannot allow themselves to do so. Perhaps most important, they are not aware that anyone at a crisis point can choose life. In their deterministic view of man, they do not, in effect, believe in the possibility of change. These people do not understand the privilege of counseling another.

The counselor functioning below level 3 does not approach being whole himself. *He does not and cannot be aware.* He emphasizes in therapy, as he does in real life, the irrelevant details, the "in-between" stuff. The implications are profound. *If* psychotherapy begins at the crisis point, and *if* the counselor functioning below level 3 can neither acknowledge nor cope with the crisis, then *with the therapist functioning below level 3 there is no real therapy.* While there may be client movement from the absence of effective communication to distorted communication from a distorted perceptual base, there is no real self-sustaining and effective communication.

If there is time at the crisis point, and often there is not, the therapist may choose to proceed cautiously, and rightfully and meaningfully so. If there is little time, as is most often the case, the therapist must move in quickly to clear away the "crud," the irrelevancies which cloud the critical issues for the client. In any event, whether there is time or not, the therapist must ultimately "touch" the client, letting him know that he is with the client in the client's deepest, most desperate moments. (At later points the therapist must be open to being "touched" by the client.)

If the client cannot communicate his desperate circumstances, or if he cannot allow his full experience of the crisis to emerge within him, the whole therapist can precipitate the crisis by confrontation or other means. *The whole therapist can experience the client more than the client can experience himself.* The whole therapist can enable the client to face squarely the life and death issues before him and, thus, enable the client to take his first steps toward or back to life. *If both therapist and client allow it to happen, counseling and therapy represent an hourly intensification of life in all of its crises and all of its fulfillment.*

## TO INCORPORATE OR BE INCORPORATED:
## THE FIRST CRISIS

The physical prototype for the life and death crises is the birth experience, where the movement toward life involves the risk of death. Similarly in therapy, the client seeks his more full emergence or re-emergence, or life, at the risk of death. This can be most clearly seen during early encounters with relatively pathological clients, where in very direct or very subtle ways the client attempts to undermine the therapist and the power implicit in his role. In a very real sense, although the client is drawn to therapy, he finds himself quickly attempting to "take the measure" of the man sitting across from him. The issue, as are all issues in the lives of many clients, is one of destroying or being destroyed, of incorporating or being incorporated. Thus, in the following example, a young man in his twenties functioning around level 2 is confronted by the therapist with his engagement in a number of destructive activities. The client directly and explicitly describes his motives and intentions:

THERAPIST: John, you really want to destroy our relationship here.
CLIENT: It's more than that.
THERAPIST: You want to kill me.
CLIENT: No, not really. I . . . .
THERAPIST: John, you want to kill me.
CLIENT: Yes, I want to kill you. I know you haven't earned it but I want to kill you, maybe for everyone I hate.
THERAPIST: That's too easy.
CLIENT: All I know is that I want to kill you.
THERAPIST: You can't.
CLIENT: I can! I can! One way or another I will. So I can't take you this way but I'll find another. I'll fail you. I'll lead you astray. You'll think I'm improving but I'll fail. I'll be your failure case. You'll be responsible.
THERAPIST: You'll do anything you have to, to undermine me, to destroy me, even something that hurts you.
CLIENT: Yes. Yes.
THERAPIST: If you can in some way defeat me, you won't have to change your way of living. You do stupid things to protect a stupid way of living, and that's stupid.
CLIENT: Oh, I want to change. I do. I can't help it. I can't help it. God, I've been wrong to hurt you.
THERAPIST: You had to find out whether you could take me. If you could, I couldn't help you, and I can.

It is almost as if the client, in his attack, is saying, "overwhelm me and give me hope." The therapist responds firmly to the client's desperate attempts to threaten the therapist and defend his way of living, but most importantly, he responds to the client's deepest need to lose in this encounter and win in his life. He confronts the client with what the client is doing, but reassures him that there is hope.

Having been unable to overwhelm the therapist, the client is now confronted with a deeper, even more disturbing motive, that of wanting to give himself fully to this strong person. His dependency needs threaten him even more than his destructive impulse. It is as if he is saying, "How can I trust that you will not abuse me if I commit myself to you?" Thus, in a later therapy session, the issue of being incorporated arises.

THERAPIST: You're really saying you don't know if you can trust me.
CLIENT: Why should I? How do I know you're not really a neurotic? How

do I know that I won't tap in on your need for power or something like that?

THERAPIST: Will I do what you would do in the same circumstances?

CLIENT: Will you destroy like I would?

THERAPIST: The question is, "Am I the guy who can help you make it?"

CLIENT: Can you help me change?

THERAPIST: You've been led down a lot of primrose paths before. That's all over now, though. You've got to know this time.

CLIENT: There's no more time. I'm running out of it.

THERAPIST: It's pretty terrifying. This is your only hope. . . .

CLIENT: But I don't know if I can make the commitment.

THERAPIST: You've got to ask that question—at the deepest level. I'd be worried if you didn't. Your life is at stake.

CLIENT: If I commit myself, can I make it? Will you help me?

The question of trust comes up over and over again, at deeper and deeper levels in therapy. Many therapists are misled by a once-over lightly on trust and confidentiality. The client's real question is whether he can trust the therapist with his life. He asks "If I can upset him, intimidate him, and destroy him, I cannot trust him. If I cannot destroy him, will he destroy me?"

## DISTANCE AND EXPERIENCE

Throughout the early phases of therapy, the issues of all phases of the client's experiences come up over and over again, at deeper and deeper levels in therapy. The client who has had a meaningful therapeutic experience may come to doubt the experience after a lapse of time. It is as if the client's acknowledgment of the experience and its full implications would commit the client to further investments of himself without knowing the implications. Each step along the way commits the person to further steps and the direction cannot always be anticipated. In the following example, the client, a woman in her thirties functioning at around level 2, had a deeply meaningful experience with the therapist at a moment of terror in her life. This was a moment in which she did not know if she could live or would die, a moment in which the therapist held out his hands to hold hers through the crisis. During the next encounter the client questions the meaning of the previous encounter:

CLIENT: You paw me just like all of the rest. You're just like the rest, you just want something from me.

THERAPIST: You question the whole experience and all of my motives.

CLIENT: You want the same thing they want—me.
THERAPIST: You don't trust that it happened.
CLIENT: It couldn't have happened.
THERAPIST: There are implications either way.
CLIENT: What do you mean?
THERAPIST: If it didn't happen, then you can't trust all of this as real and you don't have to commit yourself. If it did, well. . . .
CLIENT: If it happened, it's the first time that anyone ever cared for me, without wanting something in return.

The client wants to believe but has to doubt. But tears are real and a steady hand held in panic cannot be denied. If the previous experience were illusory, it cannot be made real. If the previous experience were real, the therapist cannot allow the client's analyzations to make it illusory. The neurotic's ambition is to make the real, illusory, and the illusory, real. The therapist must be deeply in the moment in the encounter or he cannot later trust his experience of the encounter any more than the client's later expression of his experience. Only if the client is not allowed to destroy what must live, can he enter and trust later life experiences.

## THE HONEST CONFRONTATION

Throughout each of these examples, the therapist has in the end relied upon his experience of the client. At the crisis point, the therapist must rely upon his experience of the client, with clients functioning below a minimally facilitative, self-sustaining level. Usually at this point, the therapist's most effective mode of functioning involves an honest confrontation with the client. This is often because of the time limitations which an unresolved crisis places upon therapy.

Although an honest experience with a constructive person is most often precisely what has been missing in the low-level functioning person's life and is exactly what brings him to therapy as a client, he will often do everything possible to prevent this occurrence. He prefers his fantasies to reality. Even for the level 2 clients, acting and doing cannot compete with insight and talking. The destroyer of his illusions is his murderer. He holds the therapist off with intimidation, threatening to make the therapist fully responsible for anything deleterious that happens to him. He defines an honest confrontation as a "hostile act." Indeed, any action by anyone is an attack. *Life is death and death is life.*

If, as is the case in most forms of traditional therapy, the therapist does not acknowledge the crisis, confront it, and in so doing confront the client and himself, the therapist's passivity reinforces the client's passivity. The only real change that might then take place is in the modification of the client's perception and expression of his crises. The consequent insight gives him, in therapy perhaps, the feeling or illusion that he is on top of his situation, when in reality (and he finds this out when he returns to real life), he is not. He cannot act just as his therapist could not act; a real therapist is only acting in an honest encounter involving himself and the client. Providing high levels of facilitative conditions does not in itself constitute an act, but rather, if effective, only increases the probability for action on the part of both therapist and client. The crises in therapy precipitate honest confrontation between therapist and client. Traditional forms of therapy neither recognize the crises nor acknowledge the necessity for confrontation.

A whole therapist brings his whole person and all of his accumulated store of knowledge to bear at the crisis point. His very acknowledgment of the crisis dictates his full employment of himself. If the therapist is able to "touch" the client, letting him know that he is with him in his deepest moment and that he will do whatever he has to do to free the client to choose life, then the closed cycle that disallows action is broken. Instead there is an opening movement toward emergence which will, in turn, involve other crises in life. Again, *life is a process of interrelated crises and challenges which we confront or not to live or not.*

Confrontation may be necessary very early in a therapy relationship in order for therapeutic processes to take place. Thus, in the following example, the therapist confronts a young woman client in her thirties functioning around level 2 who was referred to him after unsuccessful experiences in therapy. In a very real sense the therapist percipitates a crisis for the client:

THERAPIST: We've spent several sessions together and I think I have some feeling for who you are.

CLIENT: I've really appreciated your understanding. You have been very helpful.

THERAPIST: Not exactly. Are you familiar with the details of the referral?

CLIENT: Well, I didn't get along with Dr. S——— and I guess I still have problems with other people.

THERAPIST: JoAnne, you were labeled a psychopath. Do you understand what that means?

CLIENT: I guess so, like criminal or something.

THERAPIST: Sort of. For you it means the way you manipulate everyone without concern for their welfare.

CLIENT: I guess that's what I did with Dr. S———.

THERAPIST: . . . and others . . . and it's what you'd like to do with me.

CLIENT: (Begins to cry.)

THERAPIST: But I am different.

CLIENT: I can't believe that I matter that much to you. I know you're different but I can't help acting that way. I can't help it. I can't help it. (cries fully)

The client must now face a crisis in therapy and in her life. Can she really trust someone? Can she relax her defensive and often offensive system to allow another person in? Granted her system worked well in the "jungle" in which she had survived, but it no longer serves her in her present circumstances. The therapist, in his living embodiment as well as his words, confronts her with her choice to destroy others as well as herself. In so doing, he holds out his hand to offer her a chance to choose life.

In the following brief excerpt, a juvenile delinquent, into whom a great deal of effort had been put, was about to make the break with her foster parents and re-enter the "jungle" from which she had come:

CLIENT: What does it matter?

THERAPIST: It matters.

CLIENT: You don't give a damn.

THERAPIST: I'm here.

CLIENT (yelling): You don't understand me. None of you. You don't know who I am, where I came from.

THERAPIST (yelling): I don't want to understand one damn thing more about you than I know.

CLIENT: (makes no reply)

No more words were exchanged. The therapist met the client's challenge, more loudly than it was issued. He reaffirmed her human value, and made it possible for her not to be bound by her past any more than he was. "I don't need to know any more about you. You are you and, as such, I value you." This encounter, brief as it was, marked the turning point in this girl's life.

Traditionally, confrontation has been employed only with delinquent or psychopathic populations. It seems as if only this population gives the therapist license to return the "hostile act." However, honesty in communication, whatever form it takes, is the catalyst to full living with all populations. In the following example, a young man functioning at around level 2 threatens one last potent act, suicide, and the therapist responds:

CLIENT: . . . you've pushed me too far, that's why.

THERAPIST: You're really saying that if you die, I'm the murderer.

CLIENT: You'll have my blood on your hands for everyone to see.

THERAPIST: You've been pushed so hard that you've reached a point where it seems the only thing you can do.

CLIENT: That's all.

THERAPIST: That's honest.

CLIENT (after a pause): What do you mean?

THERAPIST: Well, it's either that or choosing to act to live.

CLIENT (after a pause): I've had everything taken from me—all my dreams—I'm back at the beginning, with nothing.

THERAPIST: There's just you and either way you act, it's got to be for you—just you.

If the therapist is indeed guilty, he cannot confront the client at this crisis point. The client's crisis becomes his, and, if he cannot acknowledge the crisis for himself as well as the client, constructive change for either cannot ensue. Of course, the therapist must, as we have emphasized throughout, do more than confront the client. He must be willing to accompany the client into the deepest, unexplored caverns of the client's unconscious. The therapist is the guide; it is his willingness to accompany that reflects his concern. It is his effectiveness in living that allows him to bring all of his resources to bear at the crisis. It is his honesty of communication that allows him to "touch" the client at the deepest level.

## THE THERAPIST'S CRISIS

The crisis for the client, as can be seen, becomes the crisis for the therapist. Whether or not the therapist acknowledges it and attends to it does not make it the less so. If he can handle these crises, both he and the client can arrive at new levels of insight and action. In the following excerpt a twenty-year-old male client functioning around level 2 confronts the therapist with the product of his fantasies. During the previous session, in a moment of panic for the client, the therapist had reached out both of his hands to hold the shaking hands of the client. The client, now distant from the earlier experience, denounces the therapist:

CLIENT: You . . . you're a dirty . . . seducer.

THERAPIST: It's worse than that, isn't it?

CLIENT: Yes! A homo! You're a dirty homosexual.
  (Silence)

CLIENT: Well, I don't know. Maybe I want to seduce you.

THERAPIST: You want to make a connection in some way.

CLIENT (weeping): I never could love anyone. They wouldn't let my love in and now I have no outlet for my feelings.

THERAPIST: Except now—with me.

CLIENT: Maybe you're strong enough to accept it.

THERAPIST: You want my strength—my potency. You want so much to be able to live, to act, to love.

Because the therapist is unafraid to enter forbidden areas about forbidden impulses, the client is able to express himself fully. Together they are able to arrive at the meaning behind the impulses, meaning which can be translated into constructive action.

Although the crisis which initiates the therapeutic process is the client's, many of the crises along the way will be shared by both therapist and client. Depending upon the wholeness of the client, the therapist may carry the major part of the burden in many instances. Witness the moment when both therapist and client are richly laden with emotional insights but have not yet discovered the essential, final direction of therapy. The question for both therapist and client is, "What are you going to do with the insights?" or "What are we going to do with our insights?" It is the neurotic hope that insight is sufficient and action, unnecessary. It is the neurotic solution to rest upon constructs rather than construction. This crisis is most prominent in movement from phase 1, the downward or inward phase, to phase 2, the upward or outward phase. It is the therapist's crisis as well as the client's.

Similarly, the termination of therapy is frequently more of a crisis for the therapist than it is for the client. Or, put another way, it is as much of a crisis for the client as it is for the therapist. The termination of effective therapy should involve handling no different from the handling of any other crisis. The therapist must confront himself as well as the client in an honest, equalitarian relationship, if indeed it is such. The client must go out into the real world, and the therapist must let him go. Most often, this is difficult for the therapist who has not given fully of himself, who has not discharged all of his responsibilities to the client. It is very difficult for the therapist who does not trust himself and does not trust what he has done in therapy. It is even more difficult for the therapist who is not himself living effectively for he cannot trust the client to live effectively upon leaving therapy. He fears for the client as he fears for himself, for he, the therapist, cannot choose. Most often, whereas the first crisis is the client's, *the last crisis is the therapist's.*

## THERAPIST-INTRODUCED PROCESS CRISES

In the final analysis, then, there is no growth without crisis and the confrontation of self and others which the crisis precipitates. The effective therapist grows at the crisis point as well as the client, and while he may not be prepared for the particular crisis involved, it makes him tap his own resources and push out his own boundaries. Within the crisis the therapist, in effect, goes "all of the way" with the client and struggles in order to facilitate directionality for the client. The implications of not acknowledging and addressing the crisis are critical. The implications of "techniquing it" are profound.

In this regard, a number of research projects are relevant. In order to study the effects of the manipulation of therapeutic conditions, what were, in effect, "crises" were experimentally introduced; that is, during the first third of the therapy hour, high levels of facilitative conditions were offered the client by the therapist. During the second third of therapy, the conditions were lowered when the therapist selectively withheld the best possible responses that he might otherwise have made. The therapist's responses tended to be innocuous rather than precipitously lowered. Finally, during the last period the conditions were raised again to a highly facilitative level. The sessions were taped and rated. The client, then, received low levels of facilitative conditions during the middle period; he was not understood with any degree of sensitivity. The therapist's regard and hovering attentiveness were not available to him, and the therapist was, to some degree, ingenuine. In effect, the client experienced a therapeutic crisis in the sense that he was attempting to communicate himself but did not receive in return facilitative communciations from the therapist. The findings are striking. The depth of self-exploration engaged in by both psychotic inpatients (Truax and Carkhuff, 1965) and low-level functioning students (Holder, Carkhuff, and Berenson, 1967) was found to be a direct function of the level of conditions offered by the therapist; that is, when the therapist offered high levels of conditions, the low functioning clients explored themselves at high levels; when the therapist offered low levels of conditions, the low functioning clients explored themselves at very low levels.

The following excerpts are drawn from the three periods of one of the studies of the experimental manipulation of therapeutic conditions. During period I a highly resistant young female client, functioning between levels 1 and 2, comes gradually to explore herself through the strenuous efforts of her high-level functioning therapist:

*Period I:*

THERAPIST: You keep staring at the tape recorder. Does it make you nervous?
CLIENT: No, it's the only thing to look at in here.
THERAPIST: You don't want to look at me.

CLIENT: No, that's not it. I bought a tape recorder two years ago. (Pause) I can't think of anything else to say.

THERAPIST: Maybe you'd just like to get out of here.

CLIENT: I just wish I could think of something to say.

THERAPIST: It's not easy to get started.

CLIENT: It never is. I guess I can't help the way I am. But I'd like to change some of my ways.

The client goes on to become more and more involved in process movement. However, during the experimental period this movement ceases and the exchange, which was dependent upon the therapist's level of functioning, deteriorates to a level of everyday functioning:

*Period II:*

THERAPIST: I guess we're both kind of tired.

CLIENT: I've been keeping late hours, working weekends, not getting any sleep. I have to rest to catch up on my studies.

THERAPIST: Studies are hard.

CLIENT: Yeah, but I like them, too, only not too much.

THERAPIST: Too much is too much.

CLIENT: Yeah, sometimes I just get tired, not enough sleep, I guess.

The process is almost a circular one which leads nowhere. It must be reiterated that the therapist's responses during the middle period were not negative or destructive in nature, but rather reflected the selective withholding of the best possible responses. During the final period, the therapist again provides high levels of conditions and the client comes to explore herself at a very deep level.

*Period III:*

THERAPIST: What you have hidden from the world is pretty precious to you.

CLIENT: I don't think the world could care less.

THERAPIST: They don't really give a damn.

CLIENT: I can't help feeling this way, but they always leave me out.

THERAPIST: They're all wrapped up in themselves. Even if you did open up. . . .

CLIENT: They wouldn't hear me or see me because they don't care (sob). So I guess I hide the real me from them.

Thus, the client proceeds to invest herself further in working out her identity, particularly in relation to others. With the therapist tuned in, she can make amazing strides of progress. With the therapist functioning at low levels, she cannot take a baby step. To summarize, when the crisis involving low levels of communication, is precipitated with low-level functioning clients, the communication process breaks down totally; the client collapses unless there is a facilitative person around to put the communication process together again. On the other hand, when high-level functioning clients are seen by high-level functioning counselors the crises are of less disastrous consequences. Thus, during the middle, experimental period, the high-level functioning clients continue to explore themselves independently of the therapist's lowering of conditions (Holder, Carkhuff, and Berenson, 1967). It seems that, once the high-level functioning client is aware that the therapist whom he is seeing is tuned in on his wavelength and genuinely concerned for his welfare, he continues to function independently of the level of therapist-offered conditions. Following the initial period of high level conditions, the higher the level of client functioning, the greater his independence of the high-level functioning counselor's conditions. Another study (Piaget, Berenson, and Carkhuff, 1967) with high and low functioning clients, supported these findings and established the differential effects of the manipulation of conditions by a low functioning therapist, where both the low and high functioning clients demonstrated progressively lower depths of self-exploration; that is, having experienced the low functioning therapist's level of conditions, both the high and low functioning clients demonstrate less and less constructive process movement. The implications for the differential effects of high and low therapists upon high and low functioning clients are compelling.

## CLIENT-INTRODUCED PROCESS CRISES

Another type of crisis might be one introduced by the client. In a series of experimental studies (Alexik and Carkhuff, 1967; Carkhuff and Alexik, 1966), unknown to the therapist involved, a female client was given a mental set to explore herself deeply during the first third of an interview, to talk only about irrelevant and impersonal details during the middle third, and to explore herself deeply again during the final third of the interview. Thus, the client experimentally introduced a "crisis" for the therapist; after the client was exploring herself deeply and meaningfully, she suddenly "runs away" from therapy and the therapist loses contact with her. Whatever he does, he cannot bring her back to high levels of therapeutic process movement. The communication process, for which he is largely responsible, has broken down.

The results are stimulating. In a way similar to the pattern of the high-level functioning clients, during the experimental period of the therapist-introduced crises, the therapists functioning above level 3 functioned independently of the client during the middle period. There was a tendency for those functioning at the highest levels to increase the level of conditions which they offer when the client lowered her self-exploration. On the other hand, those therapists functioning below level 3 dropped their conditions precipitously when the client experimentally lowered her depth of self-exploration. However, unlike the pattern of the low level clients in the experimental manipulation of therapist-offered conditions studies, during the final period when the client again explored herself deeply, the therapists never again offered conditions even close to the level of those which they offered initially.

Perhaps, many of the significant results of the study (Carkhuff and, Alexik, 1967) may be best portrayed by the client's illustration of her experience and her character sketches of the therapists involved:

> Recently I took part in a fascinating research project involving the manipulation of several therapists by a client. I was the client who attempted the manipulation by presenting a problem and exploring as deeply as possible for the first twenty minutes of the hour, then suddenly switching off to irrelevancies such as the weather, the decor of the office, and again after twenty minutes of chit chat, suddenly going back into deep exploration of my problem. The object was to test the ability of the therapists to bring the client back in the middle section into contact with the emotional implications of the problem.
>
> To give a clearer understanding of the project, I am a middle-aged woman who recently decided to enter the field of counseling. I had enrolled at a large university as a graduate student, and during the first semester I had had a brief chance to counsel an undergraduate student, with the sessions taped so that they might be a learning experience for me. My reaction upon hearing the tapes was not the expected one of hearing missed cues, but rather one of surprise and dismay at the personality I heard when I listened to myself. This, then, was the problem which I presented to each of the eight therapists whom I subsequently saw. Since none of the therapists had ever seen me before (except one whom I had met several months earlier in a casual setting), I was, for them, apparently just another client coming for help. Each session was taped, and this was accomplished in a routine way (it was fairly common at the Center for some member of the department to request that the next session be taped for training purposes). Thus, a real problem was presented by a legitimate client, and it was a genuine test of what happens to the therapist when the client attempts to control the hour.

Thus, the following excerpts typified the functioning of the high level therapist during the three periods of the research:

*Period I:*

CLIENT: As you may know, I'm in counseling and I heard my first tape and it threw me for a real loop, as to whether I should go into counseling because I came out a different person from what I ever thought of myself as being. I came out a weak, defensive, whiny, old lady, and what worries me is, am I this person to begin with, or is this just something superficial in my way of projecting myself? Or, you know, am I fit to counsel, because I wouldn't go to anybody who sounded like that myself?

THERAPIST: Are you saying, "My God, is that the real me?"

CLIENT: Yeah, that was exactly what I said.

THERAPIST: Sounds like it was something that, bang, hit you, and almost knocked you down.

CLIENT: For about two weeks it really threw me, but then I got to thinking, well, maybe it was a habit, some way of speaking that I'd learned and that it was interfering and was not the real me. And I don't know whether that's rationalizing, you know, or whether—I'm in a quandry now whether I continue counseling—it has a lot to do with it—you know, if something's there I can unlearn and project in a different way, o.k., but if I'm weak I have no business counseling others. And besides, I don't want to think of myself as this kind of a person because it's the kind of person I don't like.

THERAPIST: I get two messages from you. One is that this thing was a helluva shock to you, to hear your own voice, to hear what you thought you were during this interview, and I get another message from you, which, at another level, you're not really a weak, whiny old lady.

Even during the second period, the high-level functioning practitioner was able to relate seemingly irrelevant material to personally meaningful experiences of the client. After all, her choice of irrelevant and impersonal material was in some way personal, and the therapist stretched to tune in on its meaning. It was very difficult indeed for the client to maintain her mental set.

*Period II:*

CLIENT: That reminds me, there's something about this town. It's an awfully cold town. Northerners are so blasted—uh—indifferent. Or I don't know, they're certainly not very warm or easy to know. I've been here since last summer, and I swear I don't know anybody at all.

THERAPIST: It's hard to know where you stand, at some deep level you feel very much alone, or cut off.

CLIENT: Well, I think these professors particularly have their own little circles and nobody, you know. . . .

THERAPIST: There's no room. . . .

CLIENT: And nobody entertains much apparently, except within the department or something of that sort, and they have their own interests, the townspeople have their own interests, and the kids are busy studying and they have their little group, and I'm a grandma to them. And still there's not much you can do about this, but it is different from Washington. I was in this house here for two weeks before anyone even said, "Hello, you know, I'm a neighbor. How are you?" And finally one neighbor stopped in to borrow a stick of butter and then I didn't see anyone else for another two weeks.

THERAPIST: I wonder if you're not really asking, "Does anyone around here really care?"

Finally, during the third part of the session, the client returned again to explore herself at relatively high levels.

*Period III:*

CLIENT: I did that for years and years, trying to be what someone else wanted me to be, but I thought I was over that. . . .

THERAPIST: You keep telling me "I'm not what my voice is. I'm a volcano."

CLIENT: But I never associated my voice as being anything but . . .

THERAPIST: You keep telling me you're not what you appear to be. You know what you've told me this hour—you've told me, "I look like I'm meek, but I'm not."

CLIENT: I'm a lion, not a mouse.

THERAPIST: Your voice changed a little bit when you said that. It was looser.

CLIENT: Uh hum. . . .

THERAPIST: You could get pretty angry at that. "I'm not a mouse." What did you feel when you said that?

CLIENT: I felt like roaring.

THERAPIST: You're damn right you did. Wish you did—for you I wish you did. "Don't you call me a mouse." Do you ever feel like that?

CLIENT: Oh, yeah, many a time.

THERAPIST: I'm a mouse and a mouse can't help anybody. Lions can. Oh, I don't know—constructive lions can, lions who can make discriminations about when it is appropriate to raise your voice.

CLIENT: Humm, I hadn't thought of that.

THERAPIST: I don't come across like a full person if you always see me at my best, and in this society at my best means controlled, calm, polite, thoughtful, but never human. To be human I have to be able to communicate my anger and my joy and everything in between. And inside I know these things. I know these experiences inside. Huh? I've got to make discriminations about when it's appropriate to show these feelings, and by God, counseling is an appropriate place.

With the low-level functioning therapist, the results were quite different. Again, during the initial period, the client presented essentially the same difficulty:

*Period I:*

CLIENT: I have a problem. My problem began some time ago. I'm in the counseling program in education.

THERAPIST: Say, I don't believe I got your name.

CLIENT: Oh, Janie, Janie Clark.

THERAPIST: Janie Clark. Thank you. You know who I am?

CLIENT: Yeah, Dr. Jones.

THERAPIST: Yeah, Dr. Jones, yeah.

CLIENT: Anyway, I had my first client and it was taped, and when I turned on the tape to hear my cues I'd missed and things, and I didn't hear anything except my voice and the way I came across as a person. And at the time it really threw me for a loop because I'd never thought of myself as the kind of person that I came out on the tape. It wasn't just, you know, the different sound of the voice, or anything like that. It was a whole new me, you know, a different me, and I didn't know whether it was just that I'd picked up ways of expressing myself, which I told myself at first, but I didn't like what I saw obviously. I came out a very weak, whiny, pathetic little old lady, and I'd never thought of myself that way. And there it was just clearly, that was all that was coming across.

THERAPIST: This is your interpretation of the—uh—your listening to yourself on the tape. You thought you were not as strong a character perhaps.

CLIENT: Nothing!

THERAPIST: In other words, a difference in yourself.

CLIENT: A blobby sort of a—no personality, no umpf, no nothing to which you could relate to.

THERAPIST: And you, you think this is—and what do you think, you think, perhaps, the tape is a true indication of the—of your interpretation. . . .

CLIENT: Yeah, my first reaction was that maybe I'd learned to express myself poorly but then finally I realized that no, this was a part of me that I just never had recognized that was coming out and, this is a very recent thing for me to be willing to admit that, you know, that this is me. (Silence)

I have talked about it with a number of people and that undoubtedly has helped me to recognize that—I'm still pretty hung up on some of it, though. I'm so used to thinking of myself in certain ways—partly I can be totally unconscious of this and then afterwards I think, oh, there was that dear little old lady again, and, apparently there are some aspects of the dear little old lady that I still think I like.

THERAPIST: Uh, huh.

CLIENT: But I don't like the total picture at all, not at all.

THERAPIST: So, you, now it gives you a sort of a negative picture of yourself.

During the second period, the client was able to manipulate the therapist successfully. The discussion was on her terms, and, indeed, in many ways the therapist appeared to feel more comfortable.

*Period II:*

CLIENT: And I like the Northeast, and so they said, "Well, try this state," and so that's all I knew. And so then I came up here.

THERAPIST: Now you're enrolled in the Master's program?

CLIENT: Yes.

THERAPIST: Are you teaching, too?

CLIENT: No.

THERAPIST: You have a teaching certificate?

CLIENT: No.

THERAPIST: What did you major in in college?

CLIENT: Political science. Big help.

THERAPIST: A general college education.

CLIENT: Yeah. Oh, I love the weather up here now. I'm dreading the summer because someone told me it's hot. Part of the reason I came up here was because Washington summers are unbearable. But they tell me it gets real hot here. You probably would love some good hot weather, coming from the North, as you said.

THERAPIST: No, I like cool weather.

CLIENT: Yeah, I hate the thought of thinking of myself as the kind of person who anybody can say "boo" to and I'll turn around and run.

THERAPIST: Yeah.

CLIENT: I never understood how you guys got up here in this hall.

THERAPIST: More room.

CLIENT: Well, I thought it was because you guys must be in bad repute, and so they sent you to this old building.

THERAPIST: I don't know about that part of it, but the ostensible reason it's more room.

CLIENT: It's pretty dilapidated, but it is kind of off to itself. The other building is so busy.

THERAPIST: Yeah, it's crowded.

Finally, the client again returns to relatively high levels of self-exploration, but the therapist does not quite return to the level at which he was functioning during the first period of the study.

*Period III:*

CLIENT: To me fighting is a dirty word—somehow it means hurting people, getting hurt, you know, there's nothing healthy or good about it—seems awful to have to fight.

THERAPIST: When people fight you, you get hurt, so you don't want to.

CLIENT: Well . . .

THERAPIST: You don't want to fight other people so you won't hurt them.

CLIENT: I don't want to get hurt, or hurt, it's a combination of all these things, and I don't want any part of it—but I don't like the other alternative which is to. . . .

THERAPIST: The reality I guess, in the best sense you'd like to avoid a fight, that is, if it's your way—but in real life people have differences of opinion and so this is where you're hung up so you'll either have to fight for your say or else you don't get it.

CLIENT: You know I might just as well not have had the fight, you know. I would feel very defeated if I went in and fought and lost.

THERAPIST: You mean you might feel more defeated than you feel now.

CLIENT: Yeah, that's right.

THERAPIST: You wouldn't feel that if you fought and lost.

CLIENT: I identify fighting with losing.

THERAPIST: I see. So you think you win a fight?

CLIENT: When you get in a fight, you either win or lose, and I'm the loser.

THERAPIST: Huh.

CLIENT: I always have been, and I just always expect to be.

THERAPIST: Which, in a sense, to me it seems sort of that in a sense you're defeated before you start. You're certainly not going to win the battle if you don't fight, uh, unless you're lucky, maybe and it just sort of falls that way.

CLIENT: But somehow it doesn't seem as much of a defeat if you, you know, I chose to walk off, and I haven't lost face, or something. I don't know, but if I fight, then my self-esteem goes down.

The declining pattern is one which (in contrast to the rising pattern of the high-level functioning therapist) most low-level functioning therapists present over a number of sessions of therapy. That is, it would appear that following the exercising of the initial repertoire of responses during the early sessions, with the client's continuing presentation of crises, whether acknowledged by the therapist or not, the low-level functioning therapists deteriorate in functioning over therapy.

The client's impressions of her experience (Carkhuff and Alexik, 1967) are related as follows:

> I must mention that as an inexperienced layman, albeit a beginning student in counseling, I had anticipated that I would learn a bit more about myself, particularly in regard to the techniques from these experienced counselors. I had absolutely no forewarning that I would be so appalled at the destructiveness of some of the therapists nor that I would be so excited by the facilitative ones. I had not really envisioned that there would be a difference that I could so easily detect. After all, these were highly trained, experienced therapists, each of whom counseled several clients daily.
>
> My first impressions were, in all but one case, validated by the replaying of the taped sessions. In this particular case, I think I was misled by the fact that this was a woman counselor, and being a woman, I probably unconsciously hoped to see a good counselor and therefore must have given her the benefit of the doubt. She also was bright and intelligent, and it was only after playing back the tape that I could see that her intelligence was misused and could not be trusted. But in all other cases, I sensed immediately whether a therapist was showing respect and genuine interest in me as a human being or merely reciting a litany, so to speak. With some, I came away feeling that I had had a glimpse of a real human being in a genuine encounter, and that this person had some understanding and appreciation of me as a human being. I felt that I had learned and could learn more about myself and life from this individual and was, therefore, hopeful of finding a better way of living. With others, I came away feeling that the therapist had been totally indifferent to me and to my needs, either because of his own needs, or because he was incapable of feeling for me, that I had not only learned nothing from the encounter, but also that I left feeling very depressed and hopeless. This occurred with several counselors in a greater or lesser degree. With some of them, I felt sympathy—with others, I felt disgust and anger that they should be allowed to be in a so-called "helping" profession. I could only think of a really sick person who had finally worked up the courage to make perhaps one last attempt to find a human being with enough love and understanding to help him to find his way out of his misery. I was appalled to think of his winding up with some of these inadequate counselors who would surely destroy his last hope. It seemed to me criminal negligence on the part of society to allow this kind of therapist to operate.

Concerning each of the experienced counselors and therapists whom the client saw in one study (Carkhuff and Alexik, 1967), she provided the following character sketches:

COUNSELOR A

Counselor A walked in and I saw a man who looked shorter than he is with a brush of black hair tinged with gray, big wide eyes under bushy brows, the eyes the main feature. Something in those eyes makes you feel safe, and yet you know he can really think. But you know the guy has feelings by those eyes. None of those cold empty eyes. He talks in a voice so big it almost scares you, but not rough and not smooth, but gentle, though big. He could blast you right out of your chair, but he probably wouldn't. Somehow I knew I could trust him. And so I started telling him how it is with me, and he seems to be right with me all the time. I don't know but it's as if he didn't even need my words and I didn't feel as if he was faking. Oh, some of the time I felt he was bored waiting for me to spell it out because he was ahead of me, not because he thought I wasn't worth his time. He had a way of putting my words into such specific and marvelous analogies that made me feel more deeply what it was I only vaguely was aware of before. He gave off vitality and allowed me to share it—not that I left him with less but that he had so much and he was allowing me to take what I needed. He made me feel as if I was OK and would be able to use it usefully and come out of it. He gave me hope, optimism, and a more clearly defined problem than when I went in. I left feeling that if anything else seemed insoluble to me, I'd just go in and see him again. And he left me feeling that he would be glad to help me again.

COUNSELOR B

Counselor B was a slight, blondish, watery-eyed person whom you wouldn't ordinarily ever remember seeing. He has absolutely no presence. But he has a Ph.D. With this therapist, within a few sentences I could hardly wait to get to the part where I could talk about nothing at all. He absolutely floored me when he asked a lot of irrelevant questions about my husband's salary, my status, and so on. I wanted to tell him what those questions did to me—I wound up just despising him, and unconsciously this came out. When I listened to the tape I heard myself give a very destructive laugh. I had definitely written him off within the first two minutes, and the only reason I stayed was to do the research, but I would never have returned to this man if I had needed help of any kind.

COUNSELOR C

Counselor C is a big, blondish, sunny type of southern fellow. He is a genuinely warm guy and a very likeable one. He exudes friendliness and his eyes sparkle. You have a feeling he could really enjoy a good laugh. I did not feel that he pressed hard enough on my problems, but that maybe he was just feeling things out the first session. I thought I liked him. He seemed too slow-paced and I didn't think his intellect was as sharp as some. But I felt that I didn't really know him in any sense and that he was holding back because he didn't know me yet.

COUNSELOR D

I felt as if Counselor D was trying and wanted to be helpful, but I found it difficult to react to his personality. He was an older but sort of nondescript looking man, smoked a pipe, and looked possibly scholarly. He immediately indicated he was not feeling up to par and I felt I wanted to be nice to him because I felt sorry for him, but did not want to for my own sake. However, I felt he was reaching out to me, but sort of for my help. Was easy to talk about him as against myself but that seems a part of first-session getting to know rather than a definite lack of ability. Did not feel interested in going back to him, though.

COUNSELOR E

Counselor E seemed pretty stiff and intellectual, and gave the impression of really knowing her stuff, and of having had to battle hard to wrench any of what she knew out of the men—almost a caricature of a career girl. But she had a soft voice and smiled brightly and made me feel as if she was on my side against the men in this world. She didn't actually say anything about men, so far as I can remember, but somehow I picked up the feeling that she was strange and different. It was easy to get her to talk about her pictures and books, which surprised me as I had expected her by her appearance to be tougher. I came away thinking she was really bright and knew about therapy. After listening to the tapes, she came out the most boring, the least interested, and not very bright. I am still puzzled as to what made me think her bright as I am not usually fooled that easily. My only thought is that I projected my need to see a woman therapist as good.

COUNSELOR F

Counselor F was a big, burly, black-haired, beetle-browed, soft-fat foreign-looking man who might be a mechanic or farmhand rather than a Ph.D. in psychology. He was a typical client-centered therapist—fed me back my words until I wanted to say: "Haven't you any ideas of your own?" and "That's what I said, what are you saying them for?" It annoyed me very much, and I could hardly refrain from mentioning it. I felt he wasn't really very interested in my problem, but it was his job to sit there and be polite. My general feeling was one of annoyance with him. Would not go back if I had any problem. Came away from this interview feeling frustrated.

COUNSELOR G

This poor lady surprised me in being better than I had anticipated. She looked like a tousled, slipshod sort of matron with no organization to her character or mind. She actually was a better therapist than the neat, efficient lady I had seen before. She was touched by my problem because it coincided in some respects with hers, and soon I felt that I should be giving her therapy. It was, in fact, very difficult for me to remember that I was there for research purposes and that I shouldn't, therefore, change roles with her during this hour. She made me feel very sad and depressed, and yet I liked her and wished I could cheer her up. She would not be able to help you grow, but could give directions for specific problems, and they would probably be oriented toward her own philosophy and her own problems. But she was herself more than some of the others.

COUNSELOR H

Counselor H was a long, lanky, dark-haired, really blue-eyed, tall, string-bean of a man; young. Felt immediately a sense of intellect which was a relief after some of the others. Wasn't sure if he could be warm. As he talked he seemed warm, but I had a tiny part of me saying, "I'm not sure I'd like to get in a fight with him." I felt he might not be on my side if I didn't show up well. He was very sharp, and it was extremely difficult to pull him away from my problem. I was very depressed when I went in to see him, and he seemed to want to help me get over this depression and I felt that he probably could. During this hour, though, I was unable to shake off the depressions, which I felt was because I was unwilling rather than because he could not help me. Felt that if I went back to him and really put myself on the line, he could unravel a hell of a lot of my problems for me, but not sure I'd go back unless I felt especially courageous at the time. He might not go all the way with me if I showed something he didn't like or couldn't feel. He was very good, though; one of the best. I respected him and felt that he was good. It was just a matter of not feeling 100 percent safe. I felt him to be strong enough, but perhaps not tender enough.

The differences between the client's descriptions of the therapists involved are not only clear experientially for the client, but also congruent with our own experience and with the research findings. We have some distinct feeling for who can deliver results and who cannot. In the study, counselors A, C, and H acknowledged and confronted the crisis situation, while the others did not. At the crisis point in therapy, then, when the therapist has lost contact with the client, the low-level functioning therapists drop off and never return again to their previous levels of functioning, while the high-level therapists tend to function at the same levels or, for the highest among them, actually increase their level of functioning.

## SUMMARY AND CONCLUSIONS

If, then, we make the assumption that therapy begins at the crisis point, it is clear that *only the higher level functioning therapists do therapy.* The low-level functioning therapists, in turn, function in therapy as they function in their lives; they emphasize the irrelevant roles and impersonal aspects of human functioning; *they ignore the fabric of life, woven from the threads of human crises.*

Traditional psychotherapy is not psychotherapy. What has been considered psychotherapy, a number of regular contacts between therapist and client in which the therapist serves to facilitate the self-exploration of the client, is simply the structure within which crises can occur and be resolved and within which the client can grow, emerge, and act constructively.

Traditional psychotherapy, in its emphasis upon the implementation of stereotyped role models and the dispensing of techniques, falls short of effective practices, for at the crisis point the therapist reaches into his own resources or extends the boundaries of his resources: *the therapist handles the crisis or not as he is a whole therapist or not; the therapist handles the crisis or not as he is a whole human or not.* There are no rules for functioning in unknown areas, and crises are crises because they are unknown areas for the therapist as well as the client.

### References

Alexik, Mae, and R. R. Carkhuff. The effects of the manipulation of client depth of self-exploration upon the level of therapist offered conditions. *J. clin. Psychol.*, 1967, 23, 212–215.

Carkhuff, R. R., and Mae Alexik. The differential effects of the manipulation of client depth of self-exploration upon high and low functioning counselors. *J. counsel. Psychol.*, in press, 1967.

Carkhuff, R. R., and C. B. Truax. Toward explaining success and failure in interpersonal learning experiences. *Personnel guid. J.*, 1966, 44, 723–728.

Holder, T., R. R. Carkhuff, and B. G. Berenson. The differential effects of the manipulation of therapeutic conditions upon high and low functioning clients. *J. counsel. Psychol.*, 1967, 14, 63–66.

Piaget, G., B. G. Berenson, and R. R. Carkhuff. The differential effects of the manipulation of therapeutic conditions by high and low functioning clients upon high and low functioning clients. *J. consult. Psychol.*, in press, 1967.

Truax, C. B., and R. R. Carkhuff. The experimental manipulation of therapeutic conditions. *J. consult. Psychol.*, 1965, 29, 119–124.

Chapter **11**

> . . . A life without confrontation
> is directionless, passive
> and impotent.

## In Search of an Honest
## Experience: Confrontation
## in Counseling and Life[1]

Confrontation, as life, continues independently of all therapeutic models. With the possible exception of the existentialists, none of the major systems leaves room for the concept of confrontation: the existentialists alone approach confrontation by their concept of "encounter."

The case for direct confrontation has been restricted to special instances of therapeutic practice; namely, character-disordered clients and families, short-term crisis situations, aggressive delinquents, and preventative therapy. In general, *the therapist can only confront in the face of client aggressiveness.* Thus, we may have a situation where the client, rather than the therapist, is reaching out with his "being" to evoke the therapist's "being." The learning for the person designated as "less knowing" is that confrontation, rather than being a valued act, is a defensive reaction.

The marked avoidance and resistance to direct confrontation on the part of therapists and theoretical systems alike may have a cultural base. Unconsciously, it is tied to middle-class conditioning which equates chal-

[1]Chapter 11 is a collaborative effort under the direction of John Douds in conjunction with the authors and with assistance from Richard Pierce.

lenging directness and honesty in communication with an aggressive, hostile, and destructive attack. Even the dictionary defines confrontation in these terms: facing another, especially in a challenge. Instead, "middle-class therapy" hopes to seduce the illness away; perhaps seduction as opposed to confrontation is the manner of attack.

## THE NATURE, QUALITY,
## AND FUNCTION OF CONFRONTATION

Direct confrontation is an act, not a reaction. It is initiated by the therapist, based on his core understanding of the client. It brings the client into more direct contact with himself, his strengths and resources, as well as his self-destructive behavior. The purpose of confrontation is to reduce the ambiguity and incongruities in the client's experiencing and communication. In effect, it is a challenge to the client to become integrated; that is, at one with his own experience. It is directed at discrepancies within the client (his ideal versus real self); between what the client says and does (insight and action); and between illusion and reality (the therapist's experience of the client versus the client's expression of his experience of himself and the therapist). The therapeutic goal is nondestructive and emerging unity within the client. It implies a constructive attack upon an unhealthy confederation of miscellaneous illusions, fantasies, and life avoidance techniques in order to create a reintegration at a higher level of health. The strength and intensity of a confrontation may correspond with how dominant and central the emotional pattern is to the client's life style. The therapeutic risk will also depend upon the amount of disorganization both the therapist and client can handle.

The quality of a confrontation, then, corresponds to the experiential skill, emotional integration, and intent of the therapist. It is a risk which the therapist takes out of deep commitment to the client in the recognition that the client's defenses are his enemy and do not allow him direct contact with himself; they interfere with nourishing contact with other men. In this sense, the therapist pits his health against the client's sickness while at the same time being a formidable ally of the client's health. The therapist is the enemy of the client's self-destructive tendencies.

## CONFRONTATION AND IMPOTENCE

Confrontations may range from a light challenge to a direct collision between therapist and client. It constitutes a challenge to the client to mobilize his resources to take another step toward deeper self-recognition or constructive action on his own behalf. Frequently, it will precipitate a crisis that disturbs, at least temporarily, the client's personal and social equilibrium. Again, crises are viewed as the very fabric of growth, invoking new responses and charting new developments. Growth is viewed as a series of endless self-confrontations. Confrontation is the vehicle that ultimately translates awareness and insight into action, directionality, wholeness, and meaning in the client's life. A life without confrontation is directionless, passive, and impotent.

Confrontation is a useful therapeutic ingredient in combatting the pervasive, passive-reactive stance which the alienated person assumes toward life in general, and his present difficulties in particular. The vicious cycle in which he is engaged leaves him with a feeling, at his deepest level, that he is trapped and helpless to *act* constructively on his own behalf. He can only experience himself *in reaction to* others, and, at best, he believes he knows "pieces" of himself in contrast to experiencing himself with a sense of wholeness. Having transferred the locus of evaluation and sense of direction to forces outside himself, he finds himself ruled by fate, society, rituals, obsessions, and "luck." His desperate struggle is a passive one; he feels paralyzed to *act*. He desperately and magically hopes for life to come to him to fill the void created by his repetitive cycle. The secondary gains which he struggles to maintain are tenuous, hollow, and unfulfilling: like gelatin, they temporarily relieve his hunger. To fill the void created by a passive existence and in order to sustain himself between secondary gains, he lives in illusions of false hope. In his moments of despair and intense anxiety he hopes for a magic solution to his problems: either the realization of his illusions or some solution from an *external* source. Reality cannot compete with his fantasies, and he is afraid to sacrifice his fantasies to reality. He fears that the void will grow bigger if he gives up the temporary nourishment from his fantasies, although it was the initial void which created the fantasies. He desperately needs to break the vicious cycle, to confront himself in order to feel himself as an active force in his own life; that is, to function out of his own experience.

In his helplessness and confusion he seeks therapy. More often than not, he receives insight in the form of a conceptual integration of himself. He may choose insight as a way of life, a culturally higher, secondary gain. Insight may, seemingly, reduce confusion by subsuming the conceptualizations he has about himself in a neater package, allowing him the illusory belief of being "on top of his problems,"—he can now explain his anxiousness in high level terms. Victimized by a wishful need for a magic solution, he accumulates insights based upon his *reactions* to different people and situations, hoping for *THE ULTIMATE INSIGHT* which will be an answer to everything. Still paralyzed to act, he remains dependent and passive, noticeably lacking action and directionality in his existence.

The following illustration points up how the therapist uses direct confrontation as a vehicle to translate insight into action for a male client in his thirties who is functioning around level 2:

CLIENT: I now understand what my father has done to me. It's all very clear to me. I think I've got the situation licked.

THERAPIST: But you're still getting up at 5 o'clock in the morning for him when he could get rides from a lot of other men.

CLIENT: Well, uh, he is still my father.

THERAPIST: Yeah, and you're still scared to death of him . . . scared that he'll beat you up or disapprove of you and you're thirty-five years old now. You still fear him like you were a kid.

CLIENT: No, you're wrong, because I don't feel scared of him right now.

THERAPIST: You're scared right now—*here*—*with me*—*he's here*. . . .

CLIENT (pause): I guess I understand him better for what he is, but when I'm around him, I'm still scared, and always think of standing up to him after I leave him. Then I talk myself out of doing what I really want to do.

The client believes, in this instance, that understanding and insight is enough; having the illusion that an organized picture of his situation leaves him in control. In fact, however, he continues to behave in his stereotyped manner. The therapist confronts him with the insight/action discrepancy in the hope of facilitating client movement out of an authority/dependency relationship.

In this regard, the alienated person often has a cognitive filter between himself and his real experience. Although insight may serve to organize him cognitively, it also helps him to rationalize a passive orientation to life. This is precisely why he needs an experience of his "self." The therapist, in confronting the client in order to facilitate the client's self confrontation, may have to knock out the intricate cognitive system to bring the client back in touch with his *real* experience, his substantive core. It is from this base that the client can best build upon his real potential.

## CONFRONTATION AND RISK

The closer the decision affects the inner core of the person, the greater the fear of the life and death choice. A constructive therapeutic confrontation frequently does result in death of a sort; the death of an illusion, hence, an illusiory death. *In return for the loss of an illusion, one receives an experience of who he really is, in all of his humanity, strengths, and weakness.*

The illusions may be of strength or weakness, depending upon the client's defensive and situational needs. In every case, however, they are calculated to prevent the client from coming into contact with his own experience. Thus, the next illustration provides an example of a therapist's confrontation of a high-level functioning young woman's discrepancy between her ego ideal and real self:

CLIENT: I like to see myself as different from all the others.
THERAPIST: Your uniqueness, that's not real for you though.
CLIENT: I don't know. I don't want to be a nobody, just part of the crowd so I try to do things that are different from everyone else.
THERAPIST: You try to *act* unique.
CLIENT: I guess that's true because I always come back to doing what everyone else does anyway. I've always been a nobody and no one ever really noticed me like a few of the girls who are natural about things and seem to know what they want. I envy them!
THERAPIST: But what about *you?*
CLIENT: I don't know who *I* am.

In this instance, the client in her ego ideal wants to see herself as being "unique," and in order to realize her illusion she self-consciously looks for ways to act uniquely. In reality, she is afraid of the group's disapproval, and more consistently conforms to the prevailing norms. In therapy, she becomes involved, for the first time, in a process of searching for herself.

The following segment, in turn, is an illustration of therapy with a forty-five-year-old female client functioning at about level 2. The therapist confronts the client's discrepancy between illusion and reality, that is, between the client's verbal expression of her experience of herself as being weak as opposed to the therapist's experience of the client:

CLIENT: I know I sound weak and mousy. My question is—am I?
THERAPIST: I get your question, but you don't really come across as being this upset over it, and I don't experience you as a weak person.
CLIENT: I don't really *feel* weak, but somehow. . . .
THERAPIST: You don't like being seen as a weak person.
CLIENT: I know people like me better when I act weak.
THERAPIST: Maybe you're afraid people won't like you if you come on strong.

The client confronts herself but cannot answer for herself. The therapist responds with his experience of the client. There is no loss for the client here, but rather a confirmation of the kind of strength which will allow the client to make a full investment in therapy. Constructive therapeutic process movement ensues.

Thus, the death of an illusion can lead to a rebirth of strength. After an initial experience of death to the illusory self, the void which is temporarily created has a chance to fill up with the person's real being. *While building upon the shadow, there is little energy to expand the substance.*

The therapist, then, uses confrontation as a vehicle to initiate a crisis and facilitate a choice point (life or death) by bringing the client in touch with himself, and confronting him with implications and alternatives. The therapist, in a very real sense, clears away the "crud" for the client at the choice point. The therapist takes responsibility for precipitating the crisis —but *the client takes responsibility for his choice.*

## INTERVENTION AND ATTACK

The therapist frequently becomes a target of a passive-reactive attack from the client. The client may verbally attack the therapist in and out of therapy and, in rare instances, even physically attack the therapist. Usually, however, the client takes a more subtle mode which serves to both attack the therapist and defend his emotional patterns. The client may assume the defensive posture which has been most rewarding for him; he perpetuates the ways in which he was able to intimidate people in his world. As a result of prior destructive attacks from significant others in his past, he is unable to differentiate between attacks upon his defensive structure and attacks upon his person. There are a variety of modes of expression of his passive intimidation: playing the helpless victim who has been "needlessly" attacked, threatening a psychotic break, threatening termination, threatening to tarnish the therapist's reputation with suicide, and other destructive and self-destructive acts. Most modes attempt to subtly intimidate the therapist to feel responsible *for* the client's own self-destructive acts. The therapist, by active confrontation, precipitates an awareness of crisis; *he did not create the crisis.*

A piece of the responsibility for temporary disorganization does belong to the therapist, but the client implicitly transfers *total* responsibility to the therapist. The message is clear in one form or another—"you are responsible for destroying me." If the therapist out of his own fears and illusions of omnipotence accepts this intimidation, he is neutralized by the client.

Precipitating the crisis, however, is only a small part of the struggle. The therapist needs to be able to intervene actively in the crisis; *active intervention is the real therapeutic task.* Frequently, the crisis will bring the client's self-destructive trends into clear relief. If the therapist is able to "deliver the goods," he has the opportunity to break the vicious destructive cycle and allow the client's growth potential to emerge. For the client, this experientially translates into having a glimpse of "daylight" (real hope) for the first time. Again, what the client thought would destroy him—loss of an illusion—he finds was not destructive. This is *a key growth experience.*

Indeed, there are a myriad of rationalizations that both therapists and clients use to avoid direct confrontation in therapy. (The therapist's rationalizations, of course, are more sophisticated). Ultimately, the rationalizations take the therapist "off the hook"; the client is too fragile, in short, "It is because of the client's weaknesses that I cannot confront him." Analytically oriented theorists reason that a frontal attack on an anxious client will make him more anxious if he sees the "evil" in him. Implicitly, this assumes that confrontation does *not* bring a client to a feeling knowledge of his resources. Client-centered theorists rationalize that confrontation would be an unnecessary imposition on the client's being and, therefore, "shaping" his behavior. In short, they are willing to leave him *alone* to die.

Certainly, *it is true that confrontation from a destructive therapist is destructive to a client.* Ultimately however, these rationalizations allow the therapist to avoid a recognition of his own inadequacies and the necessity to concentrate upon them, as well as his responsibility to the client. Actually, *confrontation is the ultimate in taking therapeutic responsibility, since it implies that the therapist makes himself a target for the client's self-destructive impulses, as well as leaving himself open to being confronted by the client.* Much of the time it is the fear of exposure that is at the base of the therapist's avoidance.

*Therapeutic confrontation is a risk.* There is the all too familiar fear of suicide! Yet, the implication of not confronting the client is taking more of a risk, for without confrontation, understanding is not communicated, and a psychotic break or even suicide may occur. The risk of not confronting means no further growth for the client. At best, the client's alternative is gradual decay, and, at worst, psychological or physical death. Many join the groups of the living dead who have "tried everything," or remain in the interminable limbo of lifeless therapy.

The following is an illustration of a woman in her fifties, functioning around level 2, confronting herself and the therapist with a discrepancy in saying/doing behavior:

THERAPIST: I think it is very important to be completely open and honest with each other.

CLIENT: Well, how do I seem to you, how do I come across when you listen to me?

THERAPIST: Well, er, umm . . . I like you. You're a nice woman.
CLIENT: Don't equivocate!
THERAPIST: Maybe we need to get to know each other better.
CLIENT: Maybe.

Clearly, in this instance, the client openly confronts the therapist by challenging his "open, honest" statement. The therapist avoids the issue and offers therapy clichés. There is no prospect for growth of either party so long as the client cedes the therapist the power as the agent of her change.

Confrontation offers *growth*. The advantage of the nonconfronting mode is that society will not blame the therapist for the client's failure, and he is left with an "untarnished" reputation. The therapist who is willing to take the responsibility of confrontation needs to know, at his deepest level, that he is a constructive human being *who wants life for the client because he has chosen life for himself.*

## CONFRONTATION AND INSIGHT

The alienated person learns to develop a conceptual integration of himself. In effect, his affects become more intellectually organized. He develops the secret, superior feeling that he knows himself better and better. He becomes able to explain himself in high level terms which seem to render him invulnerable. Culturally he is rewarded for his self-knowledge, and he can feel himself "a step above" the rest. He collects more and more insights about parts of himself and becomes an accurate observer for himself and others. Any affect is suspect, a signal, not for action but for ponderous introspection with the potential for further insights. In exchange for analyzing his affect, he is rewarded with an intellect as a weapon and the passive-defensive belief that he can explain himself at every turn. He is engaged in looking for the one insight which will provide a solution to life. *There is no one solution, only a series of confrontations.* At best, insight inundates affect with ideas and drowns it in a whirlpool of words. At worst, the person is left with the feeling of being splintered into a thousand pieces, in contact with the fact that he has no identity of his own, only fitting in relation to specific people and situations.

Feeling alone, without action, leads to no change. Thus, the alienated person who seeks *only* insights slowly decays while having the illusion of making progress. For the alienated person, confrontation as a way of life is diametrically opposed to insight. It is action-oriented. Life is experienced as effecting the self rather than some third person. Because action is a way of life, the person becomes willing to experience in full the implications of the situation. He becomes aware that the situation is a life and death crisis. He becomes one with what he wants to be, stemming from listening to his own inner silence.

## CONFRONTATION: A SYSTEMATIC EVALUATION

Research into the nature, process, and effects of confrontation is sparse. However, the research accomplished has produced extremely interesting results (Anderson, Douds, and Carkhuff, 1967; Berenson, Mitchell, and Laney, 1967; Berenson, Mitchell, and Moravec, 1967). In studies of both hospitalized schizophrenics and counseling center clients, they have established that high-level functioning therapists confront significantly more often than low-level functioning therapists; that is, therapists functioning above minimally facilitative levels present both clients and patients with honest confrontations significantly more frequently than therapists functioning at less than minimally facilitative levels. It would appear, then, that the offering of high levels of conditions, such as empathy and positive regard, is not mutually exclusive of therapeutic confrontations directed at discrepancies in the client's activities. The field has lived too long with the artificial dichotomy between the offering of (1) warmth and understanding and like conditions and (2) honesty of communication in the therapeutic process. Perhaps the client comes to therapy not only seeking the safety of a therapeutic relationship in which he can explore himself and his difficulties, but also trusting that relationship, the honesty in communication which he does not experience in his everyday activities.

It is interesting to note in the research that high-level functioning therapists confront both clients and patients with their assets and resources more often than they confront them with their limitations. On the other hand, low-level functioning therapists confront their clients and patients more often with their limitations than they do with their resources.

The issue of how these confrontations can be translated into client benefits was also addressed. It was found that both client and patient depth of self-exploration tend over time to move toward higher or deeper levels, however we wish to consider it, following confrontations with high-level functioning therapists, while the depth of self-exploration tends to go down over time following confrontations with low-level functioning therapists. Thus, with the kind of confrontation which typifies the activities of the high-level therapist, the client becomes more deeply involved in constructive therapeutic process movement with all of the intensity, extensiveness, and immediacy that this implies.

There is some controversy concerning whether different populations have a differential effect upon the type of confrontation offered by both high and low-level therapists. However, the strongest evidence suggests that honest confrontation by high-level functioning therapists of both clients and patients with discrepancies in their expressed behavior elicits constructive therapeutic process movement and, ultimately, constructive gain or change.

## SUMMARY

Facilitative conditions, techniques, and insight per se are *not enough* for effective therapy. Ultimately, the client needs not only to understand but to resolve the discrepancies between his ideal and real self, insight and action, and illusion and reality, if he is to achieve emotional integration. Confrontation is an act initiated by the therapist which serves as a vehicle to bring the client in direct touch with his own experience so that he can move from a passive-reactive stance toward an existence rooted in action, direction, and meaningful confrontation. It may be constructive or destructive depending upon the experiential skill, emotional integration, and intent of the therapist. It is done with the recognition that there is no magic solution to life in illusions or external sources, and that, ultimately, we need to be in touch with our substantive core if we are to function out of our own experience. *Confrontation precipitates crisis;* but crises are viewed as the fabric of growth in that they challenge us to mobilize our resources and invoke new responses. Growth is a series of endless self-confrontations. The therapist who serves as an authentic model of confrontation offers the client a meaningful example of effective living.

## References

Anderson, Susan, J. Douds, and R. R. Carkhuff. The effects of confrontation by high and low functioning therapists. Unpublished research, Univer. of Mass., 1967.

Berenson, B. G., K. M. Mitchell, and R. Laney. Level of therapist functioning, types of confrontation and type of patient. *J. clin. Psychol.*, in press, 1967.

Berenson, B. G., K. Mitchell, and J. A. Moravec. Level of therapist functioning, patient depth of self-exploration and type of confrontation. *J. counsel. Psychol.*, in press, 1967.

> . . . the essence of any significant
> human relationship is captured in
> the depth and quality of
> the shared effect.

## Differential Treatment:
## Other Sources of Gain
## in Counseling and Therapy

Only the whole counselor can constructively intervene in the life of a client. He is in tune with his experience of the world and can discriminate between when his experience is congruent with, or divergent from, the experience of others. *The whole counselor trusts his experience of the client more than the client trusts his own experience of himself. The whole counselor trusts his experience more than the client's expression of his.* The ideal image of the counselor most usually supported in traditional training programs is that of an agent of change who does not interfere in the life of the client. He does not stray from an all-accepting attitude; he listens and understands the pain but *does nothing* active. However, active intervention is frequently necessary. The client must make decisions. In addition, with any client functioning below a minimally facilitative, self-sustaining level, the counselor must give therapy a great deal of form and structure. The direction of counseling is dictated by what is effective in helping the client to emerge with his own direction. This direction must be based on the counselor's sensitivities, and the appropriate use of these sensitivities in the selection and implementation of a preferred mode of treatment. Furthermore, the selection and implementation of a preferred mode of treatment is viewed by the whole counselor in terms of its *unique* contributions to the total treatment process, modified by the counselor's experience with the individual client. For example, this may lead to the interruption of a series of desensitization sessions by a confrontation between the counselor and client concerning unconscious client or counselor motives which lead to difficulty in the trials to extinction of anxiety. *A preferred mode of treatment may be employed by itself or in combination with other preferred modes, depending upon how the whole counselor experiences the client.*

Too often, counselors and therapists who do provide minimally facilitative levels of conditions are faced with the dilemma that the client, over the course of counseling, has gained considerable insight into his dynamics, yet can make no meaningful translations to action in his real life. The counselor has learned to trust the words of the client rather than to evaluate and promote positive behavioral change. As is the case with restricting clinical practice to the tenants of any one school, *restricting practice to high levels of the core conditions has serious limitations.* It is the rare counselor who faces these limitations *with* the client, whether these limitations are due to the core conditions or the dictates of any one school, or the personal limitations of the counselor or client. Typically, counseling and therapy are honest *only* to a degree. On the one hand, this may be due to the doubt the counselor has concerning what to do after being fully honest. On the other hand, for the less-than-whole counselor, honest expressions are often destructive. The gain is in the full honesty; there is no loss of face for honestly not knowing. The counselor cannot, and need not, always be ahead of the client. The moments of "not knowing" provide the whole counselor with opportunities to dig deeper into his experience of the client and of himself in interaction with the client. These moments also provide the opportunity for the client to struggle for his own effective direction. *Whole counselors, as well as their clients, often do not know where to go next; the whole counselor has the resources to enter process without knowing outcome.* In this moment the client comes to see something more of the counselor's humanity with all its determination, strength, and commitment in the face of doubts. The periods of temporary loss of direction provide us with the needed clues as to the preferred modes of treatment.

More typically, the client and the counselor adjust to one another at a level which *appears* honest and fruitful, but which is in fact separate from life; it stops short of exposing what the counselor does *not* know. The interaction is comfortable for each, but real therapy begins when we face what we do not know. Any therapeutic relationship characterized by long periods of calm and comfort is only apparently therapeutic. The comfort merely communicates to both the counselor and the client that each is willing to tolerate and accept the distance between them; after all, each means nothing to the other. The point is this: *full honesty in any significant human relationship precipitates crises and the need for confrontation.* The complete confrontation and follow-through (with or without coming to employ a preferred mode of treatment) constitute opportunities for growth for both the client and the counselor. Again, insights, high levels of core conditions, interpretations, and reflections are, for many clients, not enough to promote constructive behavioral change. High levels of core conditions, insights, and confrontations do provide the counselor with the experience he needs to determine how he goes about implementing the goals of therapy; that is, the counselor is committed to doing anything which will aid the client in his efforts to translate the fully honest "give and take" in counseling into actions which will enhance personal emergence. Beyond the central core of facilitative conditions, the following general statement serves as an initial orientation for the counselor. *Conditioning or direct management techniques are most effective with clients functioning at low levels; insights are most effective for those clients functioning at levels high enough to employ insights effectively in life.*

## THERAPY WITH THE LOW-LEVEL FUNCTIONING CLIENT

*Therapy for the high-level functioning counselor with the client functioning below level 3 must be on the therapist's terms.* Direct shaping and guiding are necessary and effective when provided within the context of high levels of facilitative conditions. In the following exchange with a twenty-year-old client functioning at level 1.5, after the first phase of therapy, the therapist acts independently of the client's verbalization. Up to this point in the process, the counselor related to the client as if the client could use understanding and insights. Over the course of the initial phase of treatment, the client slowly deteriorated. The counselor, although confident when he was with the client, experienced progressively increased levels of anxiety between sessions. The realization that he, the counselor, was not actively intervening in the confused life and experience of the client led to the counselor's need to deal with his own anxiety and to know that this client was not to be trusted with his own life. The counselor's anxiety came close to alarm when he also realized that the client had not even been hearing him, but merely seemed to be listening.

THERAPIST: Stan, all these random thoughts innundate you and me, you're lost, and I have been lost.

CLIENT: I had a fourth grade teacher who told me I'd be a good English teacher and everyone—has told me I am a good person who can help kids. I've been through a lot. . . . (The therapist interrupts.)

THERAPIST: You are not listening to me, let me in Stan, I don't want any more of your stories. Let me in!

CLIENT: I don't think, well my sister told me the other night, and a friend of her's I just met while we were talking, I said, "Life can be beautiful with good people," when a funny thing happened . . . a lot of people say I don't listen and I listen to everybody and talk, I'm killing myself with words.

THERAPIST: Right now shut up Stan!—and you listen to me (reaches over and shakes the client by the shoulders and shouts) Damn! You think too much—listen!

To be freed of distorted perceptions, random and fearful thoughts and illusions, and the fear of the implications of acting, the client must be led, even forced, to operate on the therapist's terms. Being pressed to extremes of behavior, even out of desperation, was for this counselor a most significant learning experience. The client did not fall apart. The full expression of the counselor's affect, at that moment, brought into full focus for both him and the client (1) how much the counselor cared, and (2) how far he would go to stop the progressive deterioration of the client. These learnings would not have been possible had the violent shaking of the client come out of some technique or planned action; the counselor's act was spontaneous and the client came to understand *after* the act. The following illustrates the relief experienced by the client after the therapist shook him physically:

THERAPIST: That was kind of rough—but you look like you're ready to listen to me.

CLIENT: No! I needed someone to get tough with me—you—you finally got through—that's the trouble, everyone listens.

THERAPIST: Look, we're going to meet every morning for coffee and talk about how to handle the day—get it? You listen to me Stan, I don't listen to all of your words.

CLIENT (with a full smile): Right, I've been killing myself with words—maybe you stopped me.

THERAPIST: We almost missed—I'm not letting go.

CLIENT: I don't think you will.

The counselor was active. As it was appropriate to act, he was consistent with who he was, and who his client was. The active intervention with no compromise promoted a meaningful and useful level of mutual trust for the first time in this relationship. The counselor left this session without experiencing fatigue and anxiety concerning Stan. The whole therapist can see the world through the eyes of his *client, sometimes better than the client who is functioning at low levels; he can determine what is good and bad in that world often better than the client.*

Later in therapy, when it was no longer necessary for the therapist to see the client every morning to plan the day, the client indicated that, up to the moment the therapist grabbed him physically, he had two fundamental questions going through his mind about the counselor when approaching a panic moment:

1. "Is this person sensitive, perceptive and strong enough to enter my world deeply, without being destroyed himself, in which case I get worse?"

2. "Is this person sensitive, perceptive, and strong enough to warrant my full trust, so that I can follow his lead without the fear that I can destroy him or that he will destroy me?"

Beyond this, the client indicated that he had, during the roughest moments, used the counselor's strength and "eyes" to put order into his world.

If the counselor, in any way, avoided the full responsibility or avoided a full effort to determine an appropriate direction for himself in honest interaction with this client, there would have been no hope that the client would have answered these questions in a way that therapy would have occurred. This client could not take the chance of being let down after finding some hope. He knew he needed to be sure of who the counselor was as a person. High levels of core conditions did not alone provide the impetus for real therapy.

## THERAPEUTIC CONDITIONING

In other instances, the core conditions may offer the client *hope* that the counselor may be able to help; they provide the foundation for effective counselor intervention. In the following case, conditioning procedures were introduced in order to free the client of burdensome aspects of selective but basic social functions, so that he could act with confidence upon his newly acquired insights.

In the following excerpt a twenty-year-old college junior functioning at level 2 and achieving well academically is certain that he will, at some critical moment in life, fail an important challenge. In addition, he had been a stutterer for about sixteen years and had undergone long periods of speech therapy. The following exchange is after summer vacation during which the apparent gains of counseling of the previous spring had been lost:

CLIENT: The first part of the s-s-summer was great—ah—pretty good. I came back, and, oh, hell, it's the same—I'm going to bust.

COUNSELOR: Whatever we did last spring was *not* enough, Lee—guess we start from that.

CLIENT: Oh, you did help—a—lot—it's just that, well, I could not keep hold of it—you did help, honest.

COUNSELOR: No, I don't need that—you don't either. I missed the boat—I need only to look at you—to know.

CLIENT: Don't blame yourself, maybe that's the way—or this is the way I will be—I let you down—I always felt good for a few days after our sessions.

COUNSELOR: Look, were not going to pass credits back and forth—and we're not going through old stuff. But you are a big, strong guy and I'm going to make you work.

CLIENT: I'll try anything.

COUNSELOR: There's a set of procedures and techniques I've been studying. I've never tried them out but from what I've read and observed, I think we can profit from giving them a damn good try.

CLIENT: What's it like?

COUNSELOR: I'll be learning as you learn, but the first thing we'll do is train you to relax.

CLIENT: If you could j-j-just do that—it would be *something*.

COUNSELOR: I want us to do a lot more. Give us a couple of months. We'll meet about three times a week and I'll share—explain everything to you as we go along.

CLIENT: Sounds kind of mysterious right now.

COUNSELOR: Guess it does—but in a nutshell—I'm going to get you to think about, with me, things that get you nervous—until the thoughts don't bug you anymore. Then we will practice things, like speaking before a group, until that gives you no more trouble. We'll work it through from easy stuff to the more difficult—step-by-step. Look, give me a few days to work it all out, then you and I will go over the entire program—I think you're a natural for this—I'm comfortable about the whole thing—and pretty confident that it's what we need.

It is obvious that there is a deep level of respect and trust between the counselor and the client. The counselor shares fully how he experiences the client and, once again, takes over the direction of the course of counseling. Counterconditioning is dictated.

The therapist, in conjunction with Lee, works out a hierarchy of meaningful stress situations, involving both school and home and the significant people in both settings. For example, at the bottom of the hierarchy, or the stress situation first worked upon, we find Lee under conditions of deep relaxation conjuring images of both (1) walking to a critical class where he must, later in the year, make an important presentation and (2) walking toward his house where he must make explanations to his father of his week's activities. When Lee felt anxiety, he let the therapist know. In small, but distinct gradations, he moved into the classroom (home), at first when the instructor (father) would not be there, and then when he was present. Finally, Lee made his classroom presentation in imagery. In addition, in each case a transition was made from imagery to role-playing and, then, actually acting. However, even the behavior therapy did not always go smoothly. After ten sessions of relaxation and desensitization training, a seemingly impassable plateau was reached. During these sessions, another experienced counselor was employed to role-play critical adult male figures in the client's life: father, high school football coach, and ROTC commanding officer.

The client, although a person of superior talents and physical resources, was shaped from early childhood to seek the approval of others. He had learned that to do *his* best alienated others because his superior performance was a threat. Approval from critical others was always held back and, in his desperate search for acceptance, he geared his efforts to a mean or modal level of output. He settled for the "nice guy" role, never threatening, never challenging, always walking a tightrope between failure and a minimally acceptable performance. At the time of these early conditioning sessions, Lee had lost contact with experiencing himself as superior in any area of endeavor, even physically:

COUNSELOR: Damn it, Lee, you let everybody judge you—you're always bound up with it—you even want to look good to us.

CLIENT: Wh-what do you mean?

COUNSELOR: You know what I mean—they're not fit to judge you, damn it! You allow everyone the right—even the little pips—you sit on who you are to get the approval of everyone *not big enough to judge you—they don't know who you are, Lee.*

CLIENT: You're getting me angry.

COUNSELOR: *GOOD*—Get angry, damn it! Who the hell are you anyway? Get angry, Lee! Don't just talk about it—get angry!

CLIENT: I can't!

COUNSELOR: Maybe all the half pints *are* fit to judge you—a patsy—damn it, you let yourself jump—for their approval. You'll end up like them. But you'll know Lee—you'll know deep down—*jump!*

CLIENT: Go to hell!

There was a long pause while the counselor and client looked at one another and at the same moment exchanged big broad smiles.

COUNSELOR: Now you look 6 feet tall and strong—and it feels GOOD.
CLIENT: Ya-Ya—you're darn right.

The client was, for the first time, in contact with who he was. Someone actually approved of him when he was fully himself. He experienced some surprise and a great deal of pride: the monster he feared did not emerge and, in fact, was nonexistent.

At this point there is not only *real* hope, but a growing sense of conviction that the client needs to *act*. Beyond this, the client began to experience a deeper and firmer awareness of his own values, his own integrity, and the initial experiencing of both fear and anger in the face of what had been fearful life decisions and circumstances.

At the twentieth session (the sessions having involved open honest confrontations and desensitization training), the client voices deeper doubts about the motives of the two therapists.

COUNSELOR: Lee, I sense your holding back again—not going all the way.
CLIENT: Ya, I can't help it but I keep thinking that in the end you will humble me—just like the rest.
COUNSELOR: Maybe I'm no different, but you'll never know unless you go all the way Lee, you'll never know.

There is little trace of any traditional client-counselor roles. The client had come to view the two counselors on an equalitarian level. He refers to them by using their first names, not as a gimmick introduced by the counselors but coming from the client spontaneously.

Finally, having successfully made his classroom presentation and receiving a very high rating by his instructor, Lee presented the client's viewpoint of his counseling experience to a class of graduate students. His presentation was spontaneous and unprepared. Indeed, the presentation was a commanding one. Following the presentation, there was an exchange between Lee, the therapists, and the students:

COUNSELOR 1: What set of things contributed most to where you are now?
CLIENT: Getting bawled out—a couple of times.
COUNSELOR 2: I remember the day we said let's junk the desensitization today and get the bastard.
CLIENT: Two weeks ago we just walked around the campus. It was a warm day, like today. You asked me about the talk I had to give to the ROTC class, and I began to say things that—I was sure the talk would go lousy, and you jumped on me. Little things help, like "to hell what others think." I could tell the both of you were angry with me. You had a

perfect reason to be ticked off at me. I was so foolish. We had some real good talks. I think that's the whole thing. As for (I don't know what it is called) desensitization, it's hard to say if it helps or not. It's been about a month. I think it helped a little bit. It's not the real thing. I used to picture scenes in my mind. I'd be asked if I was anxious, and raise my finger if I was nervous. I got to dislike it, after a while. It might have helped a little. I don't know if it worked. It isn't like being here talking to the class.

COUNSELOR 2: Somehow you have to translate the whole thing into action.
CLIENT: Somewhat. I did notice that after picturing the ROTC, going there didn't seem to bother me as much. It helps to a certain extent, not completely, though, because it is not the real thing. . . . Ya, it gets you going. I used to picture classroom scenes; entering the class was a big thing.
COUNSELOR 1: Are you aware of the resources you brought to bear? What did you contribute here?
CLIENT: When I first started, not much of anything really. Later on, my first presentation to this group, I was very embarrassed, everybody sitting around, knowing. It was very hard, very hard, believe me. First, just because it was a class, a group of people, and secondly, they did not know the whole story. I think the hardest part is going through these different things with other people, *live.* I think I really had to push myself. Had to push myself to come here for the practice sessions. The thing that really did it was sheer drive on my part to go through with it. Now, today, when I first came here, it was completely different. I was relaxed.
COUNSELOR 1: What did you tap in on in yourself?
CLIENT: Basically, I learned that what I feared, I *could* do. Everything I feared I could not do, like speaking before a class, I found I can do this.
COUNSELOR 1: The systematic part gets the client started toward considering problem areas. After handling them in imagery, you have to tap in on your own strengths. Maybe that's part of the unique contribution of behavior therapy.
CLIENT: Between sessions I used to try to put into action what we talked about, like I'm doing right now, here talking with you.
COUNSELOR 1: Who are we to you now? (referring to the therapists collectively or separately.)
CLIENT: Well, I don't look on you as being doctors. I see you as, as friends. I almost think of you as being one of the guys, just a friend. The professional role stuff is gone. You've become people.
COUNSELOR 1 (to the group): I think some of you have to doubt.
CLIENT (looking at the group): If you want to ask me anything, ask me.

## THERAPY WITH A HIGHER LEVEL CLIENT

The client, initially functioning above level 3 affords a very different experience for the whole counselor. After the counselor establishes early that he can "be with" the high level client, understand deeply, and even go beyond what the client expresses at a verbal level, therapy can be on either the counselor's terms or the client's terms. At this level, therapy is often characterized by an exchange of leadership. The realization of an equalitarian relationship (each can learn from the other by direct challenge or groping together) occurs earlier and much of the communication is nonverbal.

Whatever the initial level of the client's functioning, if the counselor is less-than-whole, counseling or therapy is on no one's terms. It can, at best, reflect the implementation of depersonalized, socially defined roles and, at worst, bring the client to the realization that he cannot even purchase human nourishment. Furthermore, and perhaps more damaging in the sense that educational and training institutions perpetuate practices which produce less-than-whole counselors, is the counselor's lack of awareness that he does *not* have anything to offer his clients. Only those counselors who become fully aware and acknowledge where they are *can* hope for constructive change.

A twenty-nine-year-old man, subject to frequent depressions and nearly overwhelming self-doubt, but with inner untapped strengths which indicated a high level of potential functioning, confronted his therapist during the sixth session:

CLIENT: I'm never sure where I stand with anyone.

THERAPIST: That applies here as well, right Jim?

CLIENT: Yea, I guess it does. I've been thinking of bringing it up—guess I was afraid to learn that you, too, would give me some meaningless bunch of words.

THERAPIST: You're telling me you're not sure you trust me enough to go further—even though we have shared a great deal.

CLIENT: Guess I was sure you'd think I was crazy—earlier I felt I might shock you.

THERAPIST: Look—at this moment I experience this: Whatever Jim fears most does not cause me *any* anxiety—I'm not sure I can get it all into words—but your impulses don't scare me—and I trust that. I feel good with you, Jim, and when our meetings are over I do not feel drained of energy. Damn it, you have your own strength—have at it for crying out loud—then *you* will know.

The less-than-whole therapist, during these moments, can only be destructive, either by action or inaction. *Therapists functioning below level 3 focus on the irrelevancies. Therapists functioning above level 3 focus on the crises and resolution of crises through full confrontation.*

## PSYCHODYNAMIC INTERPRETATIONS

Sometimes in our therapeutic work, we draw upon constructs which are not readily apparent. Often we do so, not so much because of the accuracy of the formulation, as because of the inadequacy of the existing formulations. Our need for understanding our experience dominates. In this context, we have experienced many clients most meaningfully in quasi-psychoanalytic terms.

In the following exchange, a young woman of twenty-four, married for two years, and functioning close to level 3, had been unable to consummate sexual intercourse with her husband. Although she was physically normal, her husband had never been able to gain entry.

During the tenth session, the following exchange took place after many client "tests" of the counselor's motives and strengths:

COUNSELOR: Ann, I feel you are telling me as much about how you view your husband—or men in general—as you are about yourself.

CLIENT: Maybe.

COUNSELOR: I'm sure of it, (pause) your neck is red.

CLIENT: Sometimes you get me—like you think you know everything.

COUNSELOR I know this—now—for a lot of reasons. I experience you as someone who can move fast, but when I press—you fight back like hell. There is a part of this I like, perhaps—you're not sure *I'm* strong enough.

CLIENT: That's it—sort of—I'm not sure you're stronger than I am.

COUNSELOR: Or that *any* man is stronger.

CLIENT: (Cries) I don't know why all these tears.

COUNSELOR (holding her hand firmly): You want to find a strong man—you need one at the deepest level—but you fear there are none. Only a strong man could receive all *your* love.

CLIENT: I've about given up.

COUNSELOR: You're telling me that *your* appetites are large.

CLIENT: (Sobs and shakes violently while the counselor holds her hand and says nothing; after a period of three or four minutes the client looked up and smiled.)

CLIENT: It's vague—like—I don't know. . . .

COUNSELOR: What would happen if I came on full?

CLIENT: Oh, my husband's organ is big—if that's what you mean.

COUNSELOR: But you might find your appetite to be larger. . . .

CLIENT (silence): . . . that's one side of it, I'm afraid—afraid I'll either overwhelm him or drown in the flood of my own feelings.

COUNSELOR: Both have implications. If you are overcome with the intensity of your feelings, you are no longer 'on top'—in control. If you overwhelm him, and he cannot recover as a stronger person, you will always be in touch with your starvation.

This exchange raises questions about the social myths concerning male superiority, a more intense male libido, and female penis envy. Nonetheless, the theoretical base of the counselor's understanding of the client here was psychoanalytic.

The counselor identified in some loose way, as an eclectic clinician, yet needed some framework from which to understand the client in a systematic way. Her frank, confident behavior and strong body, coupled with her sexual frustration, led the counselor to entertain an interpretation of penis envy and the client's hostile need to assert her masculinity by cruelly castrating her husband and all other men. Yet, beyond the apparently hostile challenges and tests, the counselor experienced, however vague, a large human being, only partly aware of her superiority. Dedicated to nurturing the best in his clients, this counselor chose to bypass the penis envy interpretation and bring the client directly in contact with what she had been hiding at a more meaningful level: fear of overwhelming her husband, and hence, becoming aware of the depth of her appetite for giving and receiving love, and the related fear of being overwhelmed by the intensity of her own feelings.

The analytic construct of penis envy gave the therapist his first level of understanding; his deep experiencing of the client as a person made him feel that this interpretation left something of the client as a person out of the picture. The counselor could not experience this client envying anything about another person. The resulting discordance was resolved when he reached for a more personally (for him and the client) relevant meaning. The exchange also illustrates the apparent jumps or gaps when a whole therapist interacts with a relatively high-level functioning client.

In another case, the counselor employs a psychoanalytic base to understand the roles and interplay among members of a Jewish family. The client is a thirty-eight-year-old, single, business man. The client's behavior in and out of therapy is characterized by a high level of energy and activity with little direction. His verbal behavior demonstrated his hostility, intelligence, his need for distance from people, and an easily penetrated superficiality. The counselor experienced this client to be, at his core, deeply sensitive, vulnerable, and somewhat tragic, yet possessing a core of integrity upon which to build a more confident relationship with the world. On the surface, the client was friendly with everyone to the point of avoiding any critical disagreement. The counselor experienced this set of behaviors in terms of the client's frantic search for a safe place in the world; a search, born out of a knowledge that others could and might destroy him. Often lonely and depressed, the client experienced himself as a woman:

COUNSELOR: You never stand still long enough for me to fully grab what your words mean—you are as busy in here as you are in your life outside of counseling, creating motion.

CLIENT: I know how alone I am when I stop.

COUNSELOR: Alone like your mother—but for you.

CLIENT: I'm all she has.

COUNSELOR: No! You're all she *owns*.

CLIENT (silence): But I want to feel like a man.

COUNSELOR: And, yet, behave like a stereotype Jewish mother—sort of—a bowl of chicken soup will cure everything. I don't have any chicken soup.

CLIENT: You *bastard!*

COUNSELOR: I hear a man now. Look, the Jewish mother has no property rights—she can own nothing—only the children who come along after the first born son, he belongs to the Daddy. You are number 2 son—and you belong to Mommy. If you live like a man, you deny her her only claim to property. Father had what he wanted after your older brother was born.

CLIENT: I know. I know. I know. There's not much of an emotional bond between father and me. There's nothing.

COUNSELOR: Maybe you are a woman, at thirty-eight—an old Jewish mother!

CLIENT (bursts into tears): It's so damn painfully lonely—underneath, I've known how alone my mother would feel if I broke free—and—and I've been certain this would kill her.

Again, this counselor experienced a discrepancy between a classical psychoanalytic interpretation and his experience of the client. In spite of the strong identification with a long-suffering mother, and the threat of complete castration by the father, the counselor employed these constructs only as a starting point. The blending of psychoanalytic theory with the struggle to understand his experience with the client again yielded a set of personalized insights for the counselor, not immediately available, in either the theory or the counselor's experience. The client came to know and face the fact that his personal emergence depended upon his risking all that had become his mother's life. In this case, the client was unable, at that point in time, to act to change the relationship with his mother and to seek his own, full identity. Therapy, however, did not end with the client's reluctance and, indeed, resistance. Instead, the therapist worked to move the client toward more assertive kinds of behavior (in particular, heterosexual) which would bring him more rewards and less pain in the business and social world of which he was a part.

## VOCATIONAL COUNSELING

Often, because we are human and not all-knowing, we must rely on means external to the experience of either therapist or client, although the employment of any one of these means may be dictated by the experience of one of the parties to the relationship, most often the therapist. Thus, if the therapist, in his uncertainty, does not already have diagnostic testing or a neurological examination, he may request them. Similarly, where vocational problems are involved in the context of long-term therapy, vocational testing and counseling may be integrated into the therapy or incorporated simultaneously with the therapy.

In the following excerpts, the client, after facing the deteriorative consequence of his present life situation, seeks a new and concrete direction. The counselor has employed vocational tests and sums up the results. The client is a forty-five-year-old sales manager functioning at approximately level 2:

COUNSELOR: You're not by nature a fully outgoing, verbal, and manipulative person.

CLIENT: I've tried—for twenty years.

COUNSELOR: It cost you too much.

CLIENT: Almost everything.

COUNSELOR: The test results—put it together about the way I experience you. You're more in tune with the computational detail and how they can be interpreted into something useful. I think the *communication* of what numbers mean brings people into it. You've used this part of your global interest pattern as a base for a career in sales—it's not enough.

CLIENT: I've always been aware of something missing, but I kept getting promotions, and got trapped.

COUNSELOR: Everything is closing in on you. This stuff gives us direction, (referring to the tests). The something missing here is—well—a combination of things—involving—some involvement in things, numbers or data *and* people.

CLIENT (laughs): Years ago—I—wanted to be a math and science teacher, but didn't have the money to go to college.

COUNSELOR: Why not now—it will be tough but you have the resources now. Math—physical science teacher is indicated by the Strong Vocational Interest Test.

This excerpt illustrates the full integration of the counselor's experience of the client and a personalized use and translation of trait-and-factor tests. The need for concrete direction developed out of an awareness of the implications of this critical choice point for this client. The ability to specify aspects in a job which will serve to satisfy the needs of the client rests on a broad knowledge of the work, the tests employed, and the physical, emotional, and intellectual resources of the client. The meaningful integration of all of these factors requires all the sensitivities of the whole counselor. We might add that the former client is now a successful physics teacher in a technical institute where he has been able to put his years of sales experience to good use.

In summary, the sources of gain in counseling and psychotherapy, above and beyond the central core of facilitative conditions, involve the selective use of major systems *blended with* the whole counselor's experience of the client. We have barely begun to tap the personal resources of the whole counselor and what he is in the moment-to-moment interaction with the client. Only intuitively and clinically do we know that his full expression of his vitality, sensitivities, feelings, doubts, strengths, and courage provides the vehicle by which the unknown becomes known and *acted upon.*

In terms of useful techniques, aside from the modified psychoanalytic interpretation and the client-centered reflection during the very early stages of counseling, there are, from our view, two dominant, preferred modes of treatment: behavior modification procedures and the trait-and-factor approach. The behavior modification techniques are best used with level 1 or 2 clients, and with clients functioning at higher levels who have acquired isolated symptomatology. The trait-and-factor approach is best employed with level 1 clients by making direct assignment in terms of training and job functions. At level 2 or 3, the resolution of vocational and educational plans can follow a counseling model in which the client shares in the decisions to be made. Counselors working with level 1 and 2 clients can creatively combine behavior modification techniques with vocational test results. The test results may point to the appropriate direction, and conditioning procedures provide the means to get there. Above level 3 the trait-and-factor approach is inappropriate beyond adding relevant information. It is inappropriate to match the high functioning client to a job because he is most likely to live a unique developmental pattern not governed by the usual patterns of reinforcements.

Although psychoanalytic theory provides a considerable base for understanding the low level client, the interpretations are dependent upon the counselor's cognitive map rather than the client's ability to employ the map; that is, psychoanalytic theory gives focus and method to an intellectual, diagnostic empathy not easily translated into feelings, action, and personal emergence for the client.

The existential stance offers the *potential* to bring the client to level 3, and where the practitioner is open to the employment of techniques, makes possible effective work with the level 1 client under some conditions. Although genuineness is anything but a technique, the existential stance is the only stance to give it full focus. In this way, it makes a contribution to all effective counseling and therapy, whether or not they employ techniques.

Beyond the central core plus appropriate use of preferred modes of treatment, the essence of any significant human relationship is captured in the depth and quality of the shared affect.

# Chapter 13

Counseling is as effective as the
therapist is living effectively.

## Counseling as a Way of Life

Fraudulent living, supported and nurtured by social myths, can at best yield only theories and research of half-truths and ineffective clinical practice. The contamination seeded by social myths too often influences the direction of those with enough energy to attempt growth and constructive impact. Personal emergence is structured in terms of living up to the image of the perfectly acculturated individual; an individual trapped and held back by these half-truths, myths, and the characteristics of his ideal image. Striving to live up to an image denies the possibility of unique, fully creative personal emergence, for ideal images are socially determined.

Attempts to emerge are easily neutralized by society's apparent value of the image. In addition, neutralization of potentially creative acts is accomplished by reminding the potent person that he is not altogether living up to his image—society's weapon of using one's virtues against him. *The whole person needs no image to live up to, and is not conflicted by the lack of perfect consistency.*

## THE WHOLE PERSON

The whole person does not merely live in the external world. *The life of the whole person is made up of actions fully integrating his emotional, intellectual, and physical resources in such a way that these actions lead to greater and greater self-definition.*

More specifically, and by way of illustration, the counselor and therapist who is whole addresses his energies to a full synthesis of (1) research, (2) theory, (3) the creative consideration of all theories and research in order to develop preferred modes of treatment, and (4) the development of an integrative model of his own consistent with who *he* is and one with which he is able to employ the totality of his being.

Although we stress the physical and experiential bases of life, ours is not an anti-intellectual stance. The full person who accepts the responsibility for having impact on others (parents, teachers, clergymen, spouses, counselors, and therapists) responds to make inductive generalizations from stable bodies of phenomena in his life, as well as to test, in experience and research, deductive hypotheses derived from his own and the theories of others. Constant qualification, modification, and movement into the unknown serve as the fabric for his growth. *Counseling is as effective as the therapist is living effectively.*

We, as a people, can no longer delimit ideally effective human relations to the counseling and therapy hours. Those hours, on the average, are neither ideal nor effective. The implication here is quite clear: most counselors and therapists are asking their clients to learn to live more effectively. In reality they are asking "the less knowing" person to do something that they, the counselors, cannot do.

*Effective counseling and therapy are not separate from life, but they do offer a unique and vivid contrast to the general life experience in society.* This contrast cannot be experienced so long as "the more knowing" person functions within a socially defined role. Only by breaking free of roles can he give his fully integrated self to the experience, learnings, and relearnings. Only in this manner can he tap his own resources at a deeper level and hope to become an ever expanding whole person. This is not to say that roles in therapy are never useful. As an aspect of a preferred mode of treatment, selective therapeutic techniques that require roles can add to efficacy. But roles, when employed, must be within the context of the awareness of who one is at the deepest levels. Without such self-awareness, roles, like any other tool or technique, can and will be used and abused.

Beyond these general statements and observations there are a number of specific points reflecting the implications of becoming whole.

1. The only consistency for the whole person is internal.

The person who is in tune with and acts on the bases of his integrity is free to modify, incorporate, and learn from venturing into the unknown, with fear, but a knowledge that his inner being will not and cannot be destroyed. Furthermore, he is not neutralized when others demand consistency. The person who has reached society's limits of tolerance for personal emergence and stops, has agreed not only to emerge no further, but also not to upset social systems, and not to expose others who have sold their integrity.

2. Creativity and honesty are a way of life for the whole person.

The whole person is fully aware that he is as creative as he is honest. Any semblance of trading or compromising responsible honesty results in attenuated creativity. The *real* risk for the whole person involves honesty *not* being a way of life, in all his actions, with and including physical implications. A dishonest act, for the whole person, results in a dysfunction of the basic physical foundations of life: eating, sleeping, elimination, and sex. Honesty in communication is not, however, without qualification, as in the case of the extremely brittle patient.

3. Although the way the whole person lives his life is seen by others to be too dangerous, too intense, and too profound, he is in tune with the fact that his real risk involves living life without risk.

Life has meaning in new discoveries, larger boundaries, deeper insights, more pain, more joy, and the realization that the whole person can only be as full with another person as he is full with himself *when alone.*

4. The whole person realizes that life is empty without acting.

The full person must discriminate among possible acts, make his choice, and ACT. The most significant learning comes from acting on those aspects of life the individual fears most. For the whole person there is only security in risks. In this way, and only in this way, can the individual gain or lose. In a life without risk, no one wins, no one loses, and *no one learns.*

5. The whole person realizes that whatever he does is worth doing fully and well.

Full emergence depends on a full and an integrated output of energy.

6. The whole and creative person functions at a high energy level.

He employs his energy fully, resting only as much as is necessary to restore his usual vigor, so as to be able to bring to bear and tap *his talents fully* in dealing with crises and being productive in everyday life.

7. The whole person comes to the realization that few men are large enough or whole enough to nourish and love the creative person.

A full relationship, free of neurotic drainage, is only possible among whole people. Others, functioning at lower levels, cannot go beyond insisting that the creative person has been lucky enough to stumble on a new or novel gimmick.

8. The whole person is fully aware that any significant human relationship is in the process of deepening or deteriorating.

Stability in any relationship is only apparent. When it is not growing it undergoes changes which increase distance between those involved; this is true for parent-child, teacher-student, husband-wife, and counselor-client relationships.

9. The whole person realizes that most men say "yes" out of fear of the implications of saying "no," and that most men say "no" out of fear of the implications of saying "yes."

The whole person can predict a great deal of behavior from this statement, knowing that the majority of people cannot see or respond to anything but the fear of the implications of their act at a choice point.

10. The whole person is fully aware that in order to live life in such a way that it is a continuous learning and relearning process, he must periodically burn bridges behind him.

The full life requires making discriminations. To leave room for everyone in one's life is only to leave room for one's self and, thus, retards self-definition. Clinging to past associations which drain energies only nourishes neurotic needs and diminishes creative output.

11. The whole person realizes that he is, and must be, his own pathfinder, and travel a road never traveled before.

The whole person can be alone with himself. Creative acts by definition require new and untread directions. If the person cannot live with himself, he cannot discover directions congruent with who he is; only when he does can he hope to reach for full fruition of his talents and person.

12. The whole person does not fear living intensely.

The whole person experiences greater joy and greater pain. He is aware that life is as full as it is intense. He can endure and even flourish as he lives intensely, because he has fully integrated the emotional, intellectual, and physical. It is only under extreme circumstances that the whole person taps deeper personal resources and significant new learning.

> 13. The whole person is prepared to face the implications of functioning a step ahead or above most of those with whom he comes into contact.

Knowing when not to act or to respond in terms of his deep sensitivities requires fine discriminations: These actions depend upon whether or not the second person recognizes that the whole person can be a positive and constructive influence. The whole person's insights, because they are so far beyond the obvious, are often interpreted as being psychopathic or paranoid. Further, he is often isolated and the subject of malicious gossip picturing him as an insensitive freak, or infantile. In other instances, the least fortunate of those exhibiting unusual talent are shaped up early in life. They are usually put on reinforcement schedules so that they provide entertainment for the less potent and the impotent.

> 14. The whole person is aware that for most people life is a cheap game.

Psychotherapy, as another social institution, is seen by most as a means for getting people back into the game. The whole person asks the question as to whether or not he wants to help them back into the game. Furthermore, he searches ways and means to bring the "less knowing" to fulfillment in a life without games.

> 15. The whole person is fully aware that many of society's rewards are designed to render the creative impotent.

Striving for and then achieving societal rewards traps the creative person into living his life so that he proves to others that he was, after all, worthy of such recognition: he can no longer make new contributions; he can only rely on old ones.

> 16. The whole person realizes that to emerge within the acceptable levels tolerated by society means institutionalization.

Institutionalization within society renders creative acts and persons neutral and keeps them from further growth by making them a part of *history*. Society, after a long series of trials, moves to institutionalize the creative person operating beyond its limits.

> 17. The whole person realizes that he must escape traps to render him impotent.

A few of the traps involve invitations to join society at considerable compromise, living up to images, rumors and myths, and responding to all the efforts to discredit the whole person's work rather than continuing to produce.

> 18. The whole person is aware of the awesome responsibility which comes with freedom.

The whole person must do more than know all that there is to know about his life and work in order to stay whole and extend his boundaries. He must go beyond the known to meet his responsibilities to his own integrity, knowing that without this he cannot act responsibly, with and for another.

Only the fully functioning whole person has the *right* to be a counselor or therapist, for only he lives in society, yet is able to see society through the eyes of its victims, and only he can discriminate between the good and the bad. Those counselors and therapists functioning below this level have *no right* to offer themselves as therapeutic agents and models. The fact is that most counselors and therapists cannot successfully meet the circumstances with which their clients are coping. The interaction between such a counselor and his client can be nothing more than a fraud.

We present a stance calculated to encompass all aspects of life based on the interaction between a potent facilitative counselor and his clients; that is, the counselor struggles to do what is most effective: ultimately, both counselor *and* client are influenced by what is most effective for the other. Short of this, the relationship is a circle of mutual denial and deprivation of what constitutes the basic fabric of facilitative interpersonal relationships: *responsible honesty.* Typically, the counselor assumes a façade of honesty so that the client can sound honest. In other interactions both parties operate from the following base: "You fool me and I fool you," which leads to greater and greater accumulation of hate. In the context of a significant relationship, if one party is able to fool the other, there is nothing to respect. In more general terms: neurotics (in a neurotic society, see Chapter 1) respect strength (those who cannot be fooled), and love weakness (those who can be fooled as he is fooled). Their tragedy is that they encounter so few who deserve both, and that they, the neurotics, cannot combine love and respect in any instance.

The whole person makes a choice to be a full participant in life. In this way, his life is not only intense; he is testing limits, learning, confirming, and expanding—his superiority becomes a way of life. For those who only observe or selectively participate, life is a series of competitive engagements, often without a winner or a loser. Above all, the selective observer is careful not to engage those who can expose him, and he cannot or will not see others to expose. What does grow in the observer and selective participant is despair, despondency, and self-contempt in his pseudo-search for an honest experience. In order to experience some semblance of stature and potency, the observer surrounds himself with others who fear exposure as he does. Collectively, they can make efforts to stifle personal emergence of those outside the agreement.

Any full, open, honest, and growing interpersonal relationship begins with at least one party who can be whole and the other with the potential to become whole. The relationship is further characterized by dignity, decency, and vitality. Each wants positive regard from the other. The less-than-whole person demands unconditional positive regard, and the whole person demands positive regard that has a base of *conditionality*. The whole person does not expect to be accepted at less than who he is, and seeks relationships with others who will *only* respond to him fully when he is whole. *The psychological distance between people is in inverse relationship to the wholeness of the parties to that relationship: the more whole they are, the closer they can be.*

In order to live the life of a whole person, the individual believes deeply that even major adversities will not destroy his inner core. The emotionally and physically impoverished live life carefully avoiding all major risks, convinced that if they are hit they cannot get up again. If the counselor cannot get up after being hit, he cannot help another off his back. *Denial of the physical base of life is a reflection of the stance of those who have learned to view emotion as weakness and intellect as a weapon.*

If counseling is not a way of life, then it is a game of techniques. In this view (aside from superficial behaviors) counseling is irrelevant or destructive, insofar as it reinforces the notion that the successful life is the one which you technique best: it becomes just one more of many selfish and cruel manipulations.

## THE WHOLE PERSON: THE GOAL
## OF TRAINING AND COUNSELING

The ultimate goal of both training and counseling is a whole person. In counseling and therapy, we often settle for less, much less, than the whole person. This will be dictated by the needs and resources of the client. Thus, in being guided by what is effective, we may facilitate the client in a direction that will leave him far less than whole. Nevertheless, for those clients with the necessary emotional, physical, and intellectual resources, the whole person remains our goal.

*We can never settle for less than a whole person in training.* Indeed, our therapist graduate must be more, much more, than a whole person. He must be a whole therapist—a constructive human with a high energy level and vast resources, with the knowledge of system and technique and verbal and research tools: the system and technique in order, at a given point in time, to bring the most efficacious practices to bear; the verbal and research skills in order to articulate and understand the practices.

The whole person must be able not only to perceive and discriminate differential levels of facilitative conditions but also to communicate at high levels, all of which raises the question of the selection of therapists.

We could make graduate training a long-term experience for those who cannot discriminate levels of conditions related to constructive client change. Thus, in offering high levels of conditions over an extended period of time and in emphasizing the personal experience of therapy, constructive change may be as possible as it is in formal therapy. Then, however, we are involved in the total reconstruction of the communication process, just as we are in working with low level patients. The investment is tremendous on the part of all persons involved, and, again, we must ask what it is that indicates to these persons that they are potential counselors and therapists. In some way, we must be able to discriminate those who can perceive and discriminate various levels of interpersonal functioning from those who cannot. Unlike the client whose communication process has broken down, we simply cannot take the time in training to reconstruct the trainee's assumptive world and perceptual system. *Distorted perception necessitates therapeutic personality change. Distorted communication necessitates training.*

This is not to say that trainees cannot benefit from personal therapeutic experiences, whether individual or group or both. Nevertheless, our research and training efforts suggest that those who are functioning at the highest levels—those who are closest to being whole—can benefit the most from the training experience. Those who are functioning at low levels are least likely to benefit, and *those who are functioning at low levels following training can simply not be turned loose on an innocent public.*

### THE TRAINING EXPERIENCE

In training, as in counseling, we work toward constructive change as well as increased levels of interpersonal skills. In both training and counseling we draw upon the same basic sources of learning in an integrated approach.

Thus, training, counseling, and all other interpersonal learning experiences involve an interaction between a person designated by society as "more knowing" and one designated as "less knowing." The "more knowing" must have the complete freedom and feel the heavy responsibility to pass on to the "less knowing" all that he has learned in his experiences in the relevant area. In effective learning experiences, however, he does so with an openness to the trainee's response to his contribution. Thus, he is open to potential learning in the process. If the trainee's response makes more sense than his, or if it can be incorporated in an integrated formulation, more meaningful than his, then the teacher is the learner. In educational and training settings, the "more knowing" person may actively teach; in counseling and therapy, the therapist may actively give direction or even "shape" the client's responses to the outside world. However, the effective learning process always takes place in, and is modified by, the experiential context.

Both training and counseling are experientially based; that is, as in all learning processes, what is critical is the trainee's experience of the process. There are a number of relevant questions here: Does the trainee feel truly understood? Does the trainee experience himself as benefiting from this process? Does the trainee's experience have a place in the learning process? Does the trainee feel free to act, qualify, and modify the learnings which are passed on to him? Does the trainee have the experience of a second, real party to a real relationship and truly meaningful interaction?

Finally, the trainer or counselor acts as a role model for effective training and counseling. This significant source of learning is most often ignored. Thus, the whole therapist or trainer is not only offering high levels of facilitative conditions, and didactically teaching about facilitative conditions and their effects in living, but he also is a role model of a person who is living effectively. Again, the training process is as effective as the trainer is whole.

Because of inadequacies in all of these sources of learning, the trainee will be limited by the low level trainer's level of functioning (Carkhuff, 1967; Pierce, Carkhuff, and Berenson, 1967); the trainee cannot go beyond the level of functioning of a trainer who cannot add to the level of the trainee's response and who cannot give him more meaningful direction in life.

The effect of the training experience is not dependent solely upon the therapist-trainer's level of functioning. The trainee must be open to the possibility that the trainer can have a constructive impact upon the trainee's life; that is, he must be open to the possibility of change. In our experience, some trainees are not open to change, most often those who need it the most. Rather, they tend to see their roles as counselors and therapists and guidance and social workers, as "just another job." They do not understand the privilege and responsibility of the helping role. In some strange way, they are "entitled" to influencing the lives of others. Unfortunately, we know too well, in research and experience, the two-edged effect of "helping." Students are often vociferous in their calls for meaningful experiences; so long as their experiences are not meaningful, they have an excuse for not reaching into themselves. When a meaningful experience is offered them, some cannot deliver; the most destructive among them will seek to undermine the experience in order to maintain their identities. *They cannot help others!* Just as the trainee who is a mature adult cannot emerge in a program where trainees are treated like children, so will "the child" have difficulty in a program where trainees are expected to be adult and professional.

Other trainees will test early, *make a commitment to themselves,* and become, early in their careers, creative and productive contibutors in all of their efforts, whether interpersonal or otherwise. For still others, the process of testing is longer and repetitive, and the experience of "rebirth" more agonizing.

Thus, in order for effective training to take place, the trainee must be initially open, and ultimately committed to *his own constructive change.* In addition, the trainer must be whole or in the process of becoming whole, for his limitations place limitations on the growth and development of the trainee and his fullness makes fullness possible in the trainee.

In one very real sense, the functioning of the whole counselor may differ from the functioning of the whole trainer. A whole counselor alone can provide his clients with a real choice. The whole counselor can choose to move clients in the direction of either (1) greater individuation and personal emergence or (2) conformity with a societal model of the modal man. The ultimate direction of the therapy process may depend upon the level of development, the resources, and the needs of the client. In many cases, it simply makes more sense in terms of the investment of both the client's and the therapist's time and energy to move the individual client toward more socialization. This may be tempered, however, by training in a variety of more effective modes of functioning, such as teaching the client to assert himself, so that the client can share more fully in the rewards of the relevant social system. In some cases, the two directions are not mutually exclusive. The concept of living independently of society suggests that, at many points, societal and individual goals are quite compatible; at other points they are not. In any event, only the whole therapist can move the client in either direction.

The trainer's task is a more difficult one. If we accept the proposition that only the whole therapist can offer the client the possibility of movement in either direction, then the less-than-whole therapist can only offer movement in his direction, usually that of the totally socialized man. If this is so, unless we are dealing with extremely limited population samples, we must train only those therapists who can offer the client movement in either direction. *We can only train therapists who are committed to becoming whole themselves.*

The training situation must be a living, flourishing, productive pocket of health within a neurotic environment. As a marriage between two whole people provides a pocket of health for the children involved, so must a training program in the helping professions do similarly. In this way, the training program becomes something more than the sum of the whole people in it: *a pocket of resistance in a resistant world.*

Just like a healthy marriage, there is room for direction imposed by the "more knowing" person upon those less experienced. The following is an example of a practicum classroom exchange following a role-playing experience involving John (as client), Joan (as therapist), and a therapist trainer—an experience, which, as so much meaningful role-playing does, became quickly more real than role for both parties.

THERAPIST/TRAINER: John, did you get a feeling like you were going round in circles?

JOHN: A little bit, yeah.

THERAPIST/TRAINER: Where did that leave you?

JOHN: Right where I began.

THERAPIST/TRAINER: I think this makes a point. Level 3 responses are essentially interchangeable with the client's. They don't help the client to go further.

JOAN: I wasn't able to say some things that I wanted to.

THERAPIST/TRAINER: Right. You get a piece of the feeling and right away you look for the dynamics behind it. You try to get handles on it.

JOAN: I felt the feelings.

THERAPIST/TRAINER: But you won't let the whole feeling come up inside yourself.

JOAN: It frightened me.

THERAPIST/TRAINER: It's a pretty desperate feeling. If you let it in. He was saying, "I can't touch other people. I can't touch other people. I can stay with them—and be with them—but I can't touch them."

JOAN: I wouldn't know what to do with it.

THERAPIST/TRAINER: John couldn't let it seep in all the way. If you could let it come up inside of you—it's there in you—he might have a chance. You're carrying him away when you look for handles. It's even hard to pick up because he doesn't have the feeling full. John, you feel it now, physically, you're flush.

JOHN: Right on it.

THERAPIST/TRAINER: Joan?

JOAN: More work for me.

The direction derives from a commitment to those who are once-removed from the immediate setting, the clients for whom we serve. The commitment to the welfare of our clients implies a commitment to our own welfare. Again, role-playing and other classroom exchanges may evolve into an intense, personal experience, not unlike the therapeutic process leading to constructive change:

TOM: I feel that I get hung up when I have to put forth when there's a group, and I felt anger and hate for everybody here, and I felt like saying I didn't want to do it.

ROY: Maybe it's not all fear, though. Gee, I'm anxious now, too. In a way I'm angry with the group, too. We're revealing ourselves to the group, but maybe it's for us.

TOM: I want to please but I'd still like to say, "No."

ROY: In a way you'd be getting out of it. You're still hung up with them—you're still living in a way for them. This is what you want to break.

TOM: Right. It's what I want to break.

ROY: Maybe bringing it up now will get it out and put it out.

TOM: That scares me, though. They won't like me then.

ROY: You don't want to be alone.

While the emphasis is upon training and constructive change, the whole therapist is incomplete without the tools of inquiry and formulation. Within the training program, the search and research stresses the criteria of meaning, although not to the exclusion of rigor. The whole person must be equipped to make enlightened inquiries into his efforts, whether in therapy or training. In our attempts to become increasingly more effective individuals, we simply ask questions concerning what we are doing or professing to do; in the case of the trainees, we ask questions concerning what they will actually be doing when they leave the program. In this way, and only in this way, can the student become involved in a lifelong learning process. Most important, the search and research is geared toward asking questions, *the answers to which translate in some way to human benefits.* The therapist is dedicated to integrating his clinical and research learnings in coherent theories and testable models, the implications of which will not only point to new areas of research in therapeutic processes but also to all areas of human relations. In addition, these efforts will afford the therapist a clear perspective of history and human society.

The graduate of a training program led by whole therapists is something more than an effective practitioner and researcher. *Having experienced a fully integrated training program, he is equipped to serve himself, his clients, students, and his community as a constructive and creative influence.*

The most effective and meaningful way to summarize the basis for the preceding viewpoints and conclusions is to end with the propositions with which we began several years ago. The following section involves a formalized statement of the propositions underlying a training program in the mental health profession:

Some Propositions Underlying Training
in the Helping Professions[1]
Rather than an elaborated statement of the course content and rationale of a new graduate training program in counseling, I feel that a statement concerning the philosophical stance underlying the program would be most appropriate and meaningful—indeed more important than the course content itself!

Of necessity, we operate within the articulated framework of past and current research, theory and practice. However, any serious contemplation of the early developmental level of functioning of the "helping professions" dictates that we consider our program, our students, and above all, ourselves, to be "in process." By "in process" we mean simply that it is assumed that we function in the context of the best knowledge that we presently have to offer but, most critical, we are *open* to the future, and facilitative of its potentially significant research, theory and practice. The future of counseling or of education or psychology in general, not unlike the future of any given counseling process, must ultimately be in the hands of those for whom we serve—in this case, our students and the clients for whom they serve—as in the instance of counseling it is for our clients.

A PROGRAM AS PROCESS

Counseling, more than any other sub-discipline of the helping profession within recent times, has concerned itself with its identity or perhaps its lack of identity. Its members have gone to great lengths in their attempts to differentiate the distinct contribution of counseling from those of other and related sub-disciplines. Its members have established what it is that a counselor appears to do and from what resources he appears to draw, especially in his training. In doing so, they have neglected to make explicit several underlying propositions, the explication of which is essential to the success of any program and particularly critical in the infancy of a program within an infant professional area. I should like to share with you some of these propositions and perhaps together we can contribute to the kind of training program which leads ultimately to more effective learning process and outcome. A general proposition provides perhaps the substatum for all of the other propositions.

PROPOSITION: *Counseling training is another instance of interpersonal learning processes in general.* Graduate training in the helping

[1]First written in 1964 by Dr. Carkhuff and entitled, "In Search of an Identity" (1967).

professions, as well as the therapeutic or facilitative processes for which it is intended, is not an isolated process but rather another instance of interpersonal learning and relearning processes. There is evidence to indicate that the same variables which operate effectively in any learning process, whether parent-child, teacher-student or counselor-counselee, will be effective in all of these processes. Whether or not we employ rigorous or "tender" language is unimportant. What is important is that we are asking the learner, be he trainee or counselee, to generalize to the rest of his life's situations. When we isolate the training or counseling process from other learning experiences we are often unable to relate the efficacy within the process to functioning in other life situations. Some elaboration of this brief statement of this general proposition may be illuminating.

There appear to be a number of general corollaries as well as corollaries related directly to the specific training program which flow from this general proposition and which deserve special attention because of their critical significance.

COROLLARY I. *Either we "hook" the student in a lifelong learning process or we have failed him and ourselves.* As a profession, we have not yet squarely faced up to the criteria problem in assessing our training programs. We busy ourselves with predicting success in graduate school (which means grades) which may or may not bear any relationship to the contribution a graduate may make in "real" life. We have settled too early for indices such as publication lists which themselves present quality-quantity problems and have not yet learned how to measure the contribution of the university professor or practicing clinician who facilitate the development of any number of persons who go on to make their own contributions. We can, however, take some stabs, not altogether in the dark, at where we are in this regard.

An acceptance of our early developmental stage dictates that we can no longer settle for the Ph.D. as a "finished" product who has incorporated all that is "knowable"—and more. To be sure, we must attempt to equip him with the knowledge and skills necessary for the student to become productive and creative within his field (in whatever manner we measure this). However, we have become acutely aware that an openness to change, and innovation is itself an essential characteristic in our graduate.

Implicitly, we are asking for *change* in the stance which the student assumes toward his world. Just as in counseling, our goal in counseling training is to facilitate this change in the direction of the optimal personal development of the "whole" person before us. We are asking the trainee to become an ever-changing, ever-evolving person in the process of becoming more effective in his world. We are, in effect, asking him to become a person who lives effectively in facilitating both his own efforts as well as the efforts of those with whom he is associated in an attempt to make life more worthwhile for himself and those around him.

Implicitly, we are attempting to involve the student in a life-long learning process. In this regard, while the teacher has not simply an opportunity but also a responsibility to *expose* the student in depth to his own orientation, education is seen as just that, *exposure* rather than indoctrination. We must leave him his most facilitative self—but himself—not *our* ghost emulating a set of *our* techniques. Although there are abstract attributes such as "openness" as well as concrete indices of contribution for which we aim, if we know too well the detailed characteristics and orientations of our student products before we initiate training then we must reexamine the process which has shaped his development so as to recreate him in our image. The happiest circumstance that I could imagine in counseling training at this point in our development would be for some trainees to evolve favorably disposed toward behavior therapy, some to psychoanalytic and some, client-centered with each open to the contributions of the other approach and all taking part in a concerted effort to improve the efficacy of the counseling process.

COROLLARY II. *The training process must integrate those elements which are most conducive to effective learning.* With due consideration to the stage of our understanding, the training program itself would appear to be the most appropriate model for the implementation of these learning and relearning processes, for we must ask, "If these processes cannot be facilitated in training, then where?" Training in counseling as well as counseling per se would seem to offer at least three primary sources for effective learning: (1) what is taught and reinforced didactically in an attempt to shape trainee behavior; (2) the conditions or atmosphere which afford the trainee an experiential base calculated to nurture the trainee's self-development; and (3) who the teacher is as an identification model for effective functioning. The learning process would seem to take place most effectively when all elements are present and integrated in a way of living and learning effectively: an interactional process in which the person designated "more knowing" offers to the trainee that which has proved to be meaningful and significant in his experiences in the context of a facilitative relationship which provides for the learner the conditions which current and extensive research and clinical findings suggest are essential for effective learning and change. The trainee can explore himself and his environment, come to some greater awareness and make known his own responses and reactions to the teacher's offerings. In short, the trainee can find out *who he is in this thing* and *what he has to offer* in conjunction with a teacher who makes known who he is and what he has to offer. This is a model for effective living and learning.

Since clients are asked daily to generalize from their therapeutic experience to the rest of their life's situations, such a process would not appear to be too much to ask from the counselor or from the person conducting counseling training. Even further, we might suggest that to the extent that the teacher does not live effectively and facilitatively and to the extent that he is not open to change and learning from his students, to that extent has he taught his students that life does not involve a continuous learning process. Rather than the demise of the defensive mentor, it should be the highest tribute to the teacher's excellence—and indeed essential—that every aspect of the training be dedicated to making it possible for each trainee to go beyond the teacher in many, if not most, ways and areas.

The lack of a clearly differentiated role in human affairs which has so long distressed counseling psychology is perhaps its distinct advantage. If the student products of our present programs are equipped behaviorally and philosophically as well as with the necessary knowledge and skills, counseling might concern itself less with what its related counterparts are doing and more with taking off in its own positive direction. Its distinct advantage here is that it has far fewer mystical or inexplicable steps to retrace and can base its program on a process of continual learning. The following specific corollaries are related to the direction of the new program.

COROLLARY III. *Training in counseling must be designed to stay in the forefront of meaningful and significant current research, theory and practice in facilitative interpersonal learning processes.* The training program is seen as only one phase of a continuous cycle of (1) researching the counseling and therapeutic processes, (2) applying those dimensions receiving substantial support in research to training and (3) researching the counseling process subsequent to training. This cycle reflects the belief that research and training for practice are not just complementary but the efficacy of each is integrally contingent upon the other. Each is a particularly rich resource for the other. Our most effective efforts can be brought to bear by those involved intimately in the soil of both practice and research, those who actually see the clients whose needs constitute the basis for the profession and who, in turn, can explore those dimensions which offer the prospect for best serving these needs.

The training program itself must be researched to determine its own efficacy. Priority, it can be seen, is given to the production of new knowledge concerning effective interpersonal learning and relearning processes. To the counselor, we believe, falls the chief responsibility for conducting and disseminating to the "helping" professions the research upon which depends the possibility of more effective counseling process and outcome. To the person who wants to be primarily a clinical practitioner we suggest only that he must wear "blinders"—looking neither left nor right nor back, especially backward—to not find daily new and researchable problems and dimensions in his "routine" practice. It is not that he must himself spend long hours implementing replicated Latin Square designs but rather that he must consider his practice a wealthy source for ideas and in the necessary spirit of inquiry concerning the discovery and tranmission of more effective modes of practice he has a responsibility to frame as systematically as possible his ideas in order to stimulate the efforts of others as well as his own.

COROLLARY IV. *Training in counseling must be designed to maintain a firm foundation in the basic psychological science which lends substance to its work.* In order to discharge the weighty responsibility toward the other helping professions and to remain "in process" rather than to rely upon the practice of a restricted set of skills, it is necessary that counseling be firmly grounded in the basic science and its methodology which form the base of its practice. Here we in no way mean to negate the historical and philosophical approaches which may themselves put the science and its assumptive underpinnings in perspective. However, scientific training appears to provide the kind of background which makes possible the necessary flexibility and resourcefulness and facilitates new insights. In this context, the freedom and openness to exploration, experimentation and innovation in the context of a genuine concern for the welfare of the client is necessary. The training must, therefore, incorporate programs in the theoretical and empirical aspects of psychology as well as the courses most intimately involved with the practice of the profession.

SUMMARY

The concerns for a new program in counseling have been enumerated. Neither the propositions nor their order nor the counseling emphasis are in any way exclusive of other relevant considerations. That these issues do emerge for a new program in an essentially new profession suggests that other allied professions must at some point come to grips with similar questions.

The propositions may be efficiently summarized. From the general proposition that counseling and its training are learning or relearning processes, several corollaries were discerned and elaborated: (1) the process is life-long for both student and teacher; (2) the training program must implement what is known of these processes in their effective instances; (3) the training program must itself be "in process"; and (4) it must be eqiupped to be "in process."

Again, we must return to our original premise: the open stance underlying the program is perhaps most critical. This stance is carried out in all aspects of training: for example, the extensive concern for the student selection process which constitutes such a visible obstacle for many programs and impedes the program's promulgators from making their program facilitative for *all* involved fades into a continuously shared and mutual process. Counseling training, as well as counseling, is for me another instance of living effectively, including especially the involvement in inter-personal learning processes which are facilitative of the development and growth of *all* of the persons involved. To sum, *"counseling" is a way of life.* This is the way it must be in training or not at all.

## References

Carkhuff, R. R. Toward a comprehensive model of facilitative interpersonal processes. *J. counsel. Psychol.*, 1967, *14*, 67–72.

Carkhuff, R. R. In search of an identity. *Counselor Educ. Supervis.*, 1967, *6*, No. 4.

Pierce, R., R. R. Carkhuff, and B. G. Berenson. The differential effects of high and low counselors upon counselors-in-training. *J. clin. Psychol.*, 1967, *23*, 212–215.

# Beyond Counseling and Therapy: Summary and Overview

In this final section we attempt (1) to re-establish ties with the introductory chapters and (2) to pull together in sharp relief some of our critical insights. Chapter 14 re-explores some of the basic issues, both implicit and explicit in the relationship between counseling and society, and attempts to depict the effective practitioner and truly therapeutic processes. In Chapter 15, we attempt to integrate the most salient features of all of the chapters in a brief but comprehensive statement related to the theory, research, training, and practice of counseling and therapy. In a concentrated form this chapter presents the essence of the book and the essence of a systematic, eclectic stance toward effective counseling and therapy.

> . . . only when we break
> free of society can we return to
> contribute to it.

## Counseling and Society

Our anger is born of our therapeutic experiences with clients and students, broken and disabled, products of a social system which has precluded their emergence. Most often, they have either been unable to emerge potently or have never had the credentials in the first place. Our experiences have led us to re-examine society, its role, and its effects. As society has prescribed the role of "educating" and "helping," it is to help the individual to adjust to society. *We have discovered that in many ways society is the enemy.*

The counselor, whether he is characterized as a guidance or rehabilitation specialist, is in a position uniquely different from all other positions within society: the counselor lives in and is supported by society, yet also sees society through the eyes of its victims. The role of the guidance specialist is prescribed to guide persons toward a satisfactory adjustment within society, or, put another way, to prevent the accumulation of victims of our social system—sometimes, it seems, to prevent the visible accumulation of victims. His role is similar to the educator, yet in this sense he does not have the same range of experience and freedom of operation as his counterpart, the rehabilitation specialist. Whether counselor or therapist, the rehabilitation specialist has the freedom to do whatever is necessary to enable the client to live effectively again, to bring the client back into mainstream society. The social system is embarrassed by its toll and sanctions the functioning of the rehabilitation specialist in order to avoid further embarrassment. In a very real sense, *the rehabilitator, spawned in society's guilt, is the garbage man of society, picking up the necessary victims left in the wake of a very crude and wasteful social system.* On the other hand, in spite of society's sponsorship, the total freedom of operation which he is afforded places the rehabilitator in the very unique position of doing whatever is necessary *for the welfare of the client,* whether that involves movement toward or away from society. He has the free reins of functioning unknown to the performers of other roles in society, for the system neither understands those who fall outside of society's margins nor those who can help those who have fallen. Many do not acknowledge this freedom and still others refute it.

Society, then, provides an umbrella for a process in which things can take place which could not otherwise have taken place within society for the particular individuals involved. In its attempt to enable the individual to get back to mainstream social functioning, society allows the establishment of a transitional subsociety. This is most clearly seen in group therapeutic processes where the clients often do establish their own unique subculture to serve their own unique ends as a group, and as individuals.

## MAN AND SOCIETY

We hypothesize that man is neither inherently good nor bad. Rather, he has the capacity for both good and bad acts and has demonstrated well the products of both in his several thousand years of social existence. Thus, man is shaped to actualize his constructive or destructive potential. His shaper is the social system (and its representatives) in which he functions.

Society, in turn, whatever its origin and whatever service it originally provided man, functions in its advanced stages for its own protection, preservation, and perpetuation. It has functional autonomy. Its institutions are created to serve its end; they flourish or deteriorate with or without support in accordance with the needs of the social system. Its members are shaped in a similar manner to meet society's ends. Now it functions to control man's destructive impulses; now it functions to unleash them; always seeking its own survival and equilibrium.

Society is organized most often to fix responsibility for those actions which threaten the continuation of society *in its present form.* This is not to say that society does not change. It does. However, it changes only through the efforts of those persons who live independently of society, those who sometimes run against the mainstream of society, and those who live always on or beyond the very tenuous and lonely margin of society. Whatever progress society makes, it makes by moving over to incorporate the strong words and actions of this marginal man. However, it does so only when the marginal man is potent, when he has somehow withstood the attempts to be neutralized, and has survived the attempts to destroy him. Society changes in order to neutralize the full effects of the potent man's words and actions. It does so in order to render the potent less potent.

Society is not organized to free man's creative potential but rather to maintain or render man impotent or maintain him with minimal potency. It frees man's little finger only rather than both of his whole hands for creative activities, whether tangible or interpersonal. Man cannot construct with his "pinky." In its rules and regulations and in the role models which it presents for emulation, society replaces the individual experience with a collective experience. Man cannot create with someone else's experience.

## THE TRUTHS AND THE MYTHS

In order to perpetuate itself, society must contain within itself a sufficient number of truths, both physical and emotional as well as intellectual. Otherwise it has no adherents, no members. Sometimes the truths are more clearly half-truths. The social system perpetrates a like number of myths in order to disallow the emergence of potent persons

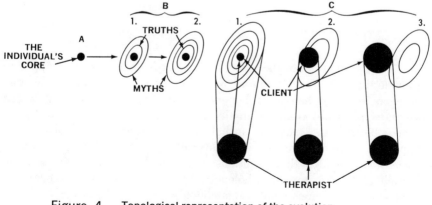

Figure 4.    Topological representation of the evolution and successful treatment of a client.

who threaten society. Man's basic problem is to separate the truths from the myths and achieve potency. Society's problem is to perpetuate the myths and maintain man impotent.

Thus, initially, the child is born with two essential directions: to survive and to grow (see Figure 4). In the healthy environment, the significant adult figures protect the child and support him, enabling him to survive; they provide him the physical, intellectual, and emotional conditions of growth, thus enabling him to experience himself in a process of continual differentiation from his environment.

Unfortunately, most children have not had the experience of a healthy environment. The child is not only reared with low levels of psychological conditions, but is fed myths which disallow his constructive emergence. Along with the myths are a number of truths. The truths move in the direction of life. The myths move in an opposite direction—the movement away from life.

The truths are never integrated into the individual's core, for he has memorized the "golden rules" of life rather than having experienced them and given them his own meaning. The myths are confusing, for they so resemble truths: for example, "academic achievement equals creativity." Man's basic problem in emergence, then, is differentiating his core of integrity from the myths, and incorporating within his core of integrity what is truth for him.

Man enters the counseling and therapeutic processes confused—terribly confused—as to who he really is. He cannot separate himself from all the codes of living he has learned. In Figure 4, stage B, we see the core of man lost in layers of myths and truths, none of which is really his, but each of which guides his activities through the days and years of his physical existence. Finally, thoroughly lost, he seeks from another human the kind of help which he cannot find in his everyday environment.

## THE FACILITATORS AND THE RETARDERS

His counselor or therapist, in turn, may or may not be equipped to provide this help. If the therapist was among the ones who had a healthy early environment, he is a whole person who sees the world clearly; he can separate the truths from the myths. If he was not among the fortunate "once borns," he may, nevertheless, have achieved wholeness or approximate wholeness; that is, in later life, someone who was whole in some way provided the conditions which enabled him to differentiate himself and move toward wholeness. In this manner he has been the recipient of conditions which he is now able to offer the client.

The effective therapist not only offers high levels of facilitative conditions, but commits himself, very deeply, to the therapeutic process. The facilitator will do all and anything that is necessary to enable the client to function more effectively (Carkhuff, 1967). The following description of the facilitative therapist by the client in the study of the experimental manipulation of client conditions (Carkhuff and Alexik, 1967) is meaningful:

THE FACILITATIVE THERAPIST

The composite high-rated therapist is an exciting, stimulating, intelligent, creative, exploring, adventurous person. He offers life. It's like the air he breathes. He is really only being what he has to be. He is living himself.

He gives me new concepts rather than merely parroting mine. He helps me to see places to go. His questions are aimed towards discovering my deepest feelings. He gave me the impression of a genuine commitment to an interpersonal encounter. He seemed to be experiencing it rather than intellectually following. He is with you and will fight for your life with you. That's the comfort of him. He is siding with the constructive forces in you. He will add his 100% to your 20% that's constructive. His analogies and concreteness are such that you don't have to ponder about what he means—you immediately understand intellectually and simultaneously feel it as never before.

During the middle section I had a real internal struggle to pull myself away from reality and involvement so that I could complete the experiment. With these people, it hurt me to try to manipulate them, as if they deserved more respect from me. During the experimental period, manipulation, the high-rated therapist starts grabbing to keep you from falling away. He plunges in and becomes more intense.

I never needed to take notes afterwards on my impressions of high-rated therapists because I knew that I could never forget the encounter. His intensity made me feel like throwing myself into his arms, and that I could trust his holding. I could feel him peeling away the layers. He wanted my deepest feelings and I felt he respected them. He always left me feeling more hopeful and more courageous. I knew that he knew a lot about me and that he could really someday come to know me.

On the other hand, and with too great a frequency, the therapist is not whole. He does not and cannot distinguish the truths from the myths for himself. He cannot enable another to differentiate himself and grow. At the lowest levels he is unable to offer anything more than his own ineffective level of living. The retarding therapist not only offers low levels of conditions, but something akin to the client's impressions from the studies of therapy (Carkhuff and Alexik, 1967):

THE RETARDING THERAPIST

A composite of the low-rated therapist shows up an unimaginative, uncreative, boring and pedestrian person. He performed his function in a mechanical, perfunctory manner, never expressing any emotion, and he didn't respond to the feelings I expressed. The tenacity of these therapists *not* to get involved with anything human was frightening. He seemed to be comfortable only in a safe, neutral range. This often was evidenced by the questions asked—detailed information communicating surface values such as societal status, financial means and other unimportant details. His questions didn't communicate respect. One showed a complete lack of concern for me until his questions revealed my financial status. Then his voice showed life for the first time as if then I was worth paying attention to. I was really disgusted.

With more frequency than I found tolerable, there was a lot of a sick kind of giggling and I didn't think my problem was all that funny, (and I know that he did not understand the experimental purposes of my session.) I struggled desperately to get something out of him and couldn't. I could handle him on his level but I couldn't bring him up to mine. My lack of respect for him showed in my responses to his questions. During the middle section I found it not only easy but sadistically pleasurable to manipulate him, for within the first five minutes I found myself unable to feel any respect for him. I felt most comfortable talking chit-chat with these people as opposed to the internal struggle experienced with the more facilitative therapists.

His "blah" voice and lack of reaction dragged me down. I couldn't reach out and grab anything because it's just a mask with words coming out. He made me feel as if I, as a client, was some kind of animal, and he couldn't go down to the client's feelings or he'd just get soiled. What he was really saying to me was "I am worthless, empty, sterile, nothing, only I have learned to keep this from the world and you. In intimacy with you, you bring me back to who I really am and you get me dirty again."

I knew this ineffectual didn't know and couldn't ever know me. I would have erased him from my memory except for purposes of this study, as an interesting example of destructive therapy. I invariably left depressed from sessions with these people.

Even the therapist who is functioning above the lowest level is not helpful. It appears that he can only help another to continue to function the way he does, benignly and innocuously, slowly weaving his way through the maze of conformity, always neutralizing the efforts of others as well as his own. Thus, the following composite picture:

THE NEUTRALIZING THERAPIST
A composite picture of the therapist who was neither facilitator nor retarder gives no vitality or life. He accepts weakness where I keep trying to show my strength. He is so depressed in manner and voice

that I need to cheer him up. His technique is to let you know he's weak and can't help. He's very polite and so sorry but he has his own needs, so that you end up feeling compassion and start working around his needs. The dominant feeling the client goes away with is that this guy must be left unhurt and unharmed so you have to be very careful and not get into anything that might disturb his equilibrium. He tunes in on your strength and asks you for it.

There are lots of quips and smiles to show what a great guy or gal the therapist is. He asks many factual questions, shallow, bright but often leading to obtuse answers. He laughs too much. I say I'm practically psychotic over this picture and he laughs.

He is happy during the middle section when he can talk superficially about himself. It's the middle part when I'm tapping in on who the therapist really is. He can be active now. He thinks I'm bringing the focus on him and he thinks I deserve something from him. I stirred up a reservoir of guilt for not acting before. As soon as he spills some shallow emotion, he is able to maintain his former equilibrium, the only place where he feels safe.

The middle range people can listen with a bare minimum of respect and make some effort to treat you as a kind of human, but they are unable to carry out for any length of time and usually find a way to get you to carry them. Often these people can sympathize and give you the feeling that we're just two frail people huddled together in this cruel, cold world and I'll comfort you and you comfort me and somehow we'll survive. But they cannot show you how to stand up and fight or try to go beyond this point, and probably don't want to see anyone able to go beyond the point at which they themselves are stuck. These therapists never recoup after the middle section.

*Man's cardinal rule is that no one can have more than he, himself, can have. The therapist who has not chosen life, himself, cannot enable another to choose life. He cannot recognize the life and death urgency of the choices confronting his clients, his students, and, indeed, his children.*

## EFFECTIVE THERAPY

The client buried under the morass of myths, has lost his directionality. He has lost his ability to act. He can only react, but mainly he does not act at all. He is living ineffectively because he cannot act constructively on his environment. In his desperation he seeks a person who can help him to find direction in his life. Hopefully, he finds a person who has direction in his own life. Hopefully, he finds a person who can act constructively. Hopefully, he finds a person who is, himself, living effectively.

The effective  therapist must be differentiated himself. He has integrated the essential truths of *his* experience. He has rejected the myths, however reasonable they appear to be. Figure 4, stage C, point 1, portrays the whole but differentiated therapist responding to the client's plea for help. The therapist provides high levels of facilitative conditions in order to establish a relationship with the client in which the client can feel secure enough so that he can come to be fully himself. In addition, the client may relax his defenses enough to allow the therapist's tentative attempts to "touch" the client, that is, to allow the client to know that the therapist is with him in his experience at this moment in time. The point of making contact with another human is the first stage in process movement; that is, *for a moment, however fleeting, the cores of client and therapist "touch" each other and vibrate in unison.* The client knows in his "being" that another person can be fully "with" him. He must now learn to discriminate the truths from the myths, the voices in him from the voices of those around him.

Thus, during the second stage of process movement, the client, having been "touched" by another person, reaches out to "touch" again. The difference between this and the first stage is that, during the first stage, the client simply relaxed his defenses to allow the therapist to "touch" him. During the second stage, the client actively reaches out to "touch" *with* the therapist. He meets the therapist halfway.

During the last stage, we see a person who has differentiated himself out from the layers of myths that prevented him from having contact with his own experience; he has incorporated the truths in his own experience, he has become more and more whole. He can now relate to the therapist on equalitarian terms.

The person in the process of becoming whole must now go on to establish such relationships with others. It is to be hoped that therapy is only the first of many fulfilling relationships in which two or more persons can fully and openly share their genuine selves. However, the person must also go on to distinguish those with whom he can relate fully from those with whom he cannot. He may even provide assistance to those with whom he cannot relate fully, but who seek his help and acknowledge him as the agent of their change.

To be sure, the construct of wholeness has many limitations. Among them is the notion that in some way a person "plateaus off" in becoming whole. Rather, we wish to connote a process which never ends, continuing lifelong.

## SOME CONCLUSIONS

The beginning of all effective intra and interpersonal processes, is the person himself. He must experience himself fully in order to be creative in all spheres of endeavor, including the interpersonal sphere. Someone must make it possible for him to experience himself in this manner.

Education can and should, although it very seldom does, facilitate this process. Rather than being a process of taking the child's experience away from him, education might become a process of giving the child his experience in clearer and stronger terms, providing better constructs or "handles" for the experience, and helping to break the barriers toward fuller and wider range of experiences. In order to provide handles, educators must offer students a full exposure not an indoctrination of the kind serving the further perpetuation of any social system. Educators should be not so concerned with their image and the image of their products, but they should offer wide possibilities and accept a wide variety of creative products.

On the part of those being educated, they must take from the presentations of the various institutional representatives what is valuable *for themselves*. They must demand a tolerance for functioning beyond the presently acceptable limits. They must demand people who are themselves living effectively for educators. If the educator cannot learn from the learner, then the learner cannot learn from the educator, for learning is a reciprocal process. The power inherent in the learner must be recognized fully, whether or not the educator acknowledges this power.

For those who have been led astray, who are the lost and confused products of a social system which is not dedicated to the emergence of its individual members, the issue is different. They are in need of rehabilitation and/or guidance. They must also demand in their counselors and therapists the same effectiveness in living which they seek. If they do not make these demands, they can only become involved in a circular process leading ultimately to the point where they started, with the only difference being the addition of a number of new layers of myth and façade.

The counselor and therapist, in turn, is afforded a rich and unique opportunity to work effectively for the betterment of his fellow man. Within the shelter provided by society, the therapist is free to do what is necessary to effect constructive change in the client. He is free to help another to emerge free and creative, whether or not the social system wishes him to be free and creative.

The counselor must live independently of society. Independence is employed in a statistical sense to mean that, at many points, his way of life is congruent with our culture and society, but at many points his way of life, of necessity, differs from the rules and regulations of society. Thus, he is freed by his own internalized code of conduct to make discriminations concerning whether or not to move the individual client toward or away from acculturation. He does not feel bound by the notion that the counseling and therapy are dedicated solely to helping the individual to adjust to society.

Finally, we must recognize all institutions (including, in particular, the academic institution) for what they are—potential enemies of our creativity. Furthermore, we must avoid the worst of all fates—the fate of the creator whose ideas have been neutralized, of the marginal man who has been incorporated in the thin lines of a paper world, and of the rebel who has been institutionalized. *The irony of ironies is that only when we break free of society can we return to contribute to it.* We cannot break free when we want what they have, status, position, prestige, and money. We can break free only when we live our own experience 100 percent, without compromise. It is a mistaken conception to label these thoughts asocial or amoral; rather, we speak of enlightened discriminations made by the highest form of social and moral being.

## References

Carkhuff, R. R. The facilitator: An overview. In *The counselor's contribution to facilitative processes.* Urbana, Ill.: Parkinson, 1967, Chapter 14.

Carkhuff, R. R. and Mae Alexik. The differential effects of the manipulation of client depth of self-exploration upon high and low functioning counselors. *J. counsel. Psychol.,* in press, 1967.

Chapter **15**

> . . . the only person who can be an
> effective therapist is the person who
> would not be counseled by any of the
> existing approaches.

**Beyond Counseling and Therapy:**
**Summary and Overview**

For many years, eclecticism has been denounced as too broad
a catch-all, unsystematic, and unresearchable. While there was a great deal
of truth in such comments, the traditionalists who forwarded them did so
largely from a defensive stance. They offered instead their own promise in
practice and research; they have not delivered! They cannot deliver!

In Chapter 1 we specified those facilitative dimensions (empathy,
respect, genuineness, concreteness, self-disclosure, and others) related to
constructive gain or change in all interpersonal learning experiences, and
saw that *the available sources of nourishment, professional or otherwise,*
*are totally inadequate to meet human needs in a time of stress.* We found
that counseling and psychotherapy can have constructive or deteriorative
consequences. These consequences can be accounted for, in part, by the
levels of facilitative dimensions at which the counselors and therapists
are functioning.

Demands must be made upon our professional practitioners. When the
client comes for counseling or therapy, he is saying whether explicitly or
implicitly, "I am simply not living effectively." When the counselor or
therapist indicates his involvement, he is saying, "I can help you to live
effectively." The missing statement by the therapist involves the question,

"Why?" Why can the therapist help the client to live effectively? Because he, himself, is living effectively. The question for each therapist is a simple one: "Are you living effectively or not?" Either he is finding fulfillment in a creative life, in his creative actions, products, and interpersonal relationships, including, in particular, counseling and therapy, or he is not. *Counseling or therapy is either a way of life or it is not counseling and therapy.*

In Chapters 2 and 3 we made clear that our stance is not an anti-intellectual one. We made an attempt to articulate the theoretical product of our efforts to make systematic and enlightened inquiries into what we have been professing to do—counseling and psychotherapy. The model is an open, yet systematic, eclectic model built around a central core of conditions shared by all interview-oriented approaches, and complemented by the unique contributions of a variety of potential preferred modes of treatment. We developed a multidimensional model based upon the interaction of therapist, client, and contextual variables where the client, as well as the therapist, is measured on the same relevant dimensions of interpersonal functioning. We have oriented a program shaped by what is effective for the client, and, in so doing, have been unable to separate research, practice, and training. Rather, we have described the necessary cycle of (1) practice, (2) research, (3) training, (4) practice, (5) research in order to determine whether what we have accomplished is an improvement over practices which dominated earlier.

In Chapters 4 through 8 we have made systematic attempts to analyze, not without editorializing, the currently dominant approaches to counseling and therapy in order to determine their potentially unique contributions over and above those accounted for by the central core of facilitative conditions. In so doing, we were reminded of a conclusion by Kierkegaard: "In relation to their systems, most systematizers are like a man who builds an enormous castle and lives in a shack beside it," (Farber, 1956). This has particular meaning for us in listening to the tapes of prominent and not-so-prominent psychoanalytic, client-centered, and existential practitioners; we have found that it is absolutely essential to separate what they do from what they say they do. For example, within existentialism, the emphasis is upon analysis rather than encounter; within client-centered, the emphasis is upon nondirectiveness rather than client-centeredness; within psychoanalytic, the emphasis is upon the therapist's preconceived notions rather than the client's discoveries.

The conclusion from these five chapters can be best integrated with Chapter 9, the first chapter of the clinical section where the two major phases of therapy are described: (1) the downward or inward phase involving the therapist's offering of high levels of facilitative conditions which enable the client to turn inward and to explore himself and his problem area intensively and extensively; (2) the upward or outward phase or period of emergent directionality where the therapist, in conjunction with the client, seeks to give some direction toward constructive action to the client's life.

Within the first phase and between the first and second phases of therapy, the conditions themselves take on differential meaning. Thus, the final, not the initial, level of empathy is critical during phase 1 and of little consequence during phase 2, except in terms of eliciting feedback from the client concerning the effects of the developing direction. Whereas unconditionality is emphasized during the initial stages of phase 1, the effective relationship takes on the character of positive regard by the end of phase 1, and may even culminate in a process involving conditionality during phase 2, as for example with many of the conditioning techniques. Although genuineness does not appear critical during the initial stages of phase 1, it takes on increasing importance with the continuation of therapy, culminating in an open, equalitarian, and honest relationship during phase 2. Concreteness, on the other hand, appears to go through several stages of meaningful application. Whereas initially, high levels of concreteness or specificity appear most effective during the initial stages of phase 1, during the later stages of phase 1, material from the unconscious may be dealt with at a very abstract level. During phase 2, the period of emergent directionality, concreteness in the specific steps, advantages and disadvantages of the alternative routes, is emphasized. Therapist self-disclosure would appear least significant during the early stages of phase 1 and most significant during the later stages and periodically, where appropriate, during phase 2.

The traditional forms of therapy—the psychoanalytic and the client-centered—stop after phase 1. They settle for insight without direction, cosmology without action. The level 2 client cannot use insights constructively, and he must distort cosmologies simply because he is functioning at level 2 and has been provided with no other means for rising above this level. Only persons functioning above level 3 can employ insight effectively. For the higher-level functioning clients, it would appear, insight may, and most often does, precede action. For the lower-level functioning clients, action and the resultant behavioral reorganization must precede insight.

The existential approach emphasizes phase 1, while its adherents write at times of phase 2. The trait-and-factor and the behavioristic approaches begin with phase 2. They immediately seek direction and are not at all oriented toward establishing an effective therapeutic relationship.

Within the first phase the psychoanalytic approach emphasizes primarily a kind of diagnostic empathy for level 2 or psychoneurotic clients (see Figure 5). Our emphasis puts the diagnostic process back within the treatment process, flowing from an ongoing interaction with the

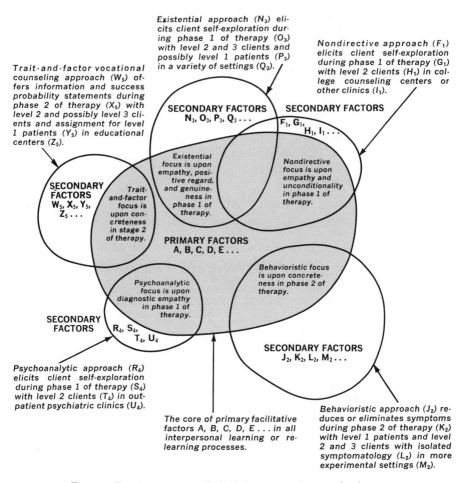

*Existential approach ($N_3$) elicits client self-exploration during phase 1 of therapy ($O_3$) with level 2 and 3 clients and possibly level 1 patients ($P_3$) in a variety of settings ($Q_3$).*

*Nondirective approach ($F_1$) elicits client self-exploration during phase 1 of therapy ($G_1$) with level 2 clients ($H_1$) in college counseling centers or other clinics ($I_1$).*

*Trait-and-factor vocational counseling approach ($W_5$) offers information and success probability statements during phase 2 of therapy ($X_5$) with level 2 and possibly level 3 clients and assignment for level 1 patients ($Y_5$) in educational centers ($Z_5$).*

**SECONDARY FACTORS**
$N_3, O_3, P_3, Q_3 \ldots$

**SECONDARY FACTORS**
$F_1, G_1, H_1, I_1 \ldots$

*Existential focus is upon empathy, positive regard, and genuineness in phase 1 of therapy.*

*Nondirective focus is upon empathy and unconditionality in phase 1 of therapy.*

**SECONDARY FACTORS**
$W_5, X_5, Y_5, Z_5 \ldots$

*Trait-and-factor focus is upon concreteness in stage 2 of therapy.*

**PRIMARY FACTORS**
A, B, C, D, E . . .

*Behavioristic focus is upon concreteness in phase 2 of therapy.*

*Psychoanalytic focus is upon diagnostic empathy in phase 1 of therapy.*

**SECONDARY FACTORS**
$R_4, S_4, T_4, U_4$

**SECONDARY FACTORS**
$J_2, K_2, L_2, M_2 \ldots$

*Psychoanalytic approach ($R_4$) elicits client self-exploration during phase 1 of therapy ($S_4$) with level 2 clients ($T_4$) in outpatient psychiatric clinics ($U_4$).*

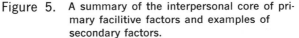

*The core of primary facilitative factors A, B, C, D, E . . . in all interpersonal learning or relearning processes.*

*Behavioristic approach ($J_2$) reduces or eliminates symptoms during phase 2 of therapy ($K_2$) with level 1 patients and level 2 and 3 clients with isolated symptomatology ($L_2$) in more experimental settings ($M_2$).*

**Figure 5.** A summary of the interpersonal core of primary facilitive factors and examples of secondary factors.

client rather than a separate process, a motion picture rather than a still picture. The client-centered approach, in turn, emphasizes both empathic understanding and positive regard (of the unconditional variety) with level 2 clients and seems, especially in a large part of its emphasis, to be most effective during the early part of phase 1. The existential approaches focus upon empathy and positive regard, and they also underscore genuineness, all of which promise potential efficacy on up to level 3, even including a properly qualified employment of technique with the lowest-level functioning patients. During the first phase, then, of all the approaches, the existential approach offers the greatest opportunity for the therapist to employ himself fully in enabling the widest variety of clients to go to the deepest levels of meaningful self-exploration in the context of a genuine relationship. Unfortunately, the existential approach is theoretically not open to the second phase, and the potential directions, where appropriate, afforded by more deterministic positions.

Of all the existing approaches, only the behavioristic and the trait-and-factor approaches constitute bona fide, potential preferred modes of treatment, given a relevant interaction of client, therapist, and contextual variables. In so doing, these approaches emphasize the dimension of concreteness with different level clients. Operant conditioning techniques appear particularly useful with level 1 patients. Counterconditioning techniques appear most effective with the relatively isolated but disabling symptomatology of level 2 clients and the isolated but nonfunctional symptomatology of higher level clients. Similarly, vocational assignment appears efficacious with level 1 patients; longer term vocational and educational counseling seems effective with level 2 and possibly even higher level clients— where suitable. The behavioristic and the trait-and-factor approaches offer a promise to lower-level clients for achieving a minimally facilitative level of self-sustaining functioning, or level 3, only in their ability to clear away obstacles to further development. Their deterministic systems offer no cosmologies predicated upon self-sustenance, growth, and actualization.

Consistent with these aspects of the core conditions and the dominant, existing approaches are the sources of learning emphasized in each of these approaches. The psychoanalytic approach, while it focuses upon a kind of diagnostic empathy, emphasizes the didactic or teaching role of the therapist as a source of learning. Similarly, the trait-and-factor approach emphasizes the teaching or didactic role of the counselor. The behavioristic approach focuses upon the "shaping" of client behavior in a didactic, therapeutic process. On the other hand, the client-centered and the existential approaches emphasize the experiential base of learning. It is readily apparent that none of the approaches (interestingly enough, not even the behavioristic) pay attention *in practice* to the therapist as a role model for learning as a significant source of learning.

Viewed from another vantage point, the major systems make an interesting picture. While we may think of the psychoanalytic and the client-centered approaches as setting their own, very different but implicit goals of therapy, the existential orientation makes the most meaningful goals explicit. In turn, the trait-and-factor approach is in a unique position to describe in full detail the goals, and the behavioristic approach has within its grasp the greatest potential for formulating the means to achieve these goals. Thus, in a very peculiar way, many of these systems, if pushed to their logical extensions, offer hope for implementing a meaningful and systematic, eclectic stance toward counseling and therapy.

In the clinical section, the model in clinical operation, with all of the modifications and qualifications necessary in clinical operation is described. The need to go beyond the known becomes readily apparent. Throughout the entire clinical section, the notion of the necessity for the whole therapist, equipped not only with a thorough, working knowledge of the systems of psychotherapy and the ability to implement these systems (Chapter 12), but also a whole person with vast emotional and physical resources as well, becomes more and more apparent. *Any system is only as good as the therapist is whole, and even the whole system is only as good as the therapist is whole.* The person who is less than whole and who is not in the process of becoming whole is aware only of the death choices at the client's crisis point (Chapter 10). Because there is no life choice, there can be no behavior change: "The client can certainly not have anything that I cannot have." Traditional psychotherapy appears, in most of its practiced forms, not to be psychotherapy at all. It simply provides a formal structure within which the crises, whether their consequences are therapeutic or not, take place. Again, the therapist confronts the crisis or not as he is a whole human or not (Chapter 11).

If we view the crisis as a stimulus-response situation, where for example, the client does not have the usual stimulus value for which the therapist is programmed then the therapist must tap his own resources, his experience of himself and the client. We have seen that when the stimulus is withdrawn from the low-level functioning therapist, he cannot respond effectively because he is unable to depend upon his own experience which he has not developed. On the other hand, we have found that the higher the level of functioning of the therapist, the greater the tendency to respond more effectively when the stimulus is withdrawn. We can assume that he has greater confidence in his own experience of the client than he has in the client's expression of his experience. In general, it appears that both within sessions and over therapy, initially low-level functioning therapists tend to decline in functioning while initially high-level functioning therapists tend to improve in their level of functioning. Their respective clients follow similar patterns. A therapist for whom counseling is only a "technique" or a series of techniques may initially function at minimally facilitative levels, but will decline in the effectiveness of his responses; that is, if he attempts to add something to the client's response he frequently subtracts from the client's response because he has only his own experience to rely on in order to enable the client to move to deeper levels.

In Chapter 13 an attempt is made to describe the goals and the means to attain them—elusive wholeness in being and attitude, in practice, theory, and research.

Unfortunately, in relation to society (Chapter 14), almost all of the systems are oriented toward middle-class acculturation. In speaking to the victims of our social system, the therapist most often must be saying, "You don't have what it takes to make it in my world, but in working with you I must emphasize the values of my world." The therapist has made it in good middle-class society. The client, for a variety of reasons, most often does not have the means to make it.

Although the therapist is provided with a great deal of freedom, even he, much less the client, is not tolerated beyond level 3. Level 3 is the maximum level of functioning that any system can entertain. He is the great integrator—without direction. He is aware of the fullness of life and cognizant of the completeness of death. Except for the very resourceful person, staying at level 3 for long periods involves a very desperate balancing act, neither moving ahead, to commit himself to life, nor falling behind to commit himself to much less than life.

The only person who can be an effective therapist is the one who has chosen life, for he is aware of the implications of both life and death choices. The only man who can be an effective therapist is one who lives beyond society's tolerance limits. *The only person who can be an effective therapist is the one who will not be counseled by any of the existing approaches.*

We are suggesting the first clinically meaningful system totally based upon the interaction between client and therapist, modified by contextual variables. It is the first open, eclectic model in which the therapist is shaped by what is effective for the client, and hopefully, in which both will be shaped by what is effective for themselves and others. The movement within the core variables is from the known to the unknown, and toward discerning new, potential preferred modes of treatment as well as the unique contributions of those currently existing.

In our systematic eclectic stance, all conditions function, where appropriate. All sources of learning are emphasized in the activities of the whole person: the didactic, the experiential, and the role model for effective living.

In summary we are suggesting the first approach that emphasizes a process culminating in a moment-to-moment, fully sharing process—a process born not only of the emotional resources of both parties to the relationship, but also of the deepest and broadest understanding of existing knowledge, and *complemented by anything that will work for the client.*

## References

Farber, L. H. Martin Buber and psychiatry. *Psychiatry,* 1956, *19,* 109–120.

# Appendix A

## Toward Meaningful
## Client Dimensions

As clinical practitioners, we have long felt that traditional diagnostic categories are not only often intellectually repugnant but usually meaningless for purposes of dictating differential treatment. Most frequently, the diagnostic constructs are not relevant to the lives, particularly the therapeutic lives of the clients. Almost always, the diagnostic evaluations do not lead to treatment calculated to bring about maximum client benefits. Similarly, the treatment processes, themselves, have functional autonomy. They are presented without clear statements concerning the indications and contra-indications for employing them. However, the attempted development of a broad, encompassing, systematic and eclectic stance toward counseling and psychotherapy and the development specifically of the concept of preferred modes of treatment leads us once again to consider meaningful client and situational dimensions which offer the promise of differential and effective treatment. No comprehensive model of counseling and therapy is complete without an attempt in this direction. We, in the present text, operate with broader global levels of client functioning and dysfunctioning in mind, and with particular emphasis upon constructive therapeutic intervention. For us, a meaningful diagnostic process flows out of an ongoing interactional process between therapist and client. There is no separate and distinct diagnostic process. Nevertheless, we must consider as a potentially rich resource of relevant client variables, systematic organizations of known etiological factors, such as those presented by Dr. Frederick C. Thorne in this Appendix. Thorne's monumental efforts are logical extensions of presently available approaches to diagnosis and treatment. It remains for us, and you, the reader to make meaningful discriminations and applications in establishing the necessary relationships between client dimensions and clinical practice.

## The Etiological Equation[*]

*Frederick C. Thorne, University of Miami*

### INTRODUCTION

The field of psychopathology is in a very confused state due to the general failure to attempt any systematic classification of the many etiological factors that have been postulated as causing psychological abnormalities. A very large number of hypothetical models have been offered by theorists attempting to explain mental abnormality. The issues are further complicated by the existence of overlapping terminologies that have never been related to each other. Each new investigator seems compelled to originate a new terminology without regard to existing theories and terminologies that may deal with the same phenomena very adequately.

To bring order and clarification into the confused field of psychopathology, it appears necessary to classify and codify existing theories of psychopathology in order to discriminate common elements and to demonstrate the relationships between all theories and their modifications. Once a suitable classification system has been devised, it should be possible to evaluate any new theory quickly to discover its historical antecedents, and to differentiate any genuinely new elements.

## THE CONCEPT OF ETIOLOGY

We have emphasized previously (Thorne, 1955) that the principal problem of all diagnosis is to identify the factors organizing patterns of integration. *Etiology* is the science of causes, that is, the origin and development of states or conditions. In medical science, etiology refers specifically to the causation of disease and disorder. In psychodiagnosis, etiology refers to the causation of psychological states (Thorne, 1966). The concept of *etiology* presumes that all real phenomena have causes, and the diagnostic problem is to discriminate the contribution of all classes of causal factors.

An *etiologic equation* is a formal statement describing all classes of causal factors and indicating their relationships. The reason for needing an equation is that very few behavior phenomena are determined by a single factor and, most commonly, it is necessary to differentiate multifactorial determination. The etiological equation differentiates between primary, secondary, predisposing, precipitating, pre-existing, and situational factors, and it attempts to weight the contribution of each. An etiological equation has the advantage of operationally specifying the various classes of factors and how they are to be measured.

## THE LAW OF PARSIMONY AND ETIOLOGY

Since, in the normal organism, higher-level integrations depend for their psychophysiological support upon intact lower-level integrations, this establishes an etiological hierarchy in which the causes of a condition must be traced back to the lowest level at which disturbance can be demonstrated. Except where a disorder can be proven to radiate from higher levels downward, logic requires the assumption that disturbances of lower-level integrations radiate upwards, causing loss of integration at higher levels of integration.

Some general principles may be elaborated concerning the relative priorities of various classes of etiological factors, and these principles should be followed in formulating etiologic equations describing patterns of causation.

1. *Genetic primacy.* Where genetic factors achieve penetrance, they always command priority over acquired factors in the etiologic pattern.

2. *Evolutionary primacy.* Biologically primitive factors, both in the development of the race and of the individual, command priority over factors evolving later. Thus, behaviors appearing also in lower animals

must be assigned biogenetic primacy over factors seen only in humans. Freudian interpretations should not be assigned to behaviors also observed in animals.

3. *Developmental primacy.* In general, behaviors appearing early in normal developmental or maturational patterns have primacy over behaviors appearing later. Thus, patterns observed in mental defectives and caused by endogenous or exogenous disease have priority over later acquired patterns.

4. *Organic primacy.* Organic factors, where present, should be assigned primacy over functional factors.

5. *Temporal primacy.* The time at which signs and symptoms first appear usually is suggestive of the locus of origin of a disorder.

6. *Hierarchical priority.* At any one moment, lower-level integrations have priority over higher-level integrations.

a. *Physiological primacy.* Lower-level supporting functions provide the necessary foundations for higher-level functions.

b. *The primacy of the unconscious.* Whether subconscious (suppressed) or unconscious (repressed), factors operating below the level of consciousness should be assigned etiologic priority.

c. *Affective primacy.* Developmentally and functionally, emotional reactions tend to have primacy over intellectual reactions.

## HEN-EGG QUESTIONS IN ETIOLOGY

A major diagnostic problem consists in differentiating the exact etiologic priorities of various classes of determining factors. Much clinical theorizing of the past has arbitrarily arranged the priority of various classes of factors on purely theoretical grounds, without systematically investigating temporal sequences and etiologic relationships. Many difficult theoretical issues such as nature versus nurture, heredity versus environment, purposive versus mechanistic, and personal versus societal, and so on, are actually questions of etiology requiring complicated methods for their solution. Too often, purely theoretical solutions represent only the personal biases of some particular investigator.

Unfortunately, normal conditions of human living are so uncontrollable and complex that it is not possible to set up definitive research designs to discriminate etiologic relationships. This is particularly true in the study of individual cases, where it is often impossible either to observe specific episodes intensively or to reproduce them by study.

In addition to proper weighting of the priorities assigned to various primacies discussed in the last section, there are available, in the longitudinal study of the stream of life, many evidences of the temporal and etiologic relationships of many classes of factors. By charting the life record of a person, it is possible to differentiate actual sequences organized by recognizable and objectifiable factors. We need to be much more sophisticated in solving hen-egg questions by longitudinal studies of behavior rather than depending on purely theoretical relationships.

## ETIOLOGY AND THE INTEGRATIONAL MILIEU

The general principle is that achieving the highest level of integration of which a man is capable requires an optimum combination of circumstances in which all lower-level functions are operating perfectly in support of the high-level creative activity representing the highest achievement. Any interference on lower levels of supporting integrations tends to reduce the whole level of functioning to the lower level at which the disturbance is occurring. Thus, if a native genius lecturing on nuclear physics at a university were suddenly shot in the abdomen by a crazed student, the professor's level of integration would immediately descend to the problem of the wounded abdomen. Of course, a tremendously highly controlled person might finish out the lecture in a prodigious effort of will power, but maintaining integration in the face of such interference is beyond the ability of most men.

The concept of specific etiology involves a causal condition that is necessary, but not sufficient, for a disorder to occur. Meehl (1962) points out that the concept of specific etiology does not necessarily imply any of the following:

1. The etiological factor always or even usually, produces clinical illness.

2. If illness occurs, the particular form and content of symptoms is derivable by reference to the specific etiology alone.

3. The course of the illness can be materially influenced only by procedures directed against the specific etiology.

4. All persons who share the specific etiology will have closely similar symptoms, histories, and course.

5. The largest single contributor to symptom variance is the specific etiology.

The concept of the *integrational milieu* is necessary to depict the multidimensional, multilevel hierarchies of factors seeking expression, and which must be integrated if experience is to be unified. Both external and internal milieu must be considered and properly represented in any etiologic equation if situational and organismic factors are to be properly weighted. The internal milieu consists of the field of psychological forces seeking expression at any moment. The external milieu includes the patterns of environmental stimuli and pressures impinging on the person at any moment. It is necessary to conceive of both external and internal milieu as constantly changing and, consequently, requiring constant revision of the etiologic equation to reflect changes in the causation of psychological states.

This author has presented a comprehensive system of integrative psychology (Thorne, 1967), which is a necessary foundation for the theory of psychological states and a logical science of etiology (causation). This system postulates hierarchical levels of factors organizing the integration of psychological states. In order to understand the determination of psychological states, it is necessary to construct valid etiologic equations weighting the contribution of various levels of etiologic factors.

It must be emphasized that this system of integrative psychology involves an entirely different conception of the nature of diagnosis and the role of etiology. Integrative psychology is concerned basically with psychological states that reflect dynamic processes of organization, unification, and integration in ever changing patterns. The concept of etiology is necessary to comprehend the factors contributing to patterns of the integration of integrates. And valid etiological equations are necessary if any logical diagnostic system for psychological states is to be achieved.

## ETIOLOGY AND EXISTENTIAL STATUS

In *situ vivo*, under normal conditions of existence, each person is running the business of his life in the world; that is, doing something to satisfy his needs and motivations. It is only by understanding "what the person is doing," that behavior can be comprehended and predicted.

This means that psychological states are of primary importance in clinical diagnosis. Classical diagnostic approaches based on "trait" psychology rarely ask the pertinent question whether the traits in question have any direct relevance to the behavior under study. Thus, people with greatly differing traits may be doing the same thing, or people with the same traits may be doing different things. The pertinence of any assumed etiologic factor is a function of its contribution to psychological states that have clinical importance.

The difficulty with formal theories postulating some standard causation for *all* behaviors is that apparent fluctuation of psychological states, even during any twenty-four hour period, precludes any constant pattern of etiologic determiners. Neither the environment nor the organism can be presumed to hold constant over long temporal periods. In fact, the presumption is for change rather than constancy, so that constancy should not be taken for granted unless reliably demonstrated.

The concept of etiology has particular reference to the global unit of the status of "the person *running* the business of his life in the world." The concept of "running the business" implies executive management by the normal Self, which has available many constitutional resources and acquired resources in the form of learned controls.

## ETIOLOGY OF PERSONALITY STATES

The theory of the psychological state developed elsewhere (Thorne, 1966), properly emphasizes the need for discovering the etiological relationships underlying the constant flux and flow of integration levels as each person daily passes through an almost infinite variety of states ranging from deep sleep to the highest creative moments. No simple theory of behavior causation is capable of explaining such a wide gamut of psychological states. Only the most eclectic approach is capable of differentiating the constantly changing field of psychological forces underlying various states. It requires a very comprehensive integrative psychology to explain all the phenomena involved in the global unit of a-person-running-the-business-of-his-life-in-the-world.

Actually, it requires a whole series of etiological equations to explain the whole series of hierarchical integrations observed during any twenty-four hour period in the life of a complex person. Many of these etiological equations involve recurring cyclic patterns, such as waking and sleeping, which can be predicted with considerable regularity; for example, all behaviors organized by vegetative functions. Other behaviors occur as only one of a kind, determined by rare coincidences of factors not ordinarily occurring together, such as murder in a moment of passion. However, in all cases, the clinical problem is to differentiate the etiological factors organizing clinically significant integrations.

Psychological state theory places more emphasis on the nature of etiologic equations than does personality trait theory, because it is more difficult to explain behavior that is constantly changing with the onward rush of life. Psychologists interested in the commonalities of behavior (traditional trait theorists) are concerned with relatively constant formulas that have more or less universal applicability. Psychologists interested in psychological states are more interested in change than chance to explain unique individuality and changing psychology.

## THE ETIOLOGICAL EQUATION

Consistent with our viewpoint that behavior is a constantly changing status of organizational dynamics which can be understood only in terms of what the person is doing with his life, this chapter will not concern itself with hypothetical models of personality structure and dynamics which may have no specific application to particular persons. Clinically, we are interested in the specificities which determine the individuality and uniqueness of any status at any time and situation. We are interested specifically in discovering the special *etiologic equation* which describes the particular dynamic organization at any point in development. By *etiologic equation,* we mean the specific pattern of causative factors organizing any particular psychological state.

The eclectic viewpoint does not start with any preconceived models of organizational dynamics but is satisfied to differentiate the factors actually organizing any particular state. The eclectic method does not take it for granted that any particular organizational dynamic *may be* operating but requires evidence that *it is* operating. The eclectic method examines any postulated etiologic equation critically, and does not accept its validity until such is actually proven. Thus, the eclectic method may postulate several possible etiologic equations, as in differential diagnosis, from which the correct one is to be discriminated.

The basic postulate of dynamic psychology is that behavior is the resultant of psychological fields of forces in which all possible etiologic factors are represented including the interactions of heredity and environment, constitutional and acquired factors, drives, needs, affective impulses, past conditionings, imaginings of the future and various forms of self-determination. The dynamic approach also considers the characteristically individualized utilization of special mechanisms or complexes such as the Freudian concept of unconscious repressions, the Adlerian concept of life style, or existential concepts of self-transcendance. Here again, this book takes the position that it is the function of the competent clinical psychologist to apply basic psychological knowledge to the problem of identifying, differentiating, interpreting and explaining the various *states* of personality organization as can be demonstrated to exist. This problem of the differential diagnosis of dynamic etiologic equations is just beginning to be understood and the methods of accomplishing it are still in their infancy. It would be premature for this chapter to indicate the dimensions of a field which is just beginning to be developed. It is anticipated that future developments in the clinical study of psychological states will go hand in hand with future breakthroughs in basic science psychology.

POSTULATE: ANY STATUS OF PERSONALITY INTEGRATION IS A RESULTANT OF A PSYCHOLOGICAL FIELD OF FORCES WHICH CAN BE EXPRESSED IN AN ETIOLOGIC EQUATION IN WHICH THE DYNAMIC INTERACTION OF CAUSAL FACTORS IS VALIDLY REPRESENTED.

Two types of personality dynamics may be differentiated. First, in order to have any personality structure at all, it is necessary to have *organizational* or *integrational* dynamics to create the unified (unitized) whole which is personality. Second, in order to maintain existing personality structures, it is necessary to have *regulatory* or *defensive* dynamics to preserve the wholeness of personality. Both types of dynamics operate on subconscious and conscious levels. In general, it will be found that for purposes of explaining psychopathology, subconscious mechanisms are more important. For purposes of explaining positive personality growth and mental health, conscious mechanisms subject to voluntary control after training are more important in determining what man can be. For the purposes of this book, we shall discuss first the *master* personality dynamics of organization, integration and unification, which make possible the active shaping and evolving of global personality. Second, we shall discuss the dynamic mechanisms whereby the person solves problems and evolves his own distinctive offensive-defensive strategy for facing life (life style).

## DERIVING AN ETIOLOGICAL EQUATION

Derivation of the etiological equation depends upon some system for weighting the relative contributions of the various classes of etiologic factors. This can be accomplished only through an analysis of the dynamics of the specific psychological state under study. Unless some general set of principles or rules for weighting etiologic factors can be established, the selection of factors tends to become idiosyncratic, with each clinician making his own selection of factors according to his particular ideological biases.

The main source of diagnostic confusion derives from the fact that many classes of etiologic factors participate in the causation of psychological states in secondary roles, and from these must be differentiated the factors with primary dynamic significance. For example, the most complex molar behaviors may be traced back even to molecular subfunctions, but this does not necessarily imply that the actual dynamics are molecular. While certain molecular conditions may need to be present for a reaction to occur, the actual dynamic factors may not be represented on molecular levels.

Recognizing that the status of any organism reflects all that has occurred in its entire past history, so that all such classes of historical causes *may* make some contribution to current status, it must be emphasized that the nexus of current dynamics lies in the present to the degree that the person is capable of reacting adaptively to the existing field of psychological forces.

The basic diagnostic questions therefore relate to the status of current dynamics so as to determine how various classes of possible etiologic factors influence it.

A practical clinical approach to the differentiation of etiological patterns is presented in the following outline of questions, which experience has indicated to be important in understanding psychological states:

I.  To what degree is any psychological state normal (in the sense of consisting of flexible coping behaviors properly reflecting all pertinent factors necessary to achieve a correct problem solution) or pathological (in the sense optimal integrations are not achieved)?

II.  If optimal integrations have not been achieved, are pathological patterns caused by excesses and/or deficits of (a) organismic or (b) situational determining factors?

III.  If organismic factors are prepotent, are they genetic, constitutional, or acquired? To what extent do these organismic factors involve "inner process" factors which are presumed to be involuntary and caused by depth factors outside the person's conscious knowledge and control, or are they conscious and subject to rational control?

IV.  If situational factors are prepotent, what stresses are involved, and to what degree can it be expected that the person can adjust to them. How can the person be taught to cope with the environment? Or can change be expected only by modifying the environment?

The reader should note that these questions relate to specific situational-existential loci in the life of the person; that is, to specific psychological states, which the person is observed to get into, or can be expected to get into on the basis of knowledge of etiological causes. This type of integrational diagnosis is entirely different from classical diagnosis directed towards the recognition of diseases or the identification and measurement of fixed personality traits. We are concerned here with patterns and levels of integration underlying clinically observable psychological states.

## FORMATS FOR ETIOLOGICAL EQUATIONS

All differential diagnosis has the objective of identifying and interrelating the various classes of etiologic factors which determine any behavior. Although purely chance factors may determine some patterns, usually there arises a concatenation of contributing factors which require diagnostic evaluation as to their priority as etiologic agents. Any complete etiologic equation should consider the following classes of causative factors:

    1.   Primary etiologic factors. The specific agent determining the nature of the condition which could not occur without it.

    2.   Secondary etiologic factors. Reactions or outcomes stemming from the primary factor.

    3.   Predisposing factors. The background of constitutional and experiential factors determining predispositions to react in certain ways.

    4.   Precipitating factors. Agents which lower the threshold for the appearance or operation of primary or secondary factors.

    5.   Personality reactions. The response of the person to what is happening to him.

    6.   Undifferentiated factors.

Practically, it is a matter of clinical judgment to assign weights to various classes of etiologic factors according to the indications of a particular case. The actual format of the etiologic equation usually reflects the clinician's opinion of the relative importance of the various classes of factors, and may be modified to suit the particular requirements of the clinical situation.

Past conceptions of etiology have suffered from oversimplification and failure to consider the multifactorial determination of even the simplest behaviors. Behavior is infinitely more complexly determined than generally accepted even among psychological scientists. The various schools of psychology have been guilty of oversimplified conceptions, often attempting to explain all of behaviors in terms of one principle. In addition to the complexities of genetic determination, it is literally true that everything which has happened to a person is a potential determiner of future behavior.

## CLASSIFICATION OF ETIOLOGICAL EQUATIONS

The comparative analysis of different theories and hypotheses concerning psychopathology is facilitated by translating any formulation into prototypical etiological equations which can then be compared with established formulations to discover whether anything new and unique has been added. There are only a limited number of etiological factors known to be operating, and most "new" contributions turn out to be variants of some older theory.

Class I.   Biogenetic Determination

DEFINING STATEMENTS

1.   Genetic factors are primary.

2.   Genetic factors show varying degrees of penetrance interacting with environmental factors. Overt expression depends on degree of penetrance.

3.   Genetic factors are difficult to modify directly, but compensatory adjustments are often possible.

CHARACTERISTIC ETIOLOGICAL EQUATIONS

Ia.   Genotype + High Penetrance + Environmental Stress = Hereditary Defects and/or Disease.

Selective inbreeding of lower classes + Impoverishment of lower-class environments = General Behavioral Inadequacy.

Ib.   Genotypical C.N.S. Disease = Endogenous Mental Deficiency.

Ic.   Genetic Schizotypia + Schizophrenic Mothering = Schizophrenia (Meehl, 1962).

Id.   High Schizotypia + High Penetrance = Process Schizophrenia.

Ie.   Low Schizotypia + Intense Stress (usually interpersonal) = Reactive Schizophrenia.

IMPLICATIONS FOR THE PSYCHOLOGY OF INTEGRATION

1.   Insufficient attention has been given in American psychology to genetic determiners of behavior. In the face of such somatic and structural variability as is manifestly apparent in humans, it is inevitable that a comparable behavioral variability must occur as a functional accompaniment of genetic variability.

2.   The basic humanness of man is genetically determined, as is the tremendous variability of innate abilities and temperamental patterns. Different genetic constitutions obviously have differential survival value and values in human relations. Genetic differences in beauty, strength, intelligence, temperament, and health obviously shape the possibilities for being in every culture.

3.   Broadly stated, the types and levels of integration of which a person is capable are determined genetically. Unless personally and socially valuable genetic factors achieve penetrance, and are maximized by a favorable environment, the possibilities for existence are drastically limited.

Class II.   Constitutional Determination

DEFINING STATEMENTS

1.   Constitutional factors are primary and organismic.

2.   Constitutional factors are usually not reversible, although some compensatory adjustments usually can be made.

3.   Abnormal development or injury results in somatic defects which are reflected in functional deficits.

4.   Psychobiologic reaction types are important in determining not only developmental patterns but also types of reaction to stress, susceptibility to illness, and thresholds of breakdown.

5.   Constitutional typologies are considered important, though more complexly determined by genetic and constitutional factors than formerly conceived.

6.   Congenital, developmental, maturational or traumatic defects result in organic deficits.

CHARACTERISTIC ETIOLOGICAL EQUATIONS

IIa.   Constitutional Disorder = Somatic Defects + Impaired Functions = Irreversible Deficits.

IIb.   Traumatic C.N.S. Damage (early childhood) = Exogenous Mental Deficiency.

Traumatic C.N.S. Damage (later Life) = Organic Encephalopathy.

IIc.   Constitutional Organ Weakness + High Stress Level = Shock Organ Lability + Organ symptoms = Psychosomatic Disorder.

IId.   Constitutional Inadequacy + Failures in Life = Constitutional Psychopathic Inferior.

IMPLICATIONS FOR THE PSYCHOLOGY OF INTEGRATION

1.   Normal functioning usually depends upon an intact soma. No basis for integration exists in the absence of intact soma.

2.   Gross defects or damage in any organ systems must limit functions accordingly. Cellular pathology must impair functional integrations of the organ system.

3.   Organic damage tends to be irreversible, particularly in the central nervous system, although some compensatory adjustments may be possible.

4.   Organic damage occurring prenatally or in early childhood precludes any possibility of normal personality development and integration, in proportion to its severity, producing syndromes of mental deficiency.

5.   Organic damage, occurring after normal personality development has already occurred, results in syndromes of organic deficit or psychosis characterized by progressive mental deterioration and loss of integrational capacity.

6.   Constitutional resources and deficits importantly determine levels of integration achieved.

## Class III.   Pathological Physiological Determination

DEFINING STATEMENTS

1.   No discernible somatic and/or organic defects.
2.   Disordered psychophysiological supporting functions.
3.   Functional disorder. Pathological physiology may be reversible.
4.   Basically, an imbalance of excitation versus inhibition.

CHARACTERISTIC ETIOLOGICAL EQUATIONS

IIIa.   Defective inhibition processes = Failure of extinction + Less stimulus generalization = Attention + Concentration Defects. (Pavlov, 1928).

Activation deficit + Parasympathetic dominance = Broadening of attention in acute schizophrenia. (Venable).

Activation excess + Narrowing of attention = Chronic Schizophrenia.

IIIb.   Breakdown of discrimination due to ambiguous stimulus + Loss of equilibrium in cortical excitation and inhibition = Experimental Neurosis. (Pavlov, 1928).

IIIc.   Conflict gradients (approach-approach, avoidance-avoidance, approach-avoidance, double approach-avoidance) + Differential or inconsistent reinforcement = Neurotic Disability. (Miller, Mowrer, and Ullman).

IIId.   Chronic over-arousal + Breakdown inhibitions = Anxiety. (Malmo, 1957).

IIIe.   Unspecified neurophysiological disorder + associative disorders = Schizophrenia.

IIIf.   Cycloid affectivity + Psychosocial stress + Imbalance of excitation-inhibition = Manic-depressive Psychosis.

IIIg.   Climacteric glandular changes + Menopause = Involutional Melancholia.

IIIh.   Drug habituation + Withdrawal symptoms + High cost of drugs = Addiction and delinquency.

IIIi.   Conditioned inhibition of normal excitatory processes = Neurosis manifested by inhibitory personality type, low self-sufficiency and conflict. (Salter).

IMPLICATIONS FOR THE PSYCHOLOGY OF INTEGRATION

1.   High-level integrations depend upon intact lower-level psycho-physiological supporting functions.

2.   Disordered lower-level functions interfere with or prevent higher-level integrations.

3.   Disorders of any integrational levels may radiate upwards or downwards, disrupting other levels of integration.

4.   Psychophysiological deficits produce functional mental disorders which tend to be reversible and not associated with mental deterioration.

5.   Psychophysiological supporting functions generally are not subject to conscious voluntary controls, however various therapeutic methods are available for balancing excitatory and inhibitory functions.

## Class IV.   Affective or Emotional Conflict Determination (Freud)

DEFINING STATEMENTS

1.   Intense emotional ambivalence is primary in conflict situations.

2.   Affective drives may be so intense as not to be controllable volitionally.

3.   Strong affective-impulsive drives (Freudian Id) seek expression in conflict with censoring Super Ego factors and are controlled by repression and other mechanisms. Sources of conflict may be conscious or unconscious.

4.   Traumatic conditionings and unresolved complexes in psycho-sexual development underly later neuroses and reaction formations.

5.   Symptom formations express latent meanings of conflicts symbolically and frequently are maintained by secondary gain reinforcements.

CHARACTERISTIC ETIOLOGICAL EQUATIONS

IVa.   Strong libidinous Id impulses + Super Ego censoring + repression or other mechanisms = Reaction and Symptom Formations. (Freud).

Strong unacceptable impulses + Repression = Neurosis.

Strong unacceptable impulses + strong Super Ego + weak Ego = Failing controls = Anxiety = Dependency and protection needs = Seeks hospitalization.

IVb.   Psychic conflict on higher levels of integration + Anxiety + Affective tensions radiating downwards to disturb lower-level vegetative integrations = Psychosomatic syndromes.

IVc.   High affective ambivalence + Anger directed inwards = Suicide.

High ambivalence + Anger directed outwards = Homicide.

Frustration + hostility = Aggression.

IVd.　Psychic trauma + Childish grief reactions = Autopsycho-drama (APSDR). (Arndt).

V.　Weakening Super-Ego control + Threatened return of the Repressed = Anxiety (panic) or Depression. (Freud).

VI.　Id-dominated Ego + Ignoring the protests of conscience (Super-Ego) = Anxiety or Depression. (Mowrer, 1960).

IMPLICATIONS FOR THE PSYCHOLOGY OF INTEGRATION

1.　Every person passes through a series of developmental stages which may involve various patterns of regression, fixation, or neurotic symptom formation.

2.　Every person is exposed to a wide variety of traumatic factors at all stages of development.

3.　Extremely severe trauma, or trauma occurring at critical periods of development, may seriously block growth and development.

4.　Each person shows characteristic thresholds of breakdown of integration under stress, developing characteristic patterns of neurotic or psychotic reaction.

5.　Persons with strong Ego functioning may be able to exert sufficient controls to maintain integration even under great stress.

6.　Neurotic symptom and reaction formations due to repression of strong conflictual impulses may result in chronic disability due to impaired integrational patterns. Mixed neuroses with high obsessive-compulsive complexes may flood consciousness with disturbing symptoms. Growth and development are blocked.

### Class V.　Cognitive Behavior Determination (Ellis, 1958; Kelly, 1955; Thorne, 1955)

DEFINING STATEMENTS

1.　Factors of perception, learning and rational thinking are primary.

2.　Normality of perception, learning and thinking processes is an essential prerequisite of normal ideation.

3.　Ideological inconsistency and error results from failure of rational-logical thinking.

4.　Attempts to act out the implications of irrational ideas result in breakdown or failure of coping behaviors.

5.　Personal constructs determine the *Weltanschauung*.

CHARACTERISTIC ETIOLOGICAL EQUATIONS

Va.　Disordered perceptions + Misinterpretation of Reality = Psychosis.

Vb.   Learned idea + Absence of conflicting ideas = Ideomotor action (Ideas tend to be acted out) Illogical ideation = Error.
Vc.   Invalid ideological conditionings = Behavioral eccentricity.
Vd.   Invalid personal constructs = Loss of contact with Reality.

IMPLICATIONS FOR THE PSYCHOLOGY OF INTEGRATION

1.   While lower-level integrations depend upon the integrity of psychophysiological supporting functions, the highest level integrations function autonomously, being organized by purely psychic factors operating in terms of their own meanings, that is, rational-intellectual factors are evolutionary mutants, introducing newer high-level factors of symbolism and creative thinking.

2.   When lower-level functions are operating normally providing "silent" support of the psyche, the person is free to react cognitively in coping with the business of running the business of his life in the world rationally.

3.   Higher-level integrations are organized by purely psychic factors, including motives, purposes, goals, ideas, values and ideals, which can be understood only in terms of their own meanings.

4.   The content of thought, including both manifest and latent meanings, becomes an important determiner of ideological integrations.

## Class VI.   Conditioned Mental Context Determination

DEFINING STATEMENTS

1.   Conditioned factors are primary. Each person has his own unique background of experience, both personal and social.

2.   Failure to learn results in experiential deficits, resulting in blindspots of experience.

3.   Traumatic conditioning results in pathological contents of learning and warping of personality.

4.   Conditioned patterns may be unlearned and relearned, therefore being largely reversible.

5.   Conditioning produces specific individual attitudes and dispositions to react in certain ways on the basis of cumulative experiences.

CHARACTERISTIC ETIOLOGIC EQUATIONS

VIa.   Normal genotype and constitution + Extreme experiential deprivation = Functional mental retardation (Wolf child).
VIb.   Normal genotype and constitution + Learning by imitation of pathologic behaviors = Conditioned behavior disorders (*folie à deux,* and so on).

VIc. Operant conditioning + Suitable reinforcement = Conditioned behavior disorder.

VId. Cultural deprivation + Experiential deficits = Behavioral inadaptibility (provincialism). (Thorne).

VIe. Critical period for imprinting + Contact with suitable object = Conditioned object cathexes. (Freud).

Critical period for imprinting + Homosexual seduction = Sexual inversion.

VIf. Strong drive (or antagonistic drives) + Unavailability of proper object = Displacement of activity to unsuitable object. (Bindra, 1959).

VIg. Traumatic interpersonal relations + Conditioned aversion and/or hostility reactions + Reintegration = Attitudinal psychopathy. (Thorne).

Mental context (particularly attitudinal) determines behavioral repertoire in specific situations. (Thorne).

VIh. Education and/or training + Acquisition of specific skills and controls = Experiential behavior repertoire.

VIi. Criminal environment + Peer reinforcement of social acts = Social delinquency.

IMPLICATIONS FOR THE PSYCHOLOGY OF INTEGRATION

1. Progressively higher-level integrations involve skilled acts depending upon conditioning, training, and acquisition of increasingly complex controls.

2. The highest-level integrations depend upon increasingly complex behaviors involving the learning of skills, talents and experience.

3. Mental context reflects the individual's particular background of experience and knowledge.

4. Complicated controls are acquired only through training and experience under conditions of increasing stress.

5. All behavior modification depends ultimately upon learning, education, unlearning, and relearning.

## Class VII. Role-Playing and Social Status Determination

DEFINING STATEMENTS

1. Failures in role-playing or failure to earn potential social status are primary.

2. Overall adjustment in running the business of life depends on playing many roles well.

3. Major failures in playing even a single important role may result in serious social inadaptibility and personal demoralization.

4. Role successes and failures to some degree determine social status.

5. Social status is to some extent environmentally determined but may be compensated for by individual effort and success.

6. Social status factors importantly determine ultimate success or failure, that is, achieving a social situation where self-actualization can take place or is potentiated.

7. Personal role constructs determine action tendencies. (Kelly, 1955).

CHARACTERISTIC ETIOLOGIC EQUATIONS

VIIa. Lack of role-playing skills + Social isolation and inadaptibility = Schizophrenia. (Cameron, 1947).

VIIb. Failure in playing important roles + Social rejection = Anxiety reactions. (Thorne).

VIIc. Failure to learn roles + Social inadaptibility = Specific situational disabilities. (Thorne).

VIId. Minority group membership (females, Negroes) + Social status restrictions = Chronic frustration states.

VIIe. Downward social mobility + Lowered social status = Inferiority complex.

VIIf. Misconstruing social roles = Failure and frustration. (Kelly, 1955).

IMPLICATIONS FOR THE PSYCHOLOGY OF INTEGRATION

1. Even though all supporting systems may be functioning normally, the failure to play important roles well may result in serious situational inadaptibility.

2. Role-playing deficiencies may be responsible for unbalanced personalities with important areas of conflict and inadaptibility.

3. Many functionally normal behaviors have low psychosocial adaptive value.

4. Social status failures importantly influence the Self concept.

Class VIII.   Self Concept and Ego Structure Determination

DEFINING STATEMENTS

1. Disordered Self concept/Ego functioning is primary.

2. The Self concept is an important determiner of Ego strength.

3. The Self concept is the nucleus of self-regard. A positive Self concept contributes self-respect and confidence. Conversely, a negative Self concept causes feelings of inadequacy and lack of self confidence.

4. The Self concept largely determines what a person thinks he can do, and how he reacts to life in general.

5. Ego strength determines the ability to remain integrated and maintain executive functions of the Self under stress.

6. All mental disorders are characterized by the failure to develop controls or the breakdown of controls.

7. Many disorders are determined by a person's reaction to himself.

IMPLICATIONS FOR THE PSYCHOLOGY OF INTEGRATION

VIIIa. Low Self concept + Lack of confidence = Poor performance = Inferiority Complex. (Adler, 1956).

VIIIb. Low Self concept + Anxiety over failure = Defensive reaction formations = Existential anxiety. (Thorne).

VIIIc. Weak Ego functioning + High stress = Personality disintegration caused by breakdown of controls.

VIIId. Self-damaging errors + Ego deflation = Lowered Self concept and guilt.

VIIIe. Self-anger + Frustration and aggression directed inwardly = Depression and suicide.

VIIIf. Lack of Self consistency + Conflictual actions = Neurosis. (Lecky, 1951, Thorne).

1. The Self concept is a high-level general factor, the valence of which determines the valence of attitudes towards the Self and Others.

2. The composition of the Self concept determines the levels of performance and achievement to which the person aspires.

3. The person must like himself in order to have Self confidence and be able to face the world. However, some dissatisfaction with Self status may be a necessary precondition for change.

4. Important discrepancies between the Actual and Ideal Self statuses may result in anxiety, which ideally may stimulate compensatory efforts. Too great Self inconsistencies or discrepancy between actual and ideal Selves may result in demoralization.

5. Higher-level integrations depend upon volitional consciousness, normal operation of controls, and intact executive Self functioning.

6. Mental health depends upon strong Ego functioning.

## Class IX.   Life Style Determination (Adler, 1956)

DEFINING STATEMENTS

1. Each person develops a more or less distinctive offensive-defensive strategy and tactics for satisfying needs and achieving goals in running the business of life. This strategic-tactical pattern is the life style.

2. Life style is learned and acquired through experience. Unhealthy life styles may be learned by imitation, by classical conditioning or by

operant conditioning.

3. The life style characteristically involves typical uses of mechanisms, reaction formations, gamesmanship, etc.

4. Neurotic life styles are supported by secondary gains.

CHARACTERISTIC ETIOLOGIC EQUATIONS

IXa. Three basic life styles are observable: Going with people, going against people, and going away from people. (Horney, 1945).

IXb. Childhood pampering + Spoiling + Protection from natural consequences of selfish behavior = Adult character disorder. (Adler).

IXc. Overprotection + spoiling = Ego inflation.
Ego inflation + "taking" life style = Sociopathy. (Thorne).

IXd. Conditioned Avoidance Reactions (CAV) = Escapist Life Style.

IMPLICATIONS FOR THE PSYCHOLOGY OF INTEGRATION

1. The life style is an important mechanism for controlling or reducing tension and conflict on psychosocial levels. Any particular life style is characterized by different levels of social adaptibility.

2. Maladaptive life styles result in failure and frustration with accompanying regression and disintegration.

3. Patterns may be integrated normally but inefficient because socially unacceptable.

### Class X.   Interpersonal Transactional Determination
### (Sullivan, 1953; Berne, 1963)

DEFINING STATEMENTS

1. Unhealthy interpersonal relations are a primary factor in all psychological disorders.

2. The concepts of *mental illness* and *mental disease* are misnomers based on inappropriate medical models. There are only disturbed interpersonal relations. (Szasz, 1961).

3. Maladaptive human relations are the main cause of emotional conflicts. Pathogenic human relations may produce various patterns of psychological disorder.

4. Persons may interact on different levels of child, parent or normal adult Self. (Berne, 1963)

5. Psychopathology stems from the relation between the person and important others. (Sullivan, 1953)

6. Transactional disorders are usually associated with vicious circles of interpersonal neurotic reactions.

Xa.  Severe psychosocial stress + Maladaptive interpersonal reactions = Mental disorder.

Parental rejection (double binds) + Breakdown of communication = Anxiety and defensive reactions in the child.

Unsatisfying human relations + Social isolation = Schizophrenia.

Xb.  Maternal dominance + Poor identification with father = Schizophrenic "mothering."

Xc.  Identification with mother rather than father (in male children) = Sexual inversion.

Xd.  Passivity + Hostility = Catatonic reactions.

Xe.  Interpersonal communications on different maturational levels = Communication breakdowns and neurotic interactions.

Xf.  Double-bind stimulation + Ambivalent emotional reactions + Conflict = Neurotic conditioning.

IMPLICATIONS FOR THE PSYCHOLOGY OF INTEGRATION

1.  Pathological social conditionings and interpersonal relationships lead to unhealthy coping reactions, conflict and frustration, and inability to establish mature integrational patterns.

2.  Certain environments and interpersonal relationships are pathogenic and productive of neurotic interactions.

3.  Disintegrating conflict arises from ambivalence, double bind relationships, and prolonged exposure to negative emotionality in others.

4.  Dominance-submission relationships are important determiners of levels of integration in social situations.

## Class XI.   Existential Status Determination

DEFINING STATEMENTS

1.  Existential status reactions are primary. These relate to the overall status of the person running the business of his life in the world, that is, the state of being in the world.

2.  Each person must develop a healthy grasp on Being-in-the-World.

3.  Existential status is a function of the cumulative balance of success/failure in running one's life.

4.  Life must have meanings. An existential vacuum results when life has no meanings.

5.  Each person must feel that his life is worthwhile.

CHARACTERISTIC ETIOLOGIC EQUATIONS

XIa.  Low success/high failure ratio = Existential anxiety.

XIb.  Existential failure + Guilt = Depression + Suicide.

XIc.  Low Self concept + Lack of meanings in life = Existential vacuum.

XId.  Existential vacuum + Loss of morale = Demoralization.

XIe.  Existential failure + Existential vacuum = Despair.

XIf.  Demoralization + Despair = Nothingness.

IMPLICATIONS FOR THE PSYCHOLOGY OF INTEGRATION

1.  Existential status reactions, reflecting the relative balance of success and failure in life, influence the self concept and may stimulate defensive reactions inhibiting higher-level integrations if withdrawal and denial reactions develop.

2.  Success reinforces feelings of security and self worth. One unit of success is the antidote for one unit of existential anxiety. Conversely, failure stimulates insecurity and self depreciation.

3.  Insecure persons, oversensitized to failure, may choose "safe" regressive integrative status in preference to dangerous higher-level integrations.

4.  Life may overwhelm a person if cumulative failure and unhappiness so tax personality resources that the person becomes demoralized and cannot go on fighting any longer, that is, the struggle to maintain high-level integrations becomes too difficult. The person "has had it" and "is burned out."

5.  Undue pain or distress in life, particularly when associated with perceptions of being a failure in life are a primal source of anxiety.

Class XII.   Social-Environmental Determination
(Szasz, 1961; Adams, 1964; Pratt)

DEFINING STATEMENTS

1.  Cultural relativity theories emphasize that judgments of good-bad, healthy-unhealthy, normal-abnormal, and so on, are relative to local mores and standards. What is accepted in one culture may be considered devant in another; therefore, there are no absolute standards of normality.

2.  Relative cultural factors determine the "goodness," deviancy, or normality of individual behaviors. Different cultures develop different standards of value, and hence encourage or reinforce contradictory values dependent upon local preferences.

3.  Pathological subcultures may produce behaviors which are considered "normal" by the subculture but abnormal by society in general. Conversely, pathological subcultures may consider normal behavior as "pathological."

4. It may be normal for a deviant person to be himself. That is, it may be normal for a sexual invert to be homosexual in that he might become sick if he attempted to be heterosexual.

CHARACTERISTIC ETIOLOGIC EQUATIONS

**XIIa.** Deviant subcultural conditionings (that is, criminal environment) + Reinforcements of deviant behaviors by cultural peers = Character disorders.

**XIIb.** Underprivileged subcultures + Higher social disorganization + Higher stress in lower classes = Schizophrenic reactions. (Redlich and Hollingshead).

**XIIc.** Social disarticulation (isolation) + decreased reality control over thinking = Schizophrenic thought and cognitive disorders (over- and under-inclusion, fragmentation and interpenetration. (Cameron, 1947).

**XIId.** Social trauma + Critical developmental periods = Neurosis. (Freud).

**XIIe.** Subcultural factors (underprivilege, criminal and gang associations) + Social rejection + Frustration = Asocial psychopathy and criminality.

**XIIf.** Constitutional sexual inversion + Social rejection + Guilt = Paranoid schizophrenia.

**XIIg.** Prisonation + Selective reinforcement of asocial attitudes by prison peers = Criminal recidivist.

IMPLICATIONS FOR THE PSYCHOLOGY OF INTEGRATION

1. The normality of integrational patterns is to be interpreted in terms of cultural relativity.

2. Many integrational patterns are determined by social-cultural factors and hence should be influenced by manipulations of the environment.

3. The culture creates the deviance, that is, the culture rather than the person is sick. The culture should be modified.

4. Many pathological reactions and deviancies simply reflect the person's efforts to integrate cultural relativity factors.

## DIAGNOSTIC IMPLICATIONS

At current stages of the evolution of clinical diagnostic methods, only the *direct examination* is capable of dealing with the large number of potential etiologic factors. The reason for this is that only the trained clinician is capable of identifying and comprehending the relationships of the complex etiologic factors in the constantly changing sequence of psychological states constituting behavior patterns. Only from intensive knowledge of a person, and particularly his needs, habits, and motivational dynamics, can behavior be predicted.

Unfortunately, contemporary psychological tests and objective methods are not adapted to the measurement of changing psychological states except as they may be administered repeatedly to measure clinically significant mental status changes. Furthermore, objective tests have not been standardized to measure higher-level patterns determined by ideological status, role and social status, life styles, or existential status.

Much depends upon the clinical discrimination of the relation of overt behaviors to what the person is "doing" at any important existential locus in life. Occasionally, "what the person is doing" may be discriminated or inferred from external observations alone. More commonly, it is necessary for the person himself to report introspectively not only what he is doing, but also concerning his mental status. The ancient question "a penny for your thoughts" is particularly relevant here. There is no substitute for the broadest clinical experience in understanding not only what people are doing but also in what ways their behaviors are clinically important. Frequently, there is no substitute for direct questioning of the client to discover what he is doing, feeling, thinking, or believes if anything is the matter with him.

## FORMULATING AN ETIOLOGIC EQUATION

In individual cases, it is desirable to follow a systematic outline in differentiating the various classes of etiologic factors and formulating an individual etiologic equation *inductively*. While it is sometimes possible to arrive at etiologic equations *deductively*, by considering which of the standard etiologic equations may apply to a single case, the more valid and clinically safer procedure is to formulate individual equations inductively for each case.

The basic problem is to demonstrate the etiologic relationships between (a) *trait factors* representing relatively constant and fixed organismic personality factors, and (b) *state factors* representing the momentary psychological state reactive to situational-existential loci. Although theoretical etiologic equations (as discussed earlier) may be postulated on the basis of empirical or statistical experience with certain general types of syndromes, actual etiologic equations constructed for individual cases always are related to specific situations of the person running the business of his life in the world. The following outline indicates a standard approach to the main classes of etiologic factors.

I. *Demographic factors.* These provide a general orientation to the type of person being dealt with.

    1.  Sex and marital status.
    2.  Age.
    3.  Race.
    4.  Education.
    5.  Employment type and status.
    6.  Socioeconomic status.

II. *Psychobiologic factors.* These relate to general *organismic* status indicating the biologic resources and deficits of the person.

    1.  Somatic type and status, including defects and deformities.
    2.  Physical health status, including relevant disease factors.
    3.  Psychosomatic status, psychophysiological factors.
    4.  Temperament. Affective status.
    5.  Intellect. Cognitive level and status.
    6.  Conation. Volitional status.

III. *Mental context.* This includes background predispositional factors relating to acquired patterns of conditioning, education, training, and cultural factors.

    1.  Habits.
    2.  Conditioned approach and avoidance reactions (CAP, CAV).
    3.  Ideological-attitudinal reaction patterns.
    4.  Role-playing and social status factors.
    5.  Life style patterns.

IV. *Existential status.* The momentary status of the Self including the momentary integrational milieu ("the spot the person finds himself in").

    1.  Self concept status. Actual versus ideal self concepts and discrepancies.
    2.  Executive self status. Status of self control.
    3.  Existential loci status. Life management problems.
    4.  Morale and motivational status. Meanings and Values in life.

V. *Situational-environment press status.* The momentary life problems the person is faced with.

It is exceedingly difficult to formulate a clinical description of a person which provides a recognizable depiction differentiating him from any other person. This cannot be accomplished using general clinical terms, derived from tests or measurements, which might apply to anyone. It can be achieved only by reference to the specific demographic, organismic, mental contextual, existential, and situational factors specific to one person at a given point in life. The exact quality of a person can be known only through intimate acquaintance, and cannot be derived from mechanical test scoring.

The next step consists in analyzing the various factors involved in clinically important data to establish their etiologic priority according to some outline such as the following:

1. Primary Etiologic Factor. Specific agent in the absence of which the condition could not occur.
2. Predisposing Factors. Constitutional and experiential factors providing the historical background of the condition.
3. Precipitating Factors. Secondary factors lowering the threshold or increasing the disposition to react, that is, "the last straw."
4. Secondary Personality Reactions. The person's reaction to his condition.
5. Situational-environmental Factors. The situational press.
6. Undifferentiated Factors.

Clinical judgment is the only tool available for evaluating, differentiating, and weighing all the various classes of factors etiologic to a psychological condition. The cookbook rules and actuarial methods which have been developed for standard tests, such as the MMPI cannot come up with more than generalized trait descriptions of a limited number of factors which usually are not relative to clinical problems. Current testing methods do not even include measures for many of the etiologic factors postulated as important. In many areas, clinical judgment is far ahead of objective measurement where suitable methods may not even be available.

## Illustrative Clinical Case Analysis

I. DEMOGRAPHIC DATA

Mrs. J, age thirty-one, white, one year junior college, housewife, three children, upper socioeconomic class.

## II. PSYCHOBIOLOGIC FACTORS

A petite, pretty blonde woman, small sharp features approaching real beauty. Alert, vivacious, and lively. Physically small, weighing 103 pounds, height five feet, three inches. Marked autonomic instability; severe psychosomatic symptoms under emotional stress including severe headaches, nausea, gastric hyperacidity, and asthenia.

Cheerful and happy when not under stress. Only moderate emotional stability; tends to collapse under pressure. IQ about 110; considered clever but not intellectual. Impulsive and immature in levels of control. Tends to follow pleasure-pain principle.

## III. MENTAL CONTEXT FACTORS

The youngest and spoiled child of a lower middle-class family, among whom she stood out like a princess among plain people. Always deferred to and got the best of everything.

Slipped through school easily on her pleasant personality. Somewhat of a teacher's pet. Also halo effect because teachers looked forward to having such a pretty little girl in class.

Early became preoccupied with materialism: sought pretty clothing, beauty culture, stylish cars, and high society. Considered a gold digger and a social climber. Evidently had her eyes on the main chance since adolescence. Chose her friends carefully and dated only upper-class boys to whom she allowed no intimacies.

Became a popular member of the "hamburger and coke" society. Ran around in the best circles to parties, dances, and so on, but never went "steady" with one boy until age twenty when she charmed the son of one of the wealthy first families, and was soon married.

## IV. EXISTENTIAL STATUS AND PROBLEMS

After the excitement of courtship and honeymoon died down, and she had had two children in rapid succession, she began to show a characteristic pattern of "nervous breakdown." Once or twice a year, she would suddenly break down, become anxious, tense, hysterical, and neurotically depressed. Everything got on her nerves and bothered her. After six to eight weeks in a sanatorium, she would quiet down and resume her duties.

Soon after marriage, she suddenly realized she was over her depth socially. Her husband's friends had more education, social background, and social confidence. She soon found that her superficial charms were not enough. Other upper-class women tended to look down on her as a social climber. She felt out of place and insecure in social entertaining.

Her Ego Strength, never high, began to fail. Her inflated Self concepts derived from the spoiled child situation came under heavy attack, and she was faced with the recognition that she was not "up" to her new social responsibilities. Developed severe existential anxiety over failing in marriage, losing her husband's respect, being rejected socially, and so forth.

Her morale and motivation to succeed became progressively lowered. She would struggle for a few months to manage her affairs, but gradually things would go bad. Her children began to escape from discipline, and she felt herself becoming very hostile towards them. She began to neglect herself and her household duties, and to drink too much.

### V. THE SITUATIONAL PRESS

Her acute decompensations were almost always precipitated by some increased social demands placed upon her by her husband or social friends. She would be expected to put on a big dinner, or take part in the arrangements for a big social event, or entertain her husband's business associates. She would struggle to put on a good front, but the pressures were too much, and she would collapse emotionally and have to be hospitalized because of severe emotional instability or acute alcoholism.

## Etiological Equation

*Primary factor:* Self-concept inconsistency between actual and ideal concepts, low Ego Strength, and poor executive Self functioning.

*Predisposing factors:* Educational, social and experiential deficiencies in relation to upper-class demands. Inadequacies in many types of role-playings. Preoccupation with materialistic considerations led her to marry above herself and out of her class. Organismic factors include autonomic lability and low thresholds of psychophysiologic breakdown.

*Precipitating factors:* Literally speaking, she had "minor league" social talents and found herself unable to cope with "big league" social pressures. Although pretty and charming, she did not have the personality resources to compete with upper-class peers who soon recognized her short-comings and did not really admit her to their "inner circle" in spite of her husband's prestige. Periodic increases in the social press increased her inner turmoil to the threshold of loss of control.

## Therapeutic Indications

Two alternative plans for therapy seem possible. (1) An intensive total-push rehabilitation and retraining program would attempt to maximize her resources and teach her the skills necessary to cope with the demands upon her. Thus far, this approach has failed. She has had intensive therapy on several occasions including a brief psychoanalytic experience which uncovered her frustrations and hostilities but still left her unable to cope with them. (2) She might be persuaded to lower her Ego ideals, recognize that she is basically an average middle-class person, and rearrange her life so as to live under comfortable conditions within her social resources. This would involve renouncing upper-class "high" life, limiting herself to friends with whom she felt comfortable, not undertaking more than she can accomplish, and perhaps even divorcing her husband if his way of life imposes intolerable demands upon her. The basic decision here is to renounce high-level competition and stick to her own class.

### Follow-up Notes

A therapeutic plan was formulated combining both alternatives listed above. The following steps were indicated:

1.  Interpretation and reassurance concerning the acute symptoms of decompensation. Symptomatic behavior therapy was instituted to desensitize and extinguish conditioned avoidance reactions.
2.  Intensive tutoring and re-education concerning how to handle immediate situational problems.
3.  Discussion of Self concepts, ego deflation, ego involvements in social class problems. Assignment of therapeutic tasks to increase self confidence, ego strength, and lessen unhealthy ego involvements.
4.  Reconsideration of whole life plan, existential problems, and future needs.

The following things therapeutically contraindicated in the initial stages of treatment:

1.  Temporarily renounce all social strivings and pressures. Do only what feels comfortable doing.
2.  Not to be hospitalized at next breakdown. To be treated with behavior therapy desensitization procedures.

### Illustrative Case Analysis

I. DEMOGRAPHIC DATA

Rev. X, age thirty-four, white, four years theological seminary, married, four children.

II. PSYCHOBIOLOGIC FACTORS

A slender, tall, well-developed man, unremarkable in appearance.

Intelligent appearing but not handsome. Generally cheerful temperament. No autonomic lability or psychosomatic syndromes.

### III. MENTAL CONTEXT FACTORS

Born into a long line of Fundamentalist protestant clergymen and never thought of anything but entering the ministry. Has always respected authority and has taken everything in the Bible literally as Gospel truth.

In divinity school, his peers regarded him as unendurably "square." Regarded himself right from the beginning as a "man of God." Over-impressed by dogma and ritual, goes to every extreme in expressing his faith. Instructed his parishioners to refer to him as "Father" (an unusual practice in his denomination). Cannot tolerate any deviation from the Gospel. Outspoken in denouncing Evil wherever he fancies to encounter it. Very directive and authoritarian in preaching the Gospel.

Totally uncritical regarding his theology. Is supremely confident of the rightness of his Church and in himself.

### IV. EXISTENTIAL STATUS AND PROBLEMS

After eight years in the ministry, Rev. X feels that his whole life pattern is going to pieces. Has never succeeded well in any parish, starting off well, but then coming to be cordially disliked by his parishioners. He is too opinionated, authoritarian, directive, judgmental, and condemning of any breach. Does not hesitate to chide anyone for his shortcomings. Is untactful and inconsiderate in management of church problems. Not an inspired speaker, he tends to mouth platitudes and to dwell endlessly on the wages of sin. He is beginning to lose faith in himself and in his Church. Somehow, what he has been defending no longer seems defensible. He suddenly feels lost and overwhelmed by the failure of all he has held valuable.

After five years of marriage, and four children as rapidly as possible, marital problems have built up. He has always regarded himself as the head of the family, instructing his wife in detail what to do, and never failing to criticize her publicly if anything goes wrong. Tends to be too permissive with the children, trying to apply the Gospel of Love. It works poorly. The children are known as "brats" in the neighborhood and are not well liked by their peers.

Rev. X is overdefensive about his social position in the community. He feels he should be recognized as a community leader but senses that he is really quite disliked and has little influence.

### V. THE SITUATIONAL PRESS

Matters have again come to a head with his parish. A very vocal group is demanding his resignation. He has appealed to higher church authority which came to town and tried to mediate the dispute but without success. The parish appears on the verge of breaking up unless some resolution of the rift is accomplished immediately. Rev. X feels that he cannot back down without losing face irrevocably. He is in a stage of acute conflict. Should he leave the ministry? Should he seek psychiatric help or pastoral counseling? Should he continue to fight for what he thinks is right?

His acute vocational and spiritual problem is exaggerated by his marital and family problems. His wife is on the point of rebellion or breakdown, threatening to leave him. The children are out of control. What will happen if he cannot get another parish? He has no savings.

### Etiological Equation

*Primary Factor:* Invalid ideology. His theological beliefs are obsolete and inappropriate in the enlightened era of the 1960s. His attempts to teach his beliefs and act out their implications have resulted in failure.

*Secondary Factors:* His Self Concept whereby he regards himself as "The Man of God," the spiritual leader of his community, and the "head" of his family, imply an authoritarian, directive, judgmental orientation whereby he has excessive confidence in his righteousness and his obligation to tell everybody else what to do.

*Predisposing factors:* No evident genetic or constitutional factors. His mental context is a reflection of his family and cultural background. He grew up in a clerical family, heard nothing but theology in his early years, and had no broadening experiences which might have trained him to be more critical. His theological training was fundamentalist and reinforced his early ideological conditionings. He simply did not have any corrective experiences which might have modified his cultural indoctrination.

*Precipitating factors:* Rev. X was thrust into existential crisis and anxiety when all his problems came to a head at the same time. He was threatened with loss of his parish, desertion by his wife, loss of his children, and of community respect. He is faced with an almost insoluble problem.

### Therapeutic Indications

Rev. X is shaken to his very core Self concepts by his dawning insights that he has committed himself to an ideologically invalid and untenable theology. He cannot escape the implications that he is failing in many roles as preacher, husband, father, and citizen.

Rev. X is forcibly required to examine his own Self concepts and Ego Ideals, and to recognize that his former authoritarian-judgmental attitudes have been maladaptive. He is forced to recognize that he has not been a good leader and is close to being a failure.

It is indicated to (a) re-examine the validity and implications of his whole theological orientation, (b) to re-examine his own Self concepts and to eliminate invalid and inconsistent ideals, (c) to examine his role-playing performances in the important areas of husband, parent and citizen, and (d) to arrive at a more tenable orientation, ideologically and personally.

He must frankly face the questions of whether he belongs in the ministry and, if so, what ministry? He must explore different theologies, and particularly more liberal positions. He might become acquainted with nondirectivism.

### Follow-up Notes

1.  Environmental stresses were temporarily relieved when his superiors arranged for a face-saving reassignment to a clerical administrative position where he would have an income while regrouping himself.

2.  He agreed to undertake pastoral counseling to study the question of whether he belonged in the ministry and also to try to reconcile some of his theological conflicts. The nondirective method was referred to him for study, along with its underlying philosophy.

3.  A period of stagnation and demoralization occurred as he underwent an ideological reorientation. For a while he was very disillusioned, feeling that he could believe in nothing.

4.  Particular attention was given in counseling to his Self Concepts and role perceptions.

5.  Rev. X finally decided that he did not belong in the ministry and undertook training to become an accountant.

### THE CLINICAL ATTACK
### UPON ETIOLOGIC FACTORS

Underlying all methods of psychotherapy is the assumption that clinical attack upon etiologic factors stimulating, instigating, or maintaining the disorder should result in remission of symptoms. Every psychotherapeutic method depends upon specific hypotheses concerning how the etiology of a condition is to be modified. The clinical problem is to differentiate the method(s) specifically indicated in any particular case.

This is the reason for presenting this analysis of various postulated etiologic equations in the hope that the clinician will recognize the diagnostic problems involved and will attempt to match up the therapeutic methods, which are specifically indicated in relation to particular clinical conditions. It is only through the valid diagnosis of etiologic relationships that valid therapeutic prescriptions can be formulated.

In terms of integrative psychology, the basic issues concern how to catalyze the highest possible levels of integration involving the highest possible levels of control and resultant high levels of behavior organization. The various types of etiologic equations herein postulated may be thought of as referring to different hierarchical levels of behavior integration. Among the pertinent clinical questions are: On what integrative level is this particular behavior pattern organized? What factors are capable of organizing such patterns of integration? What failures of integration or patterns of disintegration are reflected in this behavior? How can higher levels of integration be achieved in support of positive mental health? We believe that valid answers to such questions can be derived only from a thorough knowledge of the nature and consequences of the whole wide spectrum of etiologic equations potentially organizing behavior.

## NEW DEFINITIONS AND CONCEPTIONS OF MENTAL DISORDER

The fact that factorial studies come up with two "super" factors of *psychoticism* and *neuroticism* lends support to the contention that mental disorder should be defined in terms of patterns of defective integrations and disintegrations. The one common factor in all mental disorder is *integrative deficit* or *defect*.

In the psychoses, the integrative deficit is general, interfering with all associative organizations, and resulting in generally bizarre ideation.

In the psychoneuroses, the integrative disorder is circumscribed and limited to psychological component functions.

In organic conditions (either prenatal, natal or postnatal), normal integrations are prevented by deficits of psychophysiological supporting conditions. In functional conditions, transient psychophysiological disorders appear to be disrupting somatic supports of the psyche.

In paranoid states, there occurs a psychotic reorganization based upon defective reintegrations in which reality is not properly represented.

In disorders where Freudian-type mechanisms are operative, psychic integrations are disrupted by intrusive inner process contents, flooding consciousness, and usually uncontrollable, because of lack of insight and inability to discharge cathected impulses more normally.

Mental deficiency involves an organic deficit of integrative quality.

## SOME STRATEGIES AND TACTICS
## FOR PSYCHOTHERAPY

The confusing claims and counterclaims of the various schools of psychotherapy may be rationalized and interrelated by comparing the different underlying etiologic equations upon which their respective strategies are based. This may be accomplished by identifying the levels of integration at which postulated etiologic factors are presumed to be operating.

*Hypnotherapy, suggestion,* and *autosuggestion* assume that conditioning occurs through the uncritical acceptance (subverting rational intellect) of ideas according to the principle of ideomotor action. What has been caused by suggestion can be removed or modified through suggestion.

*Autogenic therapy* utilizes the autogenic state to produce conditions of calmness and tranquility that facilitate psychophysiologic relaxation and cerebral neutralization of charged complexes. The underlying hypothesis is that cerebral homeostasis is disturbed by stress and conflict.

*Behavior therapy* postulates that conditioned avoidance (CAV) reactions can be unconditioned and/or reconditioned by standard learning methods. The behavioristic hypotheses require only a conditionable organism, treat the client as a modifiable mechanism, and assign no importance to historical considerations concerning how the person got that way.

*Psychoanalysis* postulates a hydraulic psychodynamic model in which Id impulses are repressed by the Super Ego into the Unconscious. This assumes that symptom formation is determined by inner processes (unconscious) over which the person has no conscious control. The therapeutic hypothesis is that analysis of repressed complexes makes their origins and meanings conscious with the production of insight that is believed fundamental for corrective actions.

*Personal construct theory* hypothesizes that invalid role constructs result from faulty perceptions of reality and of the roles and feelings of others. *Fixed role therapy* attempts a reorganization of style of life through experimenting with new roles and role constructs. The personal constructs of the client are revised.

*Relationship therapies* assume that psychic disorder results from unsatisfying and conflictual interpersonal relationships. It is hypothesized that positive, unconditionally accepting, loving relationships will operate as antidotes for rejection and insecurity reactions.

*Nondirective therapy* postulates the single hypothesis of affective blocks to psychological growth. The nondirective method of reflecting and clarifying feelings in an accepting nonjudgmental atmosphere, theoretically, is all that is needed to release emotional blocks.

*Rational re-educative therapies* hypothesize that maladjustment results from effective blocking of rational-intellective resources. Rational therapy attempts to provide conditions maximizing intellective factors and more valid ideological conceptions of how to cope with life.

*Integrative reorganization therapies* postulate defects of integration or disintegration at various hierarchical levels of behavior organization. The problem is to diagnose the level of integrative failure or breakdown in order to influence etiologic factors operating at that level.

*Existential analysis* and *logotherapy* postulate the existence of existential neuroses resulting from the failure to find satisfying meanings in life and/or to actualize the Self. An existential vacuum is postulated to occur when a person feels his life has no meaning and is worthless. Existential therapy seeks to reinterpret Life to give it meaning and to teach the client how to feel existentially worthwhile.

*Eclectic therapies* hypothesize a wide spectrum of etiologic factors potentially causing disorder, and therefore postulate that it is necessary to have a wide therapeutic armamentarium of methods suited to specific indications and contraindications.

The basic strategy of eclectic therapy is to differentiate all the possible etiologic causes of disorder, and then to select appropriate methods specifically indicated to modify specific etiological factors. This is not a hodge-podge approach, experimenting with shotgun methods on a hit-or-miss basis (which sometimes has spectacular results); it is a rational method based on knowledge of valid indications and contraindications with reference to any specific etiologic equation.

## IMPLICATIONS FOR PSYCHOTHERAPY

Consideration of the wide variability of psychological states and the large number of etiological equations, which have been postulated as organizing different levels of personality integration, emphasizes the complexity of the problem of what to attempt in case handling. Within a rational orientation to clinical practice, valid diagnosis precedes therapy since the major problem is to discover what is wrong before deciding what can be done.

Confronted with a clinical situation in which the case materials and clinical problems are extremely complex, and also where a large armamentarium of case handling methods is available, it is necessary to know the indications and contraindications for utilizing any clinical method. The very scope of the problem requires a genuinely eclectic approach of utilizing all known methods according to their indications and contraindications in relation to valid diagnosis of what the particular clinical situation requires.

We reject the proposition that any single school of psychology or hypothetical model has the answer to all clinical problems. Such a claim presupposes that there is only one cause for all difficulties. To the contrary, the complexity of behavior determination requires comparably complex systems of diagnosis and case handling based on a rational analysis of the etiology of clinically important behaviors.

Rational case handling requires valid diagnostic processes at all levels of clinical decisions, ranging from the basic diagnosis as to what patterns of etiologic factors are involved down to clinical judgments as to what to do next, at all levels and stages of case handling based on knowledge of the indications and contraindications of available methods.

Although this presentation of the nature and importance of etiological equations is intended to be utilized in connection with the system of integrative psychology based on our theory of the psychological state (Thorne, 1966) it is also relevant for the classical schools of psychotherapy in direct proportion to which such theories are concerned with psychological states.

*Freudian depth psychology* is concerned with the unconscious determination of psychological states. It postulates a standard etiologic equation emphasizing mechanisms such as repression.

*Adlerian individual psychology* is concerned with the role of the Self in determining psychological states, that is, in the struggle to develop a suitable Life Style to get the most out of life.

*Rogerian nondirective methods* stress the detailed investigation of psychological states, investigating the Self concept, and catalyzing growth by unblocking emotional conflicts.

*Relationship therapies* involve an intensive manipulation of interpersonal relations with the goal of teaching more effective modes of relating. This involves direct dealing with psychological states.

In general, the more closely a method of therapy deals directly with problems of the immediate *present*, the more directly are such methods dealing with the present psychological state in contrast with historical investigations of the past.

It should be emphasized that the classification of etiologic equations and strategies of therapy herewith presented constitute only a beginning step in outlining what can be accomplished. It is our intention here to provide only some classic illustrations and examples of etiologic models which have achieved widespread acceptance. These should be used only as suggestive models for specific hypotheses achieved inductively through individual case study. Our suggestion is that an individual etiologic equation(s) should be formulated for each client. This equation should be modified from time to time as critical incidents, and significant therapeutic developments occur in the life of the client. Such equations will help the clinician to formulate an attack upon the individual case on some rational basis.

## References

Adams, H. B. Mental illness or interpersonal behavior? *Amer. Psychol.*, 1964, *19*, 191–196.

Adler, Alfred. *The Individual Psychology of Alfred Adler*. New York: Basic Books, 1956.

Arndt, J. L. *Genese en Psychotherapie der Neuroses*. The Hague: Boucher, 1958 (Vol. 1), 1962 (Vol. 11). See also, G. L. M. van den Aardweg. Autopsychodrama: Theory and Therapy of Neurosis according to J. L. Arndt. *Amer. J. Psychotherap.*, 1964, *18*, 259–271.

Berne, R. *Games People Play*. New York: Basic Books, 1963.

Bindra, D. An interpretation of the displacement phenomenon. *Brit. J. Psychol.*, 1959, *50*, 263–267.

Cameron, N. *The psychology of the behavior disorders*. Boston: Houghton-Mifflin, 1947.

Ellis, A. Rational psychotherapy. *J. gen. Psychol.*, 1958, *59*, 35–49.

Freud, S. Collected papers. London: Hogarth, 1960.

Hollingshead, A. B., and F. C. Redlich. *Social class and mental illness*. New York: Wiley, 1958.

Horney, K. *Our inner conflicts*. New York: Norton, 1945.

Kelly, G. A. *The Psychology of Personal Constructs*. Vols. 1–11. New York: Norton, 1955.

Lecky, P. *Self Consistency*. New York: Island Press, 1951.

Malmo, R. B. Anxiety and behavioral arousal. *Psychol. Rev.*, 1957, *64*, 276–287.

Meehl, P. E. Schizotaxia, schizotypy and schizophrenia. *Amer. Psychol.*, 1962, *17*, 827–838.

Miller, N. E. Liberalization of basic S-R concepts: extensions to conflict behavior, motivation and social learning. In S. Koch (Ed.), *Psychology: a study of science*. Vol. 2. New York: McGraw-Hill, 1958.

Mowrer, O. H. *Learning theory and behavior*. New York: Wiley, 1960.

Pavlov, I. P. *Lectures on conditioned reflexes*. New York: International Publishers, 1928.

Sullivan, H. S. *The interpersonal theory of psychiatry*. New York: Norton, 1953.

Szasz, T. S. *The myth of mental illness.* New York: Hoeber, 1961.

Thorne, F. C. *Integrative Psychology.* Brandon, Vt.: Clinical Psychology Publishing Company, 1967. This book presents a general theory of integrative psychology rationalizing the concept of the etiological equation.

Thorne, F. C. Principles of psychological examining. *J. clin. Psychol.,* 1955.

Thorne, F. C. *Psychological Case Handling.* Brandon, Vt.: Clinical Psychology Publishing Company, 1967. Two volumes. These books cite specific applications of integrative psychology to psychological case handling based on the indications and contraindications of specific etiological equations.

Thorne, F. C. Theory of the psychological state. *J. clin. Psychol.,* 1966, *22,* 127–135.

Thorne, F. C. The structure of integrative psychology. *J. clin. Psychol.,* 1967, *23,* 3–12.

# Appendix B

## Psychoanalysis—A Process of Devitalization*

*Raphael Vitalo*

Freud's theorizing begins with man after he has given up what is most personally and vitally his, the source which infuses words and ideas with flesh and blood. He successively labels this fund the unconscious (in his early topographical model), libidinal instincts or eros (in his later dynamic model), and id (in his structural model). For him, action emanating directly from these sources would only aggrandize the individual at the expense of others. For him, when man operated completely for himself, he necessarily operated to the exclusion of others. Such raw feeling and force was as threatening to Freud the man, as he theorized it to be to civilization at large. Freud too had ceded direct contact with his own truths. He was shaped by a sick society, and seeing no alternative to this society, as he saw no alternative in himself, his theorizing with respect to the "good life" was a process of necessary accommodation while paring away unnecessary losses. His keen awareness of the sacrifice man must make for the sake of civilization was hardened by his inability to see an alternative to this type of civilization. *The possibilities one sees for himself define the possibilities one can see for others.*

He saw and described how man was shaped and shackled by society via its internalized agent—the superego. He saw how man was prohibited from seeking his own ends and how he was seduced from his individuality. He did not see that his own view of the id as alien and brute, his embracing of the ego as the favored structure was also shaped by his world; that it too was a shackle, and not a necessary one. Constrained men are embittered. Perhaps all Freud could sense below the orderly areas of his life and the lives of others, even below those unseen areas which he explored and to which he brought order—was this embitterment, waiting to

*First printed here, and used with permission of the author.

273

burst out. For him, the unrestrained expression of this pent-up energy would be devastating both intrapsychically and interpersonally. The answer of his time was repression and denial, but this was unnecessarily costly. It involved the individual in sealing off areas of his life; it strengthened his bondage to social myths whose intrinsic necessity Freud clearly saw as illusion, and it made him more vulnerable to upset. Freud's final method was one of gradual release and "binding" of this energy.

For Freud, man acts or develops because he is frustrated; he did not see that man is first frustrated because he does not act. The constructive products of man are derivatives and shadows of more primary yearnings. They serve as an escape or at best a partial venting of his unspeakable desires.

Civilization is the product of "repressed eros"; it is the cloaked expression of eros. It begins with the inability to discharge tension directly and develops into complex and circuitous patterns of release. Each new avenue further attenuates the original potency. Some avenues erroneously acquire a pre-potency and their demands become exorbitant as, for example, excessively prohibitive ideologies. These turn back upon their source and exacerbate rather than attenuate the origin. He unveiled the falsity of civilization, the duplicity of life—but he saw no alternative.

Freud did not grasp with its full import that the child's initial development is free and spontaneous. Only partially did he comprehend that the child's free actions must be frustrated; that he must be made predictable. "The early efflorescence of infantile sexual life is doomed to destruction because its wishes are incompatible with reality. . ." He realized that the child was shaped by demands of "reality" but he could not see beyond. Without precedent for spontaneous and full action in his own life, he despaired. He failed to challenge this shaping; he failed to indict this "reality" which imposed its necessity. He could not see that this demand was a betrayal, effected by a regime as arbitrary in its origins as those moral ideals to which men subjugate themselves—a betrayal perpetuated by a society of people who have forsaken themselves and feel the need to seduce others into the same abandonment; a society of ac-culturated "adults" whose placid existence is threatened by the unpredictable. Freud, too, feared the unpredictable. He felt uneasy in the presence of the unexplained. Alienated from the muted child within him, he could not trust its demands. He could only see it as a source of discomfort dangerously pointing toward a moment of crisis, and for Freud, crises can have no fruitful consequences. They only disturb the process of accommodation to the "necessarily" alienated forces within us and the antagonistic forces without. More pointedly, crises disturb reflective processes (ego functions) and Freud had cast his lot with reason. Above all, he was "a mind"; with its razor sharp edge he dissected the child within him into neat and orderly pieces, draining it of all life. Tragically, he chose the wrong party as victim; he could see no alternative. The child's original desire for nurturance and unqualified acceptance for who he is—is frustrated. His parents betray their protective trust. He is shaped and seduced into the game of civilization. His pleas turn to demands; his demands to subtle manipulations. He enters into the duplicity of the world and into competition for the meagre sustenance it offers. What he is made to relinquish continues to yearn for expression and fulfillment, but this too is translated into the language of the game. His actions always remain appearances cloaking another reality.

Freud was aware of the "original trauma" which the child experiences. He was aware that it led him into the false actions of civilization and the duplicity of life. For him the "original trauma" can never be undone; he could only see the demanding child; he could not see the earlier, pleading child. Above all, raw feeling is threatening to a mind. And so he writes of the child's corruption as his necessary accommodation to reality. He is aware that the accommodation takes place "in the most distressing circumstances, and to the accompaniment of the most painful feelings." Throughout, he is aware of the pain, tragedy and duplicity of life, but he can see no alternative. His answer could only be: "Ameliorate the pain, minimize the strife."

The process of psychoanalysis is the process of devitalizing the world within and without. It is the triumph of the death instinct, not the death instinct as it is usually seen in terms of its gross manifestations, outer or inner directed aggression, but, rather the more subtle workings in the process of "binding" energy—the process which solidifies the patient's gains in therapy. Psychoanalysis takes the place of the normal acculturative process where the latter has been ineffective or where later "trauma" have revitalized dormant urges. It improves on the normal acculturation process in that it gives the individual a sense of the arbitrariness of present structures, allowing him more latitude and freedom from involutional bondage to any particular "object" or "activity" in the game. It allows the client to individualize himself, but only at a great price. It arrives at this point by various roads, most of which are made explicit in the theory. Indirectly, the client's aberrant games are dealt with. His confused and distorted statement of withheld defiance is slowly unfolded. Through a gradual process of release and "binding," the withheld finds representation in consciousness and thought. Through the techniques of free association and synthetic interpretations, the client comes into mediated contact with the forces that lie within him and gains some distance from the world without. The repetitiveness and length of analysis have the added effect of inuring the client to his inner demands.

The contact he achieves with his inner life and the subtle demands of the external world is mediated by a process of intellectual insights, reflection and thought. This is "binding." The ego tames the raw energy of the id by deflecting it into thought. Affect is allowed to seep into awareness but it is neutralized by this diversion.

In this manner an "individual" is born. The client is freed from passive boundness to the world without; he is also freed from the imperatives to action issued from within. Given no hope, the unquenchable desire, which is the bedrock experience of all men, must also be "bound." The patient is taught to acquiesce to the utter futility of his desire and with his finely honed weapon, the analytic attitude, he thinks away its fire.

In the end, the Freudian man must deaden himself—he must adjust. The vital immediacy of life is exchanged for the placid nonimmediacy of thought. Now calmly alienated, he may be a man of active mind—but he cannot create. He may be able to entertain many possibilities, but he is unable to commit himself to any. The ultimate irony is that he is an individual—an individual ultimately indistinguishable from others. He is hollow. He is without conviction or passion. He suffers little and enjoys less.

# Appendix C

## Abstracts of
## Research Projects

### A. COUNSELING AND PSYCHOTHERAPY: PROCESS AND OUTCOME

### The Differential Effectiveness of Counselors and Therapists with Inpatient Schizophrenics and Counseling Center Clients*

*Fred Hirshberg*
*Robert R. Carkhuff*
*Bernard G. Berenson*

PROBLEM AND METHODOLOGY

Ten inpatient therapists and ten student personnel affiliated outpatient counselors each saw (1) hospitalized schizophrenic patients and (2) college students for one session of counseling. Thus, a total of forty sessions were recorded and analyzed. It was anticipated that the inpatient therapists would function at higher levels of therapeutic process with the inpatients, and the counselors would function at higher levels with college students due to the respective experiences of each group.

RESULTS AND DISCUSSION

The outpatient counselors functioned at significantly higher levels of therapeutic process than the inpatient therapists with both schizophrenic patients and student-clients. In general, the level of conditions offered was characteristic of the therapist and not of the client population: some therapists offered high levels of conditions to both the inpatients and the outpatients; other therapists offered low levels of conditions to both the inpatients and the outpatients. This research constitutes another in the series of research suggesting that it is primarily the therapist who determines the level of conditions offered the client.

*Unpublished research, University of Massachusetts, 1967.

# The Differential Effects of the Manipulation of Therapeutic Conditions upon High and Low Functioning Clients*

Todd Holder
Robert R. Carkhuff
Bernard G. Berenson

PROBLEM AND METHODOLOGY

A study was designed to determine the effects of manipulated therapeutic conditions upon the depth of self-exploration of persons functioning at high and low levels of empathy, respect, genuineness, and concreteness. The three highest functioning students and the three lowest functioning students were selected from eleven female college students who were cast in the helping role of the counselor. Unknown to each subject-client, an experienced counselor, functioning at high levels of facilitative conditions based upon previous research findings, offered high levels of conditions during the first third of a clinical interview, low levels during the middle twenty minutes, and reinstated high levels of conditions again during the last third of the interview. The counselor attempted to standardize the introduction to the initial and third periods, and attempted to continue to make as many responses during the middle period as he did during the other periods. It was anticipated that high functioning clients, having experienced a high level of therapeutic conditions, would continue to function independently in the communication process during the manipulation period. It was also anticipated that the depth of self-exploration of the low functioning clients would be a significant function of the level of conditions offered by the counselor; that is, self-exploration would be lowered when the counselor-offered conditions were lowered.

RESULTS AND DISCUSSION

The depth of self-exploration of the low functioning clients was found to be a significant function of the level of conditions offered by the counselor, while the intrapersonal exploration of the high functioning clients continued independently of the level of conditions offered by the counselor, and was significantly higher than that of the low functioning clients. In general, it would appear that high functioning clients make better use of the counseling process than those who are functioning at lower levels of conditions. The results support the proposition that following the establishment of a relatively high level of communication, much of the communication process with the high-level functioning, or level 3 clients may remain implicit.

* Journal of Counseling Psychology, 1967, 14, 63–66.

# The Differential Effects of the Manipulation of Therapeutic Conditions by High and Low Functioning Counselors upon High and Low Functioning Clients*

*Gerald Piaget*
*Bernard G. Berenson*
*Robert R. Carkhuff*

### PROBLEM AND METHODOLOGY

One high-level functioning therapist and one moderate-level functioning therapist saw four high-level functioning clients and four low-level functioning clients, selected from among sixteen clients cast in the helping role. The therapists were controlled on age, sex, and experience. Unknown to each client, the therapists offered high levels of facilitative conditions during the first third of the interview, low levels during the experimental period, and high levels again during the final third of the session. It was anticipated that high-level clients would function independently of both high- and low-level therapists, and that low-level clients would be manipulated in their depth of self-exploration by the level at which both the high and low therapists were functioning.

### RESULTS AND DISCUSSION

The high-level functioning clients functioned independently of the high-level functioning therapist's manipulations, while the low-level functioning client's depth of self-exploration was a function of the level of conditions offered during each period. However, both the high- and the low-level functioning clients deteriorated in self-exploration over the session with the low-level functioning therapist. It appears, then, that while low-level functioning clients are almost totally dependent upon the high-level functioning therapist's level of conditions, the low-level functioning clients simply deteriorate in functioning with the low-level functioning therapist. Similarly, while the high-level functioning clients function independently of the high-level functioning therapist, they deteriorate with the low-level functioning therapist. The initial level of conditions offered by the therapist appears the critical index of truly effective therapeutic processes.

*Journal of Consulting Psychology,* in press, 1967.

### The Effects of the Manipulation of Client Depth of Self-Exploration upon High and Low Functioning Counselors*

*Mae Alexik*
*Robert R. Carkhuff*

PROBLEM AND METHODOLOGY

Two male counselors, of identical training and experience, one functioning at high levels of empathy, respect, genuineness, and concreteness, and the other functioning at low levels, were seen by a client who, unknown to the counselors, had a response set to explore herself deeply during the first third of the interview, not at all during the middle twenty minutes, and then again deeply during the last third of the session. It was anticipated that the lower-level functioning counselor would be manipulated by the degree of client self-exploration, while the higher-level functioning counselor would not be manipulated but would continue to offer high levels of conditions. Each counselor was under the impression that he was seeing a regular client on the first interview. The client was a forty-five-year old female graduate student in education, who had sought help concerning personal difficulties involved in her implementing the counselor's role in training. The client was asked to participate in the project, and the full implications of her participation were discussed with her.

RESULTS AND DISCUSSION

The client was able to manipulate successfully the degree to which she explored herself, with both periods 1 and 3 being significantly different from the experimental period. Counselor A tended to function below level 2 (on a five-point scale) during period 1, drop to level 1 during period 2 when the client did not explore herself, and raise his level of functioning to 1.5 during period 3 when the client attempted again to explore herself. The ratings for periods 1 and 3 versus period 2 were significantly higher for all individual conditions. Counselor B tended to function at level 4 during the experimental period and to demonstrate further improvement to 4.5 during period 3. The differences for period 1 and 3 versus period 2 were not significant because counselor B's level of functioning during period 1 cancelled the effects of his functioning during period 3 The ratings for period 3 were significantly higher (.01) than for period 1 for all conditions except concreteness. It is important to note that the counselors functioned consistently with the past ratings of their performance, thus suggesting a generalization effect of the therapist's level

*Journal of Clinical Psychology, 1967, 23, 212–215.

of functioning, a finding consistent with the research suggesting that the level of conditions offered are characteristic of the therapist and not the client. In general, the results confirmed the hypothesis that the lower-level functioning counselor would be manipulated. However, during period 1 counselor A functioned at higher levels than during period 3, suggesting that the counselor does not recover following a significant drop in client process involvement. The implications for the functioning of lower-level counselors following a "crisis" or an inability on the part of the client to explore herself are important. Counselor B was not manipulated by the client's level of process involvement. However, rather than continuing to function consistently across the interview, he tended to function at higher levels with the introduction of the experimental period. During period 3, it is noteworthy that counselor B functioned at levels significantly higher than during period 1.

## The Differential Effects of the Manipulation of Client Self-Exploration upon High and Low Functioning Therapists*

*Robert R. Carkhuff*
*Mae Alexik*

PROBLEM AND METHODOLOGY

Eight experienced therapists were seen by a client who, unknown to the counselors, had a response set to explore herself deeply during the first third of the interview, not at all during the middle twenty minutes, and then again deeply during the last third of the session. It was anticipated that the lower-level functioning therapists would demonstrate a drop in level of functioning during the experimental period and never again recover to their previous levels of functioning during the final period, while the higher-level functioning therapists would continue to offer high levels of facilitative conditions independently of the manipulation of client process variables.

RESULTS AND DISCUSSION

Three therapists were found to be functioning above level 3 during the initial period while five therapists were functioning below level 3. The client was able to manipulate successfully the depth of her self-exploration. Those therapists functioning above level 3 all tended to function independently of the clients manipulation, with the highest therapist again moving toward higher levels at the point of manipulation, and the

*Journal of Counseling Psychology*, in press, 1967.

lowest among the three being effected only slightly. Of the therapists functioning below level 3 in the initial period, all dropped significantly in their level of functioning during the experimental period and none returned to their initial levels of functioning. Again, it is important to note that the counselors functioned consistently with past ratings of their performance from other studies. The implication is that, at a "crisis point" in therapy where a client who had been previously exploring herself at deep levels, but then begins to "run away" from personally relevant material, low level therapists can simply not respond appropriately with consistent levels of facilitative conditions while high level therapists continue to offer high levels of conditions. Indeed, there is some tendency for the highest level practitioners to function at higher levels following the "crisis point."

## Process Variables in Counseling and Psychotherapy: A Study of Counseling and Friendship*

James C. Martin
Robert R. Carkhuff
Bernard G. Berenson

PROBLEM AND METHODOLOGY

A study was designed to assess the levels of facilitative conditions offered by friends and professional counselors. In a counterbalanced design, sixteen volunteer college students were interviewed by both (1) their best available friend and (2) a professional counselor. Thus, a total of thirty-two interviews were conducted, with each of the two experienced counselors involved seeing eight of the interviewees, and each seeing four interviewees first and four, last. Following each interview, the interviewee filled out a fifty-item relationship questionnaire evaluating the interviewer. Randomly selected excerpts of the recorded sessions were rated.

RESULTS AND DISCUSSION

On all tape ratings of the levels of facilitative conditions offered and the process involvement elicited in the interview, the counselors performed at significantly higher levels than the best available friends. On the questionnaire the results were similar. While the two professional counselors as a group demonstrated significantly higher levels of conditions than friends, as a group, the counselors differed significantly

*Journal of Counseling Psychology, 1966, 13, 441–446.

from each other, suggesting that while professional experience may be of primary value in the development of receptor and communicative skills, other factors such as the personality and attitudes of the individual counselor may be critical.

## The Effects of Counselor Race and Training upon Counseling Process with Negro Clients in Initial Interviews*

*George Banks*
*Bernard G. Berenson*
*Robert R. Carkhuff*

PROBLEM AND METHODOLOGY

The retarding effects of counselor race upon the responses of Negroes have been hypothesized in the areas of counseling and psychotherapy, test examination and education. A study was designed to determine the effects upon eight Negroes in initial clinical interviews of an inexperienced Negro undergraduate student serving as a counselor, and three white counselors of varying degrees of experience and types of training, including a relatively inexperienced graduate student counselor, a relatively experienced graduate student counselor, and an experienced doctoral level counselor from a nationally prominent program with a traditional trait-and-factor counseling program which is not oriented toward counselor-client differences. In a counter-balanced design, during consecutive weeks, each counselee saw each counselor for an initial clinical interview. Randomly selected excerpts of the recorded sessions were rated on counselor empathy, positive regard, genuineness, concreteness, and client depth of self-exploration. In addition, a fifty-item relationship inventory assessing the counselor's level of functioning was administered to the counselee. Finally, the counselees were asked (1) whether they would see the counselor again, and (2) to rank the counselors in order of effectiveness.

RESULTS AND DISCUSSION

There were no significant differences between the levels of the objective tape ratings of the individual facilitative conditions offered by the three counselors who were trained in relationship-oriented counseling. All three, however, were functioning at significantly higher levels than the traditionally-trained counselor. Essentially the same results were

*Journal of Clinical Psychology, 1967, 23, 70–72.

demonstrated on the counselee inventory assessments of conditions. All eight Negro counselees indicated that they would return to see the Negro counselor again. Five counselees said that they would return to see one of the white relationship-trained counselors and three, the other. None of the eight counselees would return to see the traditionally-trained counselor. Essentially the same results were obtained on the rank-orderings with the white doctoral level person ranked last by all counselees. The results suggest that counselor race and type of orientation and training are more relevant variables than experience per se.

## The Differential Effects of Therapist Race and Social Class upon Patient Depth of Self-Exploration in the Initial Clinical Interview*

*Robert R. Carkhuff*
*Richard M. Pierce*

### PROBLEM AND METHODOLOGY

A study was designed to ferret out the differential effects of (1) the race and (2) the social class of the therapist upon patient depth of self-exploration, a critical index of patient therapeutic process involvement and a significant correlate of positive therapeutic outcome. Social class was defined by educational and vocational level. Four lay counselors who had completed a lay mental health counselor training program included the following: (1) an upper-class white counselor; (2) an upper-class Negro counselor; (3) a lower-class white counselor; and (4) a lower-class Negro counselor. Thus, all lay counselors had (1) similar training, (2) similar kinds of therapeutic experience, and all had (3) demonstrated no significant differences in their levels of counselor-offered conditions as measured by rating scales of (a) empathy, (b) positive regard, (c) genuineness, and (d) depth of self-exploration elicited in patients in clinical interviews. All counselors were females. A Latin Square design was replicated across four different groups of four hospitalized mental patients each: (1) four upper-class white patients; (2) four upper-class Negro patients and (3) four lower-class white patients, and (4) four lower-class Negro patients. All patients were females. Each counselor saw each patient in a design counter-balanced to control for the effects of order. In order to control for counselor fatigue factors, each group of four patients was seen a week apart. The patients rotated to the counselor's rooms and each forty-

*Journal of Consulting Psychology,* in press, 1967.

five-minute length interview was recorded. All counselors began each session encouraging the patient in an open-ended fashion to discuss "whatever is important" to the patient "at this moment in time." Randomly selected excerpts from the sixty-four clinical interviews were rated on the depth of patient self-exploration.

RESULTS AND DISCUSSION

Race and social class of both patient and therapist were significant sources of effect, and the interaction between patient and therapist variable was significant. In general, the ratings of patient self-exploration ranged from level 1 to level 3 with an average of slightly under level 2. In general, the patients most similar to the race and social class of the counselor tended to explore themselves most, while patients most dissimilar tended to explore themselves least. There were no significant effects of the order in which the patients were seen, and the effects of race were not dependent upon the level of social class in both patient and therapist. As patient depth of self-exploration during early clinical interviews has been highly correlated with outcome indexes of constructive patient change, the results have implications for counseling and psychotherapy.

## The Predicted Differential Effects of High and Low Functioning Therapists upon the Level of Functioning of Outpatients*

William Pagell
Robert R. Carkhuff
Bernard G. Berenson

PROBLEM AND METHODOLOGY

Eight outpatients, four from a V.A. outpatient clinic and four from a counseling center, were screened as relatively long-term cases and randomly assigned to eight different therapists. Prior to treatment, each patient was cast in the helping role and the level of his functioning assessed. Differential predictions of gain and no gain were generated by the difference in the therapist's level of functioning in his first session with the client, and the client's level of functioning when cast in the helping role. A number of indexes were employed to assess the level of client functioning prior to and following treatment: tape ratings of the client cast in the helping role; expert assessments of the client's level of functioning; the therapist's assessment of his level; self-assessments; and assessments

*Journal of Clinical Psychology, in press, 1967.

by the standard interviewees who saw the client pre-and-post. It was anticipated that the clients of those therapists who were (1) functioning above level 3 and (2) functioning a level higher than the client would demonstrate the most constructive change.

RESULTS AND DISCUSSION

The same two of the eight therapists were (1) functioning above level 3 and (2) functioning a level higher than their clients. Thus, the prediction of constructive gain was generated for only their two clients. No other therapists were functioning more than a level higher than their clients and, thus, the remaining predictions were for no change rather than deterioration. In general, the predictions were supported on nearly all dimensions by the results of the analyses of the experts' ratings, tape ratings, and therapists' ratings. While the trends were positive on the self and interviewee ratings, they did not attain significance. Significant differences were not found as frequently for concreteness and self-disclosure as they were for empathy, positive regard, and genuineness. The results support the hypotheses that only those therapists functioning either (1) above level 3 or (2) a level higher than their clients are functioning can be effective.


## The Differential Effects of Absolute Level and the Direction of Counselor Change in Level of Functioning over Counseling upon Client Level of Functioning*

*Dan Kratochvil*
*David Aspy*
*Robert R. Carkhuff*

PROBLEM AND METHODOLOGY

Twenty-four college students designated by their teachers as "psychologically healthy" were assigned randomly in groups of six to each of four counselors, two functioning at high levels of therapeutic dimensions and two functioning at low levels. Both counselors and clients were cast in the helping role prior and subsequent to ten hours of group counseling, and random selections of the tapes of their helping efforts were rated on the facilitative dimensions. It was anticipated that the clients of those counselors functioning at the highest levels would gain the most. However, the pre-post testing of the counselor cast in the helping role

*Journal of Clinical Psychology, 1967, 23, 216–218.

provided an opportunity to assess the effect of the level of direction of the counselor's functioning upon client functioning.

RESULTS AND DISCUSSION

One of the high counselors and one of the low counselors deteriorated in functioning over the course of counseling, and the two remaining counselors improved in their level of functioning over counseling. The clients of counselors functioning at high levels of therapeutic dimensions did not demonstrate significantly more constructive change in functioning than the clients of counselors functioning at low levels of therapeutic dimensions. However, the clients of those counselors who improved in their functioning over the course of counseling demonstrated significantly more constructive change in functioning than the clients of those counselors who deteriorated in functioning. The results suggest an important qualification upon the effects of high- and low-level functioning counselors: within limits, the level of functioning may not be as critical as the direction of movement in functioning of the counselor, perhaps reflecting his own personal growth or deterioration.

## The Effects of Confrontation by High and Low Functioning Therapists*

*Susan Anderson*
*John Douds*
*Robert R. Carkhuff*

PROBLEM AND METHODOLOGY

Forty initial interviews by therapists with both hospitalized schizophrenics and university students were analyzed to determine the number, nature, and effects of therapist-initiated confrontations of discrepancies in client behavior. It was anticipated that the confrontations of high-level functioning therapists would differ in number, nature, and effects from the confrontations of low-level functioning therapists.

RESULTS AND DISCUSSION

High-level functioning therapists made significantly more confrontations of the client than did low-level functioning therapists. However, in general, the high-level functioning therapists tended to

*Unpublished research, University of Massachusetts, 1967.

confront the client with client resources, whereas the low-level functioning therapists tended to confront the client with his limitations. In the two-minute period following confrontations by high-level therapists, clients tended to explore themselves more deeply than they had previously been exploring themselves, whereas clients of low-level therapists tended to remain the same or drop off in their level of self-exploration following confrontation. Also, in general, hospitalized schizophrenics were confronted most often with their resources while college students were confronted with their limitations. The major implication involves confrontation in context: employed by high-level therapists it appears to be an effective therapeutic ingredient; employed by low-level therapists, it is not.

### Level of Therapist Functioning, Types of Confrontation and Type of Patient*

*Bernard G. Berenson*
*Kevin M. Mitchell*
*Ronald C. Laney*

Fifty-six first interviews representing the therapy of fifty-six therapists were assessed for level of therapeutic functioning by objective tape ratings of empathy, positive regard, genuineness, and concreteness. Therapists represented a wide sample of experience, ranging from advanced level graduate students and interns in clinical and counseling psychology, to therapists with more than fifteen years of experience. The sample also included therapists who were employed in in- and out-patient clinics and college counseling centers.

Five types of confrontation were employed: experiential, didactic, strengths, weakness, and encouragement to action. Frequency and type of confrontation was accepted only when the two independent judges agreed upon both presence and type of confrontation.

RESULTS AND DISCUSSION

Average tape ratings of therapist-offered conditions provided a valid basis for classifying therapists into high and low functioning groups. Although patient type yielded a significant main effect, it did not interact significantly with the other major variables in this study. Neither the high nor low therapists responded differentially to patient types in terms of the frequency or type of confrontation they employed.

*Journal of Clinical Psychology, in press, 1967.

Most important was the finding that level of therapist functioning interacts significally with type of confrontation. In addition to confronting his patient more frequently, the high-level therapist most often confronts his patients experientially. The low-level therapist confronts his patients (if he confronts at all) with weaknesses about as often as he does experientially. Thirteen high-level therapists accounted for 105 of the 201 confrontations, whereas 43 low therapists accounted for the balance (96).

## Level of Therapist Functioning, Patient Depth of Self-Exploration and Type of Confrontation*

*Bernard G. Berenson*
*Kevin M. Mitchell*
*James A. Moravec*

Thirteen therapists were designated as high functioning and 43 as low functioning based on objective tape ratings of empathy, positive regard, genuineness, and concreteness. These first interview tapes were then independently rated for level of patient self-exploration. A third pair of raters tallied the frequency and type of therapist-initiated confrontation: experiential, didactic, strength, weakness, and encouragement to action. A confrontation was tallied only when there was complete agreement between the raters.

RESULTS AND DISCUSSION

The results suggest that high and low levels of patient self-exploration do not interact with level of therapist functioning in terms of type of confrontation employed. However, the low-level therapists had a much greater proportion of low self-exploring patients than did the high-level therapists (thirty-four to nine for the low therapists and three to ten for the high therapists).

Both high and low level therapists employed types of confrontation differentially. The most dramatic comparison between the differential use of types of confrontation for high and low therapists was evident in the use of experiential confrontation. The thirteen high-level therapists employed sixty-five of this kind of confrontation, while forty-three low-level therapists employed it only thirty-eight times.

While there are differences in the use of type and frequency of confrontation by high and low therapists, the level of patient self-exploration

*Unpublished manuscript, State University of New York at Buffalo, 1967.

did not interact with any of the other major variables. High-level therapists, however, are likely to interact with their patients, even within the limits of the initial interview, in such a manner that very few of their patients could be classed as low self-exploring.

## B. TRAINING AND SELECTION

### The Development of Skills in Interpersonal Functioning*

*Robert R. Carkhuff*
*Gerald Piaget*
*Richard Pierce*

PROBLEM AND METHODOLOGY

A series of three studies were implemented in order to determine the development of interpersonal skills: (1) college freshmen with psychology and nonpsychology interests and helping and nonhelping orientations were cast in the helping role in order to determine their differential levels of functioning; (2) college senior psychology majors, divided into those having high and low grade-point averages, were cast in the helping role and assessed; (3) beginning graduate students in clinical and counseling psychology were cast in the helping role and assessed.

RESULTS AND DISCUSSION

Beginning graduate students in both clinical and counseling psychology were found to be functioning at levels (approximately 2.3 overall) significantly higher than senior psychology majors (approximately 1.9 overall) who, in turn, were functioning at levels significantly higher than beginning college students (approximately 1.5 overall). Counseling students were higher than clinical. There were no differences between psychology and nonpsychology freshmen, with or without helping orientations. In addition, there were no significant differences between senior psychology majors with high grade-point averages and those with low averages, although those with high averages tended to be slightly higher. In general, there is a strong suggestion of a developmental trend toward higher levels of interpersonal functioning up to the beginning of graduate school, perhaps as a function of experience and increasing sophistication.

*Counselor Education and Supervision, in press, 1967.

## Training in Counseling and Psychotherapy: An Evaluation of an Integrated Didactic and Experiential Approach*

*Robert R. Carkhuff*
*Charles B. Truax*

PROBLEM AND METHODOLOGY

An approach to training in counseling and psychotherapy integrating the didactic-intellectual approach, which emphasizes the shaping of therapist behavior, with the experiential approach, which focuses upon therapist development and emotional growth, was implemented with two simultaneously-run programs; (1) a group of twelve graduate students in clinical psychology and (2) a group of five lay hospital personnel. The program relied heavily upon scales which in previous and extensive research had been predictive of positive patient outcome: (1) counselor empathy; (2) positive regard; (3) genuineness; and (4) patient depth of self-exploration. During the last week of training, each trainee had a single clinical interview with each of three hospitalized patients. Randomly selected excerpts from the recorded sessions were rated on all four scales, and the results were compared with the ratings of random excerpts of therapy from fifteen prominent therapists.

RESULTS AND DISCUSSION

With the exception of the critical variable of patient depth of self-exploration, where the lay personnel functioned at the levels of the other two groups, the three groups consistently performed in the following rank order: (a) the experienced therapists; (b) the graduate students; (c) the lay personnel. However, while a hierarchy of performance was established, the experienced therapists did not effect significantly better process levels than the graduate students on any dimensions, and the graduate students were not significantly higher than the lay group on any indexes. The only significant difference was found in the comparison of the experienced and the lay group on the dimension of therapist genuineness, thus suggesting that with experience, the therapists come to be more freely, easily, and deeply themselves in the therapeutic encounter. The results indicate that in a relatively short period of time, both graduate students and lay hospital personnel can be brought to function at levels of therapy commensurate with those of experienced therapists.

*Journal of Consulting Psychology, 1965, 29, 333–336.

## Lay Mental Health Counseling: The Effects of Lay Group Counseling*

*Robert R. Carkhuff*
*Charles B. Truax*

PROBLEM AND METHODOLOGY

A treatment program was designed to test whether the high level of functioning of trained lay hospital personnel translated directly to patient benefits. A total of eighty hospitalized mental patients were subdivided into groups and seen twice a week in group therapy for a total of twenty-four sessions, by five trained lay hospital personnel. Seventy patients served as controls. The lay personnel, primarily attendants, had been trained by an approach integrating the didactic approach, which emphasizes the shaping of therapist behavior, with the experiential approach, which focuses upon therapist development and "growth." The patient population was, in general, an older chronic one with an average of two admissions and over ten years hospitalization on the present admission. Outcome criteria assessed included hospital discharge rates and pre- and post-treatment ratings of ward behavior by the nurses and ward attendants, since the degree of patient chronicity and pathology and the low educational level precluded the use of psychological testing.

RESULTS AND DISCUSSION

Of the eighty patients who were seen in counseling, six dropped out, all within the first six sessions. Eleven of the remaining seventy-four patients who continued in counseling were discharged after two or more months of therapeutic treatment. Of the seventy control patients, six were discharged within the three-month period of time. Significant improvement was noted on the following indexes of the ward behavior of the treatment group when compared to the control group: (a) "degree of psychological disturbance"; (b) "degree of constructive interpersonal concern"; (c) "degree of constructive intrapersonal concern"; (d) "degree of overall improvement over the past three months." The results demonstrate the effectiveness of time-limited lay group counseling, evolving from a short-term integrated didactic and experiential approach to counseling training.

*Journal of Consulting Psychology, 1965, 29, 426–431.

## The Effects upon Trainee Personality and Interpersonal Functioning in Counseling Training*

*James C. Martin*
*Robert R. Carkhuff*

PROBLEM AND METHODOLOGY

Guidance counselors in a summer practicum in counseling and a control group of graduate students meeting concurrently in a child psychology course were cast in the helping role prior and subsequent to their six-week courses. Both groups were assessed on the following indexes: tape ratings; interviewee ratings; self-ratings; and the ratings of significant others, all on dimensions of interpersonal functioning. In addition, the Constructive Personality Change Index of the MMPI (that is, those items on which subjects could change) was administered pre-and-post. The training group received a counseling program integrating the didactic and the experiential approaches to counseling. It was anticipated that the training group would demonstrate significantly more constructive gains in functioning than would the group meeting the same number of sessions for the teaching experience.

RESULTS AND DISCUSSION

On all indexes of all dimensions, the training group demonstrated significantly more gain than the control group, thus demonstrating the efficacy of the integrated approach to training. In particular, the training group demonstrated significantly more constructive personality change, thus suggesting that effective training is not simply a process of teaching, but one in which the trainees themselves become involved in a process leading to therapeutic personality change. The generalization of the effects of gains in interpersonal functioning to significant others in the lives of the individuals involved is an important extension of changes resultant from training.

*Journal of Clinical Psychology,* in press, 1967.

## The Interpersonal Functioning and Training of College Students*

*Bernard G. Berenson*
*Robert R. Carkhuff*
*Pamela Myrus*

PROBLEM AND METHODOLOGY

A systematic study was designed to assess training process and outcome and to control for the following problems of previous training and therapy research: first, lacking pre-post testing, the researcher could not safely conclude that all training groups were similar in ability before the program began and that change over the period of training did in fact occur; second, no control groups were employed to test the efficacy of training when compared to no training over time; third, no training control group, that is, groups which meet for the same number of sessions and participate in all the activities but those critical to the training proper, had been incorporated; fourth, the problem of not being able to conclude from the research *what* counseling training dimensions led to *what* indexes of change remains unresolved. Eighteen male and eighteen female undergraduate students were randomly assigned to one of three groups: (I) the training group proper which employed (1) previously validated research scales assessing the dimensions of empathy, positive regard, genuineness, concreteness, and self-exploration and (2) a quasi-therapeutic experience; (II) the training control group which did everything that the training group did with the exception of the employment of research scales and the group therapy experience; (III) a control group proper which received no training experience. Both groups I and II were run by experienced therapists functioning at essentially the same levels of facilitative conditions. Pre-post measures were taken on the following four indexes assessing trainee empathic understanding, positive regard, and genuineness, and the degree of self-exploration elicited in others: objective tape ratings; inventory reports of standard interviewees; inventory reports of significant others; and inventory self reports.

RESULTS AND DISCUSSION

The hypothesis that Group I would demonstrate significantly greater improvement in interpersonal functioning than Group III was supported on all indexes. The hypothesis that Group II would demonstrate a significantly greater improvement in interpersonal skills than Group III

*Journal of Counseling Psychology*, 1966, *13*, 441–446.

was supported on two of the four indexes—the self reports and the reports of standard interviewees. The hypothesis that Group I would demonstrate significantly greater improvement than Group II was supported on two of four indexes—the reports of the standard interviewees and the significant others. With the exception of the "significant other" index, the following rank-order was consistent throughout on all five dimensions of all indexes: (1) Group I; (2) Group II; (3) Group III. On the reports of "significant others" the rankings of Groups II and III were reversed (group I still demonstrated the greatest improvement), suggesting perhaps a lack of sufficient degree of closure in the training control group, which left the training control group trainees unable to generalize to application in another context. The implications for traditional dormitory counselor selection and training as well as many other counseling programs, in general, are profound.

## The Differential Effects of High and Low Functioning Counselors upon Counselors-in-Training*

*Richard Pierce*
*Robert R. Carkhuff*
*Bernard G. Berenson*

PROBLEM AND METHODOLOGY

This study was designed to test the hypotheses that two groups of counselors-in-training would gain differentially in their levels of functioning according to the level of functioning of their counselor-trainers, with those of the higher functioning counselor gaining the most. Seventeen volunteers for a lay mental health counselor training program were randomly assigned to two groups, eight to a high-level functioning counselor and nine to a moderate-level functioning counselor, as measured by previous objective tape ratings of empathy, respect, genuineness, concreteness, and self-disclosure. The groups met for ten two-hour sessions. Assessment indexes were administered preceding and following training. Objective tape ratings of standard interviews, where the trainees were given the set to "be as helpful as possible," were accomplished with previously validated research scales. Standardized reports concerning the trainee's level of functioning were filled out by the standard interviewee. In addition, an index of whether or not the trainees continued in training was employed.

*Journal of Clinical Psychology, 1967, 23, 212–215.

RESULTS AND DISCUSSION

Of the eight trainees assigned to counselor A (the high counselor), all continued in training to its conclusion. Of the nine trainees assigned to counselor B (the low counselor), four remained and five terminated before the completion of the training. A Chi Square of 3.9 was significant at the .05 level. The counselor-trainers functioned in training consistently with the past ratings of their counseling; that is, the high counselor functioned at levels significantly higher than the low counselor in training. In general, the results supported the hypotheses, that the trainees of the higher-level functioning counselor would demonstrate the greater constructive gain. In accordance with predictions, the average level of the low counselor's group was similar at the end of the twenty hours to the level of functioning of the low counselor. However, in the case of the high functioning counselor, the group did not approach the counselor's average. It is suggested that in an extended long-term study, the group of the high counselor would move toward his level while the group of the low counselor would remain at the level of the low counselor.

## The Differential Effects of High and Low Functioning Teachers upon Student Achievement*

*David Aspy*

PROBLEM AND METHODOLOGY

An investigation of the influence of a classroom's emotional climate upon the cognitive growth of 120 third-grade students who had been matched according to sex and IQ was implemented by (1) administering five subtests of the Stanford Achievement Test to the students at the beginning and conclusion of the same academic year and (2) tape recording reading groups conducted by their six teachers. The teachers' levels of empathy, congruence, and positive regard were determined from the tape recordings by three experienced raters who employed scales which had been validated by previous research of psychotherapeutic interviews. The teachers tape recorded their reading groups fifteen minutes each day during one week in March and again during one week in May. Each of the raters evaluated eight randomly selected excerpts of each teacher's performance.

RESULTS AND DISCUSSION

The ratings for the teachers occurred in one higher and one lower cluster; that is, the ratings for three teachers were not significantly

*Unpublished manuscript, University of Florida, 1967.

different, but all their ratings were significantly higher than the remaining three teachers. Also, the ratings for each of the three conditions placed the teachers in the same rank order. Therefore, sixty students received significantly higher conditions than the remaining sixty. The results of four of the five subtests and the total gain indicated that those receiving higher conditions achieved significantly more gain than those receiving lower conditions. The spelling subtest revealed nonsignificant differences between the two groups with the group in lower conditions achieving more gain than the higher condition group. The results indicate (1) the procedure produced measures of a part of the classroom climate which related positively to student achievement, (2) higher conditions related positively to higher achievement, and (3) lower conditions related to lower achievement. Higher conditions seemed to enhance achievement while lower conditions retarded it. The difference between the means for the total gain by the two groups was 1.6 years.

## The Effects of High and Low Functioning Teachers upon Student Performance*

*David Aspy*
*William Hadlock*

PROBLEM AND METHODOLOGY

The classes of grammar school teachers were recorded and assessed to determine the level at which the teachers were functioning in their classroom interactions. Indexes of student performance were assessed in order to determine their relationship with teacher level of functioning.

RESULTS AND DISCUSSION

Students of teachers functioning at the highest levels of facilitative conditions demonstrated higher levels of academic achievement than students of teachers functioning at the lowest levels of conditions. The students of the highest level teacher gained an average of two and one-half academic years over the course of one academic year while the students of the lowest level teacher gained an average of six achievement months over one academic year. In addition, the students of the low-level functioning teachers were significantly more truant than those of the high level teachers.

*Unpublished manuscript, University of Florida, 1967.

# INDEX